SHE'S GONE

Five Mysterious Twentieth-Century Cold Cases

Kathleen Brunelle

Prometheus Books

Essex, Connecticut

Prometheus Books

An imprint of Globe Pequot, the trade division of
The Rowman & Littlefield Publishing Group, Inc.
4501 Forbes Blvd., Ste. 200
Lanham, MD 20706
www.rowman.com

Distributed by NATIONAL BOOK NETWORK

British Library Cataloguing in Publication Information Available

Library of Congress Cataloging-in-Publication Data Available

ISBN 978-1-63388-958-3 (cloth : alk. paper) | ISBN 978-1-63388-959-0
(ebook)

∞™ The paper used in this publication meets the minimum requirements of
American National Standard for Information Sciences—Permanence of Paper
for Printed Library Materials, ANSI/NISO Z39.48-1992

CONTENTS

AUTHOR'S NOTE

She's Gone is a work of narrative nonfiction. The stories in this book have been recreated through many hours of research into court transcripts, newspaper articles, genealogy records, police evidence, and hundreds of other documents pertaining to these cases. Some of the conversations in this book are based on verbatim conversations found in these records. Other conversations and scenes are recreations based on records, transcripts, and interviews. During the research for this book, I interviewed family members and detectives where possible to establish both the family and the investigatory angles of the case.

Through years of working on these five cases, I have come to know each of the women in this book. In Anna's case, though her vocal neighbor and Anna's family did their best, there was no one to speak out for Anna. More than a century after her disappearance, I feel a great sense of responsibility to do right by Anna by finally telling her story. I am honored to do so. Though Dorothy and Jean's stories have been told before, I chose to include and repeat them here. Both of these women, born in different decades, were ahead of their time. Their stories, and the lessons within them, bear repeating. Agnes's tragic disappearance has been touted as a honeymoon horror story, but it's a deeply personal and cautionary tale of family devotion. Agnes is the story with which I started the book. Finally, from the moment

I heard about Simone's case, I knew I needed to include her in *She's Gone*. The more people who can share her story, the more chance we have to bring Simone home where she belongs.

1

DOROTHY ARNOLD, 1910

She bought half a pound of sweets at one place and a light novel at another and from that moment was gone from the ken of her whole circle of acquaintances as completely as though she had never existed. —Evening Times

JANUARY 16, 1911: FLORENCE, ITALY

"Where is Dorothy?" John repeated the question, lengthening each word as he raised his voice in frustration and anger.

Junior denied knowledge of the young woman's whereabouts. John could feel his rage rising, his fist uncontrollably clenching.

In his peripheral vision, John glimpsed his mother, looking so small in her black veil, so overwrought with fear.

His twenty-five-year-old sister, Dorothy, had been missing for more than a month. And although the man before him was almost twenty years her senior and useless as far as Dorothy's family was concerned, Dorothy had been caught sneaking around and exchanging letters with him in recent months. It was true that Junior was in Italy when Dorothy disappeared in New York. Still, the family felt that Junior was hiding something from them.

Dorothy Arnold, press photo. *New York Times, 1910*

John steadied his voice and looked Junior full in the eye before asking one last time.

"Where is Dorothy?"

But Junior only repeated his incessant denials. John could no longer contain his anger. He punched Junior square in the jaw and watched him fall to the floor. Searching Junior's pockets, he found what he wanted—his sister's letter.

Moments later, John and his mother exited Junior's hotel room, letter in hand, hoping to find a clue about Dorothy's whereabouts. Little did they know that its contents would only spark more questions and lead to one of the greatest unsolved missing persons cases in New York City's history.

A SECRET GETAWAY

The lobby of the Hotel Lenox filled with the low and pleasant laughter of a smiling young woman. She was decidedly good-looking, with grayish-blue eyes and dark brown hair swept up in a stylish pompadour. At twenty-five years old, she had never booked her own hotel room away from her family before. She was both giddy and nervous with excitement. Now as she perused the grand lobby, with its ornate columns and chandeliers, Miss Dorothy Arnold glanced at her escort.

George Griscom Jr. was a decidedly older, portly man in his early forties. A regular at the hotel whenever he stayed in the Back Bay, Mr. Griscom had already reserved a room with a private bath for Miss Arnold. He was excited to share the city of Boston with Dorothy, but he meant to treat her respectfully. He planned to stay at the nearby Hotel Essex.

Dorothy's parents did not approve of George, who went by "Junior," so the couple met secretly. His family came from old money and old New England stock like her family. Dorothy's father respected men who made something of themselves; Junior, however, seemed content to vacation with his parents and enjoy leisurely club lunches.

Whether she was simply itching for a taste of freedom or whether she truly held romantic feelings for Junior, Dorothy made a deliberate decision to deceive her parents in September 1910 in order to spend a weeklong secret getaway with him. Although Dorothy was not a teenager, she was treated as such during the time period in which she

The Hotel Lenox, ca. 1900–1906. *Detroit Publishing Company Collection, Library of Congress*

lived, and she felt the need to lie about her plans. Certainly, her parents never would have allowed such a clandestine encounter.

Their attitude was not considered strict in 1910. When a man was interested in a woman romantically, he traditionally visited her home under the watchful eyes of her family. Couples were encouraged to get to know one another in this way before they married. Unmarried women who accompanied men in public without a chaperone, however, were considered at worst whores and at best "charity girls"—girls who "put out" without payment. The idea of dating had been introduced only within the previous decade.

Dorothy's social position made her secret plan with Junior even riskier. She could cause great embarrassment for her family, damage her own reputation, and risk future marriage opportunities. At twenty-five years of age, Dorothy surely knew better, and forty-two-year-old Junior definitely knew better. Regardless, the pair decided to meet.

One of Dorothy's good friends and college chums, Theodora Bates, lived in Cambridge, a suburb of Boston. Dorothy's plan was to secure her parents' permission to spend the week visiting Theodora in Cambridge and instead meet Junior at the Lenox. Her parents agreed. Moreover, they sent Dorothy without a chaperone.

The clerk behind the desk welcomed Dorothy and showed her where to sign the ledger. She provided her family's home address while bellhops whisked her luggage to her room. At the time, rooms with private baths cost today's equivalent of about $75 per day. With her allowance—a healthy sum of more than $3,000 per month in today's economy—Dorothy could certainly afford her stay. She also pawned jewelry at the Collateral Loan Company on Boylston Street. For a gold watch and chain, two diamond rings, and two bracelets, they paid her today's equivalent of $9,604.

Dorothy and Junior enjoyed a carefree and indulgent week. They dined at the hotel and local restaurants, enjoyed nightly theater outings, and visited city shops. Witnesses claimed that the couple appeared cheerful and relaxed. Junior's behavior toward Dorothy, according to hotel owner Lucius Boomer, "was beyond reproach." He was a complete gentleman and never visited her hotel room.

Dorothy checked out on Saturday, September 24, never divulging her secret week away. But secrets have a way of surfacing.

THE PERFECT LIFE

Born Dorothy Harriet Camille Arnold on July 1, 1886, in New York to Francis Rose Arnold and Mary Martha Parks Samuels, she boasted an impressive pedigree. Her father was a direct descendent of *Mayflower* passenger William Brewster, and her father's sister married Supreme Court Justice Rufus Peckham. Her family's money came from her father's inheritance and his business, F. R. Arnold and Co. Perfume & Cologne Imports. The Arnolds were considered part of New York's high society and listed on the New York *Social Register*. The family made their home on fashionable East Seventy-Ninth Street. They employed a live-in cook and two live-in maids.

Dorothy was the second of four children: older brother, John; younger brother, D. Hinkley; and younger sister, Marjorie. Educated at the best schools, Dorothy spent her primary years at the Veltin Day School for Girls on West Seventy-Fourth Street, where French immersion started in kindergarten, and attended college at Bryn Mawr in Pennsylvania, where she graduated with a bachelor of arts in literature and language in 1905.

MCCLURE'S

Always a voracious reader and lover of language, Dorothy developed a passion for writing her own poems and stories while still a student. Upon graduation, she had become serious about a possible writing career and had tried writing various poems and short stories. In early 1910, she prepared a piece for publication.

That spring, she submitted the completed story, "Poinsettia Flames," to *McClure's*—a political and literary magazine edited by Willa Cather. After receiving a quick rejection, Dorothy felt disheartened and dejected. She shared the disappointing news with her family, who teased her about her literary ambitions. Their mocking made Dorothy feel even worse.

Undaunted, Dorothy began work on a second story. From then on, she conducted her writing correspondence through the general delivery window on Thirty-Fourth Street, away from the prying eyes of her family. She also decided that she needed her own writing space in order to perfect her craft. When Dorothy's parents returned from their summer vacation in Maine that October, she asked her father to rent her an apartment in Greenwich Village—a bohemian section of the city known for housing the creative set. Her father said no.

"A good writer can write anywhere," he told her.

Dorothy knew better than to ask again. Instead, she continued to work in secret on her second short story titled "Lotus Leaves," which she submitted to *McClure's* in late October.

BOOKS AND CHOCOLATE

By early December, Dorothy was planning her sister's debut. Her eighteen-year-old sister Marjorie's party was a week away, and Dorothy still needed a dress for the event. That Monday, December 12, 1910, she decided to walk along Fifth Avenue to peruse the sales.

A cold and bitter wind blew from the north. All along Fifth Avenue, icy sidewalks glistened in the morning sun. Recent temperatures had remained in the low twenties, and that day was no different. The high would reach only 21 degrees in the city by afternoon. The ponds in Central Park boasted twelve-inch layers of ice—ideal for skating.

Dorothy chose her navy-blue suit complete with a hobble skirt and serge jacket from her wardrobe. Her long coat flowed past her hips and promised to keep her warm during her trek. She wore her hair as she usually did, swept up in the full pompadour style of the day with a tortoiseshell comb. She selected a favorite pair of blue lapis lazuli drop earrings to match the suit and slipped on her signet lover's knot ring. Her low black heels, though not ideal for the morning ice, worked well with the suit and the black velvet hat that she chose to complete her outfit. She affixed her Baker hat with a matching lapis lazuli hat pin that also complemented the two blue velvet roses adorning the hat.

Dressed for her shopping trip, Dorothy exited her bedroom and checked in with her mother. Mrs. Arnold offered to accompany her, but Dorothy gently assured her mother that she needn't come.

"No, Mother, don't bother. You don't feel just right, and it's no use going to the trouble. I mightn't see a thing I want, but if I do, I'll phone you."

Costume worn by girl on day she disappeared. *(New York) Evening World, January 1911*

Mrs. Arnold acquiesced, and Dorothy grabbed a black cloth handbag in which she carried about $20 to $30 ($650–$1,000 today) and a large black fox muff before leaving. It was the last time Mrs. Arnold would ever see her daughter.

An hour later, around noon, Dorothy arrived at Park and Tilford on the corner of Fifth Avenue and Fifty-Ninth Street. The salesgirl recognized Dorothy immediately, as she was a regular customer. Before leaving, Dorothy charged a half pound box of chocolates to her father's account. As she stepped back onto Fifth Avenue, she slipped the sweet purchase into her large fox muff.

She stopped after another half mile at Brentano's—an upscale bookstore on Fifth Avenue and Twenty-Seventh Street. Dorothy liked to take her time and check out the new titles before selecting a book. Salesclerks noticed Dorothy browsing through the new fiction section. She chose a current bestseller titled *Engaged Girl Sketches* by Emily Calvin Blake—a series of lighthearted short stories about young girls and their engagements. She charged her purchase to her father's account, leaving behind a traceable record of her stop and the time she left the store.

Outside the bookstore, Dorothy ran into her friend Gladys King. The girls chatted about Marjorie's debut. Gladys had received her invitation the day before and handed her response to Dorothy, joking

results have more than answered
this expectation.   The company's progress has been

Corner of Fifth Avenue and Twenty-Seventh Street, where Dorothy was last seen.
Mechanical Curator Collection, the British Library, Library of Congress

about saving the postage. Gladys described Dorothy as "carefree" and
"in good spirits." By the time the girls finished talking, it was nearing two o'clock. Dorothy told Gladys that she planned to walk home
through Central Park. As they parted, Dorothy turned around to
wave goodbye to her friend before heading in the direction of Twenty-
Seventh Street, never to be seen again.

NO POLICE OR PRESS

Dorothy always arrived promptly for meals, and if she was going to be
late, she called. When Dorothy did not return home that afternoon,
her family became concerned. When she didn't call, they became worried. When she missed dinner, their worry turned to fear.

After dinner, they phoned two of Dorothy's friends—Elsie Henry
and Edith Ashley. Neither girl had seen or heard from Dorothy.
They asked the girls not to tell anyone about their phone calls.
When Elsie called later, Mrs. Arnold stalled, saying that Dorothy
had come home. Elsie asked to speak to Dorothy, but Mrs. Arnold

said that Dorothy had just finished dinner and gone to bed with a headache.

The following morning, Dorothy's older brother, John, consulted his friend and attorney John S. Keith, a junior partner in the law firm Garvan & Armstrong. A friend to both John and Dorothy, he had taken her to dances and viewed her as a younger sister. The Arnolds apprised him of Dorothy's disappearance, and they began to search through her room.

Dorothy's mother and sister confirmed that she had not taken any of her clothing. Sifting through Dorothy's personal correspondence, Keith found letters with foreign postmarks. He also found European travel brochures on her desk. Keith then inspected the burned remains of Dorothy's fireplace; John surmised they were probably part of a writing manuscript.

The family found that the mass of Dorothy's foreign correspondence came from Junior. They realized she had been using a general delivery window to secretly access mail. They also realized the seriousness of Dorothy and Junior's relationship. Keith suggested they contact Junior, who was vacationing in Italy.

Keith sent the following cable: "Dorothy Arnold missing. Family prostrated. Cable . . . if you know anything of her whereabouts."

Junior's response was short and disappointing: "Know absolutely nothing. Junior."

That afternoon the Arnold family met with Francis P. Garvan, former assistant district attorney for New York City and head of the law firm where Keith worked. Garvan suggested that Arnold hire the Pinkerton Detective Agency to aid in the investigation.

Considering the windy and icy weather conditions on December 12, the family wondered if Dorothy might have slipped and injured herself during her walk home. Keith checked all of the area hospitals while Mrs. Arnold and Marjorie worked out a detailed description of the suit, accessories, and jewelry Dorothy wore the day she disappeared. The rest of the Arnold family drove through the city, checking streets and morgues.

THE INITIAL INVESTIGATION

During the first ten days of the investigation, Pinkerton agents searched the globe for Dorothy Arnold. The Pinkerton Detective Agency was a private detective and security agency that became famous in 1861 for successfully thwarting a plot to assassinate President Abraham Lincoln. Under the direction of George S. Dougherty, head of the agency, Pinkerton agents executed searches for Dorothy in New York, Pennsylvania, Washington, DC, Boston, and Europe. Using the new wireless radio system, they monitored outgoing steamers and railroads. They conducted hundreds of interviews. Mr. Arnold told them to spare no expense.

There were moments of hope, when one of the Pinkerton agents cabled, "I have the girl!" It wasn't Dorothy, however, just a student on her way to Paris to study fashion. After ten days it was clear that even with the best detectives on the case, the family was no closer to finding Dorothy.

Garvan implored Francis Arnold to seek the help of the New York Police Department. Reticent at first, Mr. Arnold eventually assented. Garvan and Arnold visited the station for the first time three days before Christmas. Commissioner Flynn detailed twenty-five detectives to the case, including the famous NYPD detectives "Camera Eye" Sheridan and Peter Beery. They canvassed not only hospitals and morgues, but also asylums, hotels, and boardinghouses. They conducted house-to-house searches, sifted through marriage records, and searched every exit out of the city.

They even spent days combing "every clump of bushes and every thicket in the heavily wooded parts of Van Cortlandt Park and in the woods which border it," based on Mr. Arnold's theory that Dorothy may have gone there to read the book she had purchased that day. She was fond of Cortlandt Park and often went there to read under a favorite tree. Perhaps, thought the family, she had gone there on December 12 and been attacked.

Finally, they cabled Junior again, demanding that he turn over any letters from Dorothy, especially the final correspondence he received from her on November 26th. "Letters received. Dorothy still missing.

George "Junior" Griscom Jr. *Los Angeles Times, February 1911*

Cable . . . if you can suggest possible plan or if further developments. Send letter Nov. 26 or anything else."

John Arnold traveled to Cambridge to investigate Dorothy's fall visit, which eventually led him to the Hotel Lenox. From there, he pieced together the details of his sister's September getaway with Junior—she had signed for the room and provided her address. John was shocked and angered. He cabled his father and returned to New York with this new information.

During the Christmas holiday, detectives focused their resources on the Washington, DC, area. Dorothy spent many Bryn Mawr holidays with her father's sister, her Aunt Harriette Peckham, in Washington, DC. The Arnolds considered the possibility that Dorothy had traveled to see her aunt and somehow had gotten lost. The family remained at home together during the holidays—perhaps hoping that at that time of the year, more than any other, Dorothy might come home to them.

The new year came and went, however, with no sign of their beloved Dorothy. Their hopes dashed, the family began the next phase of their private investigation into her disappearance. Dorothy's mother was frantic. After learning about Dorothy and Junior's Boston getaway, Mrs. Arnold believed that there was a very real possibility that Dorothy had eloped with Junior. She felt that if she could just see Dorothy, she could talk her into coming home. It was decided that Mrs. Arnold would accompany John on a trip to Italy to confront Junior.

They secretly sailed for Florence on January 5, 1911. Mr. Arnold informed reporters that John had gone to Europe on company business and that Mrs. Arnold, under the strain of losing her daughter, had traveled to New Jersey to rest.

When they arrived in Florence on January 16, Mary and John Arnold wasted no time. They went directly to Junior's room at the Anglo-American hotel. According to the often-sensationalized news articles of the day, Mrs. Arnold, heavily veiled to avoid detection, spoke first. She demanded to know what Junior had done with her daughter. Junior pleaded ignorance. He swore he had not heard from Dorothy since her November 26 letter.

The letter itself was cheerful and chatty, but the end of the letter was worrisome. Dorothy informed Junior that *McClure's* had rejected her second submission: "Well it has come back. McClure's has turned me down. Failure stares me in the face. All I can see ahead is a long road with no turning. Mother will always think an accident has happened."

The Arnold family most likely all read the contents of this letter. The family now had to consider the idea that Dorothy, frustrated by her writing career, meant to harm herself. Though it was possible that she was merely venting her frustration, the family had to take Dorothy's statement seriously in light of her disappearance. John prepared to return to New York, but his mother decided to remain in Italy in case Dorothy was there. Meanwhile, Mr. Arnold's attorneys had convinced him to go public with Dorothy's case.

THE MISSING HEIRESS

On Wednesday afternoon, January 25, a full six weeks after Dorothy's disappearance, Francis Arnold stood stoically in his lawyer's office surrounded by a sea of reporters. Francis still abhorred the idea of bringing the press into the investigation. Still, after six weeks with no leads, Francis Arnold was desperate to find his daughter.

And so, flanked by his counsel, Francis Arnold remained silent while Garvan spoke to the assembled reporters: "We have run every clue to earth and find ourselves today confronted by a stone wall. . . . We have searched in vain for six weeks among the hospitals and morgues. Mr. Arnold has offered to pay a substantial reward for news that will lead to finding her."

Francis Arnold stepped forward. He got right down to the ugly business: "Assuming that she walked up home through Central Park, she could have taken the lonely walk . . . along the reservoir. There, because of the laxity of police supervision over the park, I believe it quite possible that she might have been murdered by garroters, and her body thrown into the lake or the reservoir. Such atrocious things do happen."

Having made his statement, Francis prepared to turn the meeting back to his attorneys. The reporters, however, shot off a barrage of

One of three photographs of Dorothy Arnold initially released to the press.
Wikimedia Commons

questions at the old man: "Did you object to your daughter keeping company with men?"

Shocked, Francis Arnold responded. "It is not true that I objected to her having men call at the house. I would have been glad to see her associate more with young men than she did, especially some young men of brains and position, one whose profession or business would

POLICE DEPARTMENT

CITY OF NEW YORK,

LOOK FOR==MISSING

Miss Dorothy H. C. Arnold
Of No. 108 East 79th Street
New York City

Dorothy Arnold's missing poster. *New York Police Department, January 1911, Wikimedia Commons*

keep him occupied. I don't approve of young men who have nothing to do."

Francis Arnold's tone conveyed his frustration. He clearly spoke from experience, and reporters learned more than they needed from his unspoken words. They surmised that Dorothy Arnold had in fact been seeing a man "who had nothing to do" and that her father did not approve. From the moment the press became aware of the case, they investigated the possibility of a love gone wrong and the role it could have played in Dorothy's disappearance.

To redirect the reporters, Francis Arnold insisted that his daughter's actions had nothing to do with her disappearance: "It was an act of Providence and not by her own will that my child was lost and it will be an act of Providence that will restore her to me."

He also announced a $1,000 reward (just over $32,000 today) to anyone who could supply information leading to the return of his daughter. Garvan produced a description of Dorothy and the outfit she was wearing when she disappeared. He also provided three photographs of the missing heiress.

Francis Arnold ended the interview. He was no fool. He very likely saw the clouds on the horizon, but he had exhausted every other avenue. He and his family would endure assaults on their character, their privacy, and their very sanity. What was to come would, in fact, break some of them. It was inevitable.

The following morning, news of Dorothy's disappearance made national headlines. Within a week, the world was talking about the missing heiress who disappeared in broad daylight while shopping on Fifth Avenue. People were fascinated by the mystery. Journalists described the way she vanished as if she had been "swallowed by the grave." They remarked that her case "had all of the baffling elements of a Sherlock Holmes mystery."

What seemed to fascinate and perplex people most of all was that Dorothy had disappeared in the middle of the day in a city full of people and law enforcement.

Dorothy's Bryn Mawr classmates immediately set up a letter chain to spread the necessary information concerning her disappearance. Papers interviewed Dorothy's friends about her plans that day. One, who wished to be anonymous, told reporters, "I think she had no definite aim at all. Things are very much reduced in the stores at this time of year, and I have the idea that she was going to do exactly what she and I have often done together—walk along down Fifth Avenue and stop in wherever she saw anything she liked."

Sightings of Dorothy began pouring into police headquarters. Garvan's team prepared for this inevitability with a corps of detectives. The moment a sighting or clue came in, they dispatched a detective from the area to investigate. On the first day, detectives investigated twenty different sightings throughout the country. A man reported seeing Dorothy just after midnight in a downtown restaurant. Another caller insisted that Dorothy was living in a boardinghouse on a Brooklyn side street under an assumed name. A third said she tried to pawn a watch to book passage on a Hamburg-American steamer.

Many people tried to help the Arnold family, but some tried to take advantage of their misfortune. The day after the case went public, the family received two ransom notes. The search team was not inclined to take these notes seriously, for if someone had been holding Dorothy, her captor would have tried to make a deal weeks before. Francis Arnold told reporters that one of the letters demanded "more than he could possibly raise." Throughout the ordeal, writers demanded today's equivalent of $150,000 to more than $64 million. They threatened to blow up the family home and shoot members of the family.

DOROTHY ARNOLD, AGAIN

Since her case broke, there were so many sightings of Dorothy Arnold that newspapers began titling their reports "Dorothy Arnold, Again." Most people, however, legitimately believed that they had seen the missing woman.

Due to the Baader-Meinhof phenomenon, also known as the frequency illusion, once readers saw Dorothy Arnold's images in the newspaper, they began seeing women who looked like Dorothy Arnold everywhere. Dorothy was spotted in hotels, rooming houses, apartments, health resorts, hospitals, rescue missions, sanitariums, bus stations, and train depots. The young heiress was seen making calls in telephone booths, purchasing wool hose, wandering the streets, browsing a cigar store, collecting mail, and encamped with a band of gypsies. People claimed to have spoken to Dorothy in train stations, sat across from her in restaurants, and cared for her in hospital settings. A German rigger thought he spotted Dorothy boarding a steamship with a group of schoolteachers. Another man called to say that his best friend had arranged to take Dorothy to the theater. Even the Boston Museum of Fine Arts staff thought that they had spotted Dorothy when a woman contacted them about modeling.

People called the Arnold home with detailed stories of their sightings, like the man who had seen Dorothy on a ferry with a "shabbily dressed man" en route to Philadelphia. Sometimes Francis Arnold investigated these sightings himself. Other times, his sons John and D. Hinkley traveled to meet "Dorothy Arnolds."

One of the most important sightings from Philadelphia was reported by a postal worker, W. J. Moore, on February 7, 1911. Moore was hesitant to come forward until the postmaster encouraged him. He told papers about the sighting: "A young woman called at my window one day about the middle of December and asked for mail addressed to Miss D. H. C Arnold. There was a letter here for a person of that name, and I gave it to the young woman who called for it. The day the disappearance of the New York girl was advertised and her picture was published I said to the man who works at the next window: 'I have waited on that young woman.' I remembered the circumstances instantly when the case was made public. In the first place, women very seldom, I have found, have their initials before their names. When the young woman asked for a letter for Miss D. H. C. Arnold, not Miss Dorothy H. C., as I remember very clearly, I had her go over the D. H. C. part of it several times. As I say, the combination of letters was unusual for a woman, and I did not understand first what it was she said."

Whereas most people simply noted and then phoned in their sightings, some attempted to "capture" Dorothy Arnold, which made for some frightening situations. A woman staying in an Atlantic City hotel registered under her real name, Mrs. Arnold from New York. The poor woman had to cut her vacation short to escape the hounding reporters.

A second woman endured a horrific and frightening experience in Spokane, Washington, when the deputy and sheriff mistook her for Dorothy Arnold. C. D. Robbins was captured from her home and taken against her will to the sheriff's office where she was ordered to fess up. She and her husband sued the sheriff and deputy for $3,000 ($96,000 today) for humiliation.

A less intimidating example took place in Chicago, where four detectives followed a woman they thought was Dorothy Arnold. She was actually Dorothy A. Hayes, from Newark, New Jersey. When she exited a train station, four plainclothes detectives noticed her resemblance to Dorothy Arnold and her luggage inscribed with the initials "D. A." They followed her to her hotel, loitered in the lobby, and then followed her to a drugstore before she confronted them. When they accused her of being Dorothy Arnold, she laughed and asked a police officer to follow her to the hotel, where she gave them her identification to prove otherwise.

Some women who were mistaken for Dorothy Arnold and followed by the press were forced to hold interviews to confirm their identities. Marjorie Brown of Atlanta, Georgia, told reporters once and for all that she was the daughter of Edward F. Brown of the law firm Brown and Randolph. In other words, back off or my father will sue you.

If you had the unfortunate circumstance of being a young woman who was named Dorothy Arnold and who looked even slightly like the heiress, you went into hiding. One woman named Dorothy Arnold was pursued all over Europe. She registered as Pauline Arnold on her passage back to America to try to escape reporters, but they were waiting for her at the docks. She finally told them, "I am Dorothy Arnold but not the Dorothy Arnold. And now that I'm home I hope I won't be bothered anymore with that question. I've been asked it all over Europe for six months and my patience is nearly gone."

Another woman was staying in a hotel in Enid, Oklahoma, when she was followed by a group of seven detectives who mistook her for Dorothy Arnold. She was so disturbed by their behavior that she left the hotel and opted to stay at a private residence. When detectives followed her to the residence, the woman asked them why they continually followed her. They told her that she was Dorothy Arnold. When she insisted that she was not Dorothy Arnold, they told her she would have to prove it. She countered, "Well, if I am Dorothy Arnold, you will have to prove it, something which you will not find so easy as you think, perhaps."

Perhaps the worst and most horrifying instance is the story of Mrs. L. J. Smith. She was simply changing trains on her way to the theater when a man forcibly grabbed her by the arm and shouted, "I know you, Dorothy Arnold. I've got you at last."

The man began dragging her toward the stairs. She cried out for help, but the man told the other passengers that he was a detective and she was Dorothy Arnold. The crowd simply looked on as he dragged the woman, who was crying out in pain, closer to the stairs. With tears, she promised to go with the man if he would let go of her and let her walk. Once he did, she pleaded with passersby to help. He assured them, however, that he was a detective. The result was that the crowd simply followed them while Smith continued to scream and beg.

The man, with the crowd following behind, brought her to a police station where he told officers that she was Dorothy Arnold. At that point, the woman was hysterical. Luckily, the police believed the woman and gave her a place to rest before sending her home in a taxi. They sent the "detective" to Bellevue for observation.

Even Dorothy's sister, Marjorie, was not safe. When she accompanied friends to Flower Hospital in mid-February 1911, the papers widely reported that Dorothy Arnold was a patient there. Mr. Benjamin Arnold, the girls' uncle, was a practicing intern at the hospital. Marjorie simply stopped to say hello to her uncle while there with friends who were visiting a relative.

After the press announcement, many callers went to the Arnold home with strange stories to tell the family. Edward Legg of Philadelphia informed Mr. Arnold about a ransom situation that he was positive concerned Dorothy Arnold:

"I was in front of the Hotel Bellevue-Stratford, Philadelphia, one night in December when two chauffeurs ran their cars together by accident almost at my side. The cars were not much damaged, and the chauffeurs turned out to be old acquaintances.

"One said to the other: 'I brought a girl over from New York last night.'

"'How did you do that?' the other asked.

"'Why, I pretended that a woman had fainted in my car and asked the girl if she would step in and see if she could do anything for her. Then I sped away.'

"'What are you going to do with her?'

"'I am going to keep her a while and see if I can't make someone pay me for the trouble.'"

Francis Arnold took the man's address and asked his attorneys to investigate the clue.

Other letters offered the chance to communicate with Dorothy in exchange for money. In these instances, writers usually asked the family to drop the correspondence with money at an assigned location from which they would deliver the correspondence to Dorothy.

Over the years, many women—perhaps swept up in the publicity or looking for an escape of their own—professed to be Dorothy Arnold. In 1914, Emily O'Dell of Los Angeles claimed to be the missing heiress until her husband and detectives showed that she was born in LA and had never even been to New York. In Honolulu in 1917, Dawn Moore claimed that she was the missing heiress. Irma Munsell (though probably not her real name) claimed multiple identities, among them Dorothy Arnold. A young wife living in Muskogee professed to be Dorothy Arnold as well.

Another interesting case centered around a woman who left her husband. He and his mother went to the press, claiming she was Dorothy Arnold and had left them to return to her New York family. After weeks of press, the woman came forward to say that she was not Dorothy Arnold. She suspected that her husband concocted the story with his mother to try to find out her whereabouts and ask her to return. She did not go back to her husband.

There were sightings that appeared to be legitimate. For example, one of Dorothy's Bryn Mawr friends was living in Italy. Unaware of Dorothy's disappearance, she wrote home to her sister that she had run into her old school chum Dorothy Arnold at a Florence restaurant. Her sister immediately told their father, who reported the sighting to authorities on March 3, 1911. The Arnold family suggested that the young lady meant to write that she saw Mrs. Arnold instead of Miss Arnold. The girl's father retracted his statement and the story died out.

The most significant sightings include those on the day that Dorothy disappeared. She purportedly visited the steamship office to inquire about schedules and the general delivery window to check for mail.

IDLE YOUNG MEN

While reporting sightings and clues, newspapers were still determined to find out about Dorothy's love affairs. The Arnold family did their best to quash this notion straightaway. Garvan and Keith crafted a careful statement for reporters about Dorothy's love life: "Miss Arnold's family quickly satisfied themselves that her disappearance had nothing to do with her acquaintance with any young man, for the only person they turned to in their search had not seen her since last September. She was not engaged and had no men friends paying more than ordinary attentions to her. She had always preferred the company of her girlfriends."

Meanwhile, plucky reporters sought statements from her girlfriends and her sister-in-law. The *Evening World* asked Keith for Dorothy's mother's opinion on the matter. He said, "The Mother, who shared her secrets, is positive that 'Dot,' as she calls her, is not in love."

The *Washington Post* sought its information from the description of Dorothy's room and posted the following on the front page of its January 27 edition: "There were letters from a man whose admiration was plainly evident and who, so far as could be inferred from his own letters, believed that his love was reciprocated in part at least."

Slowly out of this narrative developed the tale of a forbidden love that pitted Dorothy against her parents. People who had known the family were only too glad to contribute to and feed the gossip.

John Jessen, the Arnolds' former grocery clerk, told papers that Mrs. Arnold got "wrought up" over a young man of whom she disapproved who had been paying attention to Dorothy.

Reporters hounded Keith about the possibility that Dorothy quarreled with her parents over a love interest. Keith quipped, "Oh, that is nonsense. Miss Dorothy was fond of her father and mother. She kept nothing from her mother. When she left home it was a terrible blow to Mrs. Arnold and she was as much at a loss to account for it as the father."

Keith's denials did little to dampen the flames of public curiosity. Papers fed these flames with rumors that Dorothy had "frequent quarrels with members of her family" and that she had been "crossed in a love affair." The press contended that Dorothy might have even eloped. Journalists quoted Commissioner Flynn as saying that he believed that a love affair was at the bottom of the case. Francis Arnold had considered this theory himself, but he no longer put any stock in it. Not after six weeks of intense investigation. And he resented the commissioner's comments.

The press, however, continued to investigate the story. The *San Francisco Examiner* reported that Dorothy was extremely "friendly" with a wealthy or noble foreigner or a young man who was living abroad. They based their information on Dorothy's foreign correspondence. Only hours later, they would put a name to the description—Griscom.

When Junior's name was suggested as a possibility, the Arnold family came forward through their attorneys to "emphatically deny" that he had ever been one of Dorothy's suitors. Within twenty-four hours of the public announcement marking Dorothy's disappearance, the world was looking for Dorothy Arnold *and* her lover.

BLIND TRAILS

The Arnold family wanted to keep Dorothy's relationship with Junior private because they were still investigating it themselves, and they certainly didn't want the world knowing about Dorothy's Boston trip.

By denying the relationship, though, they tarnished their own credibility. The press had already tied Dorothy to Junior, and it was only a matter of time before they ferreted out the juicy details.

To keep the affair secret, the Arnold family also covered up the true nature of John and Mary Arnold's trip to Italy. Again, it was inevitable that journalists would uncover the truth. Almost immediately, reports leaked that the family was holding back pertinent information. The *Chicago Tribune* quoted a high police official as saying, "Reporters are being led along blind trails because the family does not wish to have all the truth revealed." The *Morning Post* told its readers: "The police are still inclined to believe that the family has not been frank in telling all that is known about the disappearance of the young woman."

To control the storm of innuendo, Francis Arnold made a statement that ran in numerous papers: "Any insinuation that my family is withholding anything is cruel and uncalled for. There is no scandal. Before God, I declare that we are hiding no skeleton in a closet." He hoped that would quiet the gossip mill. He could not have been more wrong.

Trouble began with John Arnold's return from Italy on January 28. Unaware that his sister's disappearance had been announced, John was blindsided at the pier by reporters' questions. "This is the first I have heard of the strange disappearance of Miss Arnold," he told them. "I don't care to say anything about the matter until I reach my home."

Soon papers were reporting that John had sent a secret cipher to his brother the evening before. At the day's press conference, Keith assured reporters that the message simply alerted the family of John's arrival. He refused to discuss the message further.

John Arnold went directly to the law offices of Garvan & Armstrong, where he learned that his sister's disappearance had been made public on the afternoon of January 25. He addressed reporters, "I am sorry my father should have seen fit to give out the story. I do not care to say anything more until I shall have had a chance to consult with my family."

A reporter asked John whether it was true that he had knocked out George Griscom to get his sister's letters. Arnold refused to answer the question.

With John Arnold back in New York, the family discussed the state of Dorothy's case. They doubled down on their story about John Arnold's trip to Europe. Keith met with the press: "The trip of John Arnold, the missing girl's brother, to Europe . . . had nothing to do with the search. The young man went abroad in the interest of his father's business."

No sooner had they quashed the story behind John's European trip than questions about Griscom intensified. The press was not thrown off so easily. The family decided that it was time to come clean about Junior.

Keith finally admitted that Mr. Griscom had been one of three suitors who had paid attention to Miss Arnold during the previous summer. He also divulged that there were letters from Mr. Griscom in Dorothy's desk. He further admitted that Miss Arnold received letters from Griscom at a general delivery window. He was quick to point out, however, that there were also letters from two other gentlemen among her papers. Finally, Keith told reporters that the family had been surveilling all three men since the correspondence was discovered. He assured them that the family had investigated Mr. Griscom thoroughly and that they were satisfied that he had no role in or knowledge of Miss Arnold's disappearance. Keith concluded, "He [has been] eliminated from the case. No suspicion attaches to him whatever."

Although Francis Arnold had agreed to divulge information concerning Junior Griscom, he was adamant that they not reveal his wife's location in Italy to the press. She suffered under a great nervous strain, and Mr. Arnold felt that it was imperative to give her space from the constant worry that pervaded their Manhattan home. They decided to downplay her absence to the press and redirect questions concerning her whereabouts.

The Arnold family was fighting a losing battle. By Monday, newspaper headlines read, "Mrs. Arnold Missing." They based this report on an earlier interview with Marjorie Arnold, Dorothy's younger sister, as well as records of outgoing steamers. When asked for her mother's location, Marjorie told reporters that she did not know where her mother had gone. It was all a mystery to her. The *Buffalo Courier* had an idea.

After reporting that Mrs. Arnold had disappeared under mysterious circumstances like her daughter, the paper reported that Dorothy's mother had booked passage for Europe on or around January 1. They also pointed out that John Arnold sailed a few days later. Their theory was that Mrs. Arnold had received information about Dorothy and traveled to Europe to find her. They surmised that John Arnold went to Europe in search of both his mother and sister.

Keith attempted to control the narrative. He explained that Mrs. Arnold was in hiding to avoid the "turmoil" surrounding the case and that the family would not divulge her location. He reiterated that Mrs. Arnold did not know Dorothy's whereabouts and that the disappearance was a mystery to the whole family. Within days, however, the press discovered that Mrs. Arnold was in Italy. Soon the whole story surfaced.

EARLY THEORIES

With each passing day, Francis Arnold became more and more convinced that his daughter was dead. Whether her death was accidental or intentional, by her own hand or another's, he could not be sure. He was sure, however, that she was no longer alive, even if he was alone in that belief.

The NYPD was certain that Dorothy had run away and would return home eventually. When asked how he could be so certain, Commissioner Flynn told reporters that he had a lot of experience with such cases and in most instances the person came home when ready. Since they had not found her body or any of her belongings, the NYPD felt certain that Dorothy would return.

From the time Dorothy's case went public, journalists reported a similar narrative. The Friday after her disappearance, the *New York Times* ran a front-page headline announcing that Dorothy would arrive home that day. The article cited an anonymous source who worked on the case and said that people had seen her in the city in the past fifteen days.

The possibility that a beautiful young woman of means could have been attacked and murdered in the middle of the day in downtown Manhattan was an ugly reality that nobody wanted to face. It did not fit with any sort of "meaningful design," to borrow a phrase from Truman Capote. It meant that they were all vulnerable and mortal. It was more palatable, even exciting, to believe that she had found forbidden love and defied her family. This was certainly easier for the readers of the *New York Times* and news outlets throughout the country, but the Arnold family were the ones living the nightmare day in and day out.

Francis Arnold felt angry and betrayed. He was certain that Dorothy would communicate with her family if she could. She would not torment them. The family lived in a constant state of anxiety. Francis told the press, "It would be bad enough if the daughter I loved so well were lying beside her grandmother in Greenwood Cemetery, but this suspense and uncertainty are a thousand times worse."

Though the strain of those initial days had severely weakened Dorothy's seventy-three-year-old father, he spoke to the press about his theories. He was exhausted mentally and physically. When he met with reporters on January 28, he told them that the police department's position was "unkind," for he believed his daughter was dead, the victim of an attacker.

When reporters approached Francis Arnold later that day for comment, he was silent. He appeared exhausted and beaten. As reported by the *New York Times*, Mr. Arnold turned round to reporters, tears streaming down his face, and quietly said, "Boys, it is the silence of death."

THE FAMILY MOURNS

On Tuesday, the final day of January, Francis Arnold and his two sons met in lawyer John Keith's office. At three o'clock in the afternoon, John Arnold emerged from the private session and addressed reporters: "I am sure my sister is dead. I have felt that she was dead all along, and now I am sure of it. I have given up all hope of ever seeing my sister again."

A reporter from New York's *Evening World* asked, "What news have you heard that could influence you to think this?"

"I must refer you to Mr. Keith. He will tell you all that there is to tell."

John Keith stepped forward and spoke. "There is no doubt now in my mind that Miss Arnold is dead."

"What inspires you to reach such a conclusion?" pressed another reporter.

"I cannot give you my reasons at this time. I can only tell you that we are sure she is dead and add for the sake of her family and her good name that even if she is dead—as we are morally convinced she is—no scandal of any sort has played any part whatsoever in the case."

On February 6, ten days after releasing Dorothy's story, Mr. Arnold received a postcard written in a hand that looked like Dorothy's that said simply, "I am safe." Convinced it was the work of a crank and distressed over the loss of his daughter, Mr. Arnold suffered a "nervous collapse" under the strain and was bedridden.

JUNIOR SPEAKS

While papers published reports that Dorothy and Junior had their picture taken together in a Fifth Avenue studio, Junior and his family sailed home across the Atlantic. A reporter from the *World* surprised Junior and his parents aboard the steamer *Berlin*. The family, who had yet to endure the full scrutiny of the press, was taken back by the intrusion.

Junior refused to discuss Dorothy's disappearance, simply telling the reporter, "I only wish I could give you some news of her, or that you could bring me some."

The reporter continued to fire questions at Junior: "Was Dorothy Arnold with you in Florence?" and "Did Dorothy Arnold visit you in Florence?"

Junior responded, "She was not at Florence, and I did not see her."

Junior's father, George Griscom Sr., was perturbed by the intrusive reporter. He and his wife appeared anxious and unsettled.

"I have no information on the subject," Mr. Griscom told the correspondent. "I am going home in the ordinary course, not for any special reason."

Mrs. Griscom added when asked, "I can offer no explanation whatever for Dorothy Arnold's disappearance. So far as I know she is not now and was not in Florence."

Little did they know that this uncomfortable impromptu interview was the first tempest in a media storm that they would endure the moment they set foot in the United States.

Prior to Junior's return to the country, Mr. Arnold alerted the press that he and his son would meet with Junior before he disembarked to apologize to Junior and his family for involving them in the case. Skeptical reporters asked Mr. Arnold why he couldn't apologize to Junior in the comfort of his own home.

Mr. Arnold simply replied, "The sooner the better."

Mr. Arnold clearly wanted to get to Junior before anyone else could speak with him, and it certainly wasn't to apologize. What they discussed, we'll never know. Junior provided hints during his first official interview, given just after his meeting with Mr. Arnold.

"I feel confident that Miss Arnold is alive and I hope to see her soon. The last letter I received from Miss Arnold came to me in Florence only a few days before the receipt of the cable message telling of her disappearance."

Reporters asked Junior if there was anything in Dorothy's letter that would make him suspect she was suicidal.

"That I cannot answer. I will not discuss the contents of the letters which have passed between Miss Arnold and myself, simply because her mother has requested me not to do so."

"Is it not true, Mr. Griscom, that you asked Mr. Arnold to give his consent to your marriage to Miss Dorothy?" a reporter asked.

"If I did, that is a matter between Mr. Arnold and myself. I must decline to answer the question."

"When did you last see Miss Arnold?"

"Just before my departure for Italy on the steamship *Cincinnati* on November 3."

"Did you see Miss Arnold in Boston or in one of the suburbs of that city the latter part of last August?"

"No, I will not discuss that with you."

"Why did you come back to New York?"

"Why did I come back? Simply because it was the only manly thing for me to do under the circumstances. I am not the villain that I have been painted, and I sincerely trust that people of New York will withhold judgment until the mystery of Miss Arnold's disappearance has been solved. There are many things which I cannot say now, but I am here to cooperate with Miss Arnold's relatives in every way I can to find her and restore her to her parents. It is only right, however, that I should get into communication with members of the Arnold family before I talk too freely. I will say, however, that I believe Miss Arnold will soon be found."

"Do you expect to confer with members of the Arnold family?"

"Most assuredly. I expect to see Mr. Arnold and his sons tomorrow."

Reporters then asked Junior about the "encounter" between him and John Arnold at the Anglo-American hotel.

"These are matters of which I cannot talk. I am certain you gentlemen understand the position in which I am placed as a result of Miss Arnold's strange disappearance. I want to be frank with you, but there are questions I cannot answer."

"Do you believe Miss Arnold will be found in Philadelphia?"

"Really, I don't know, but I am certain she is not dead. I have been hoping and praying all the way over from Italy that the mystery would be solved before the *Berlin* reached here. It is a great disappointment to me that you gentleman did not bring the encouraging news which I really expected."

At that point, Junior's father spoke: "We intend to remain in New York for some little time before going to Pittsburgh, and my son will visit the Arnolds tomorrow. Until we have seen them, we must decline to discuss the case further."

Junior's first interview provides some interesting information. He declined to answer questions to which the answer was "yes": Did he meet Dorothy in Boston? Did Dorothy say anything that could be construed as suicidal in her last letter? Did he and John fight at the Anglo-American? He declined only one other question—whether he asked Dorothy to marry him—which implies that he did. John Arnold was also asked that day if Junior and his sister were engaged, and he also declined to answer that question.

Later that afternoon, Junior and his father hurried from their hotel to catch a waiting taxi. An *Evening World* reporter intercepted them before they could enter the car. He questioned Junior, "Regardless of any intention you may or may not have of marrying Miss Arnold, when she is found, can you not of your own knowledge settle the question whether she is living or dead?"

"I—I have nothing to say," stammered Junior.

His father, sick of the media attention, slammed the car door as the taxi drove off. The *Evening World* reporter promptly followed the Griscoms and reported their movements: the elder Griscom bought Junior two ties at a department store and then Junior departed on a fast train to Atlantic City, where his parents later joined him. Rumors began to circulate that the Arnold family had booked rooms at the same Atlantic City hotel and that Junior and Dorothy were to be secretly married there.

The following day, Junior invited reporters to his hotel room at the Chalfonte. He paced the room excitedly before making the following statement: "I had not intended making a statement at this time, but I am placed in a bad position if I do not. I would much rather be kept out of it, but I see you construe my coming here as being intended to mislead you and that I know where Dorothy is. As soon as Dorothy Arnold is found I will marry her, providing the Arnold family consents. I cannot place my hands upon her right now, but I feel positive that as soon as Mrs. Arnold arrives in this country tomorrow . . . the whereabouts of Dorothy Arnold will no longer be a mystery."

"Is she fond of you?" one of the reporters asked.

Junior slapped the table in laughter and looked toward his father. "What do you think of that, father?"

Another reporter asked, "Were you and Miss Arnold engaged last summer at York Harbour, Maine, when you were there as a guest?"

"That is a delicate question to ask, don't you think? I guess I wouldn't say I would marry her and there had been objections unless there had been an understanding, do you think?"

Junior's father, who was at his side, gently encouraged his son: "Now, George, the best thing to do is to tell them all you know and have it ended."

Junior continued, "You fellows have bothered me to death about whether I will marry Miss Arnold. I guess you must know that there has been an attachment between us, and so that you won't ask me again, I will tell you that I will marry her."

"When?" reporters asked.

"As soon as she is found. Now, believe me, fellows, I don't really know where she is. The fact is, I was terribly upset to find that we were here before Mrs. Arnold got here, and that made it decidedly unpleasant, for you know I could not say things that I would like to, and I wanted to tell you I would marry her, but then I had to keep silent. Now understand me. I don't know where she is to the extent that I could lay my hands on her at this minute, but I am positive she will be found soon, say when her mother gets here, which I understand will be tomorrow. Understand me, too, I was in no way responsible for her going away. Before I marry her, I must get the consent of the Arnold family, and I will tell you now that there have been objections to the marriage on the part of the Arnolds."

The elder Mr. Griscom spoke, "One reason why neither my son or I would talk in New York yesterday was that we wanted to see Mrs. Arnold before we made any statement. We expect to see Mrs. Arnold. While we expect to stay here a day or two or more, George may receive a message to leave at any minute."

"Will the message be from New York or Philadelphia?"

Junior told his father that he would answer that question: "You know I can't say where the message will come from, but I expect one. I'll let you know when it comes. I didn't come here to meet anybody. Merely came down for a rest, for things were too exciting in New York. I don't intend to do anything to deceive you fellows, and to show that I am sincere, I will permit you to delegate one of your number to follow me night and day."

Junior's father was much more relaxed that evening and conversed in the lobby of the hotel with an old friend. He also shook the hands of the reporters stationed in the lobby, telling them, "I would, of course, consent to the marriage of my son to Miss Arnold, but I hope to be able to impress the public with the fact that myself and my wife are not in any way seeking an alliance with the family of Miss Arnold for any personal reason. George wants to see you fellows. We want this thing over with and don't want you to think we are concealing something."

The Griscom family wanted to end the publicity nightmare. Junior was so nervous in his Atlantic City room that he refused to use his telephone or answer his door, even for room service. They were beginning to get a very small taste of what the Arnold family had been dealing with for weeks.

The following morning, Junior sat down with reporters again. Though he and his family were exhausted, they realized that trying to hide from the press only made matters worse. The Griscoms decided to be as transparent as possible.

Junior, who was cheerful but a little defeated, admitted that he and Dorothy had been engaged, though they had to postpone the wedding due to parental objections. He and his father believed it was better for the Arnold family to discuss when the engagement took place and for how long. When reporters asked if Dorothy might be in Philadelphia or Atlantic City, Junior looked to his father. The two agreed that it would be better for the Arnolds to answer that question.

Junior expected that Dorothy's whereabouts would be announced after Mrs. Arnold's arrival from Europe and that he would marry Dorothy thereafter. His father cut in, "But you don't know anything about it of your own knowledge."

Junior agreed with his father. They knew nothing about Dorothy's whereabouts. Nor were they certain that Mrs. Arnold had any such knowledge. When Junior last spoke to Mrs. Arnold, they had discussed the idea of Junior putting personal advertisements in the newspaper to attract Dorothy's attention, but they had decided against it.

In fact, at the beginning of the investigation, Dorothy's mother had placed secret personals in the newspapers asking Dorothy to come home or to write. She signed them "Mary Martha," her children's pet name for her. She figured that they might induce Dorothy to come home or communicate with her.

In fact, when reporters searched through the personals for communication between Junior and Dorothy, they found an example in that morning's paper: "Everything is going all right. You may expect to hear from me Tuesday, signed Junior."

Junior denied writing the message. More messages followed, and Junior continued to deny his involvement. Sure enough, these messages were written by a convicted forger who was using the personals to communicate his prison escape plan.

Junior discussed his letters with Dorothy, his cables with the Arnold family, and their theories about her disappearance (that she and Junior had eloped).

Griscom asked newsmen for their views about the case. They believed that the Arnolds had called off the search and feigned Dorothy's death so that she could resurface when things cooled. Reporters asked Griscom if there was anything wrong with that theory.

Griscom said no, but his father jumped in: "There's too much in that of which we can know nothing."

His father impressed upon him that he should not share his opinion, only facts.

Upon learning of Junior's statements to the press, the Arnold family issued a press release saying that the only grain of truth in Junior's entire interview was that "he was made to promise to go from Florence to New York as soon as he could so as to be on hand if Miss Arnold was found."

Francis Arnold spoke with reporters: "Griscom, in his sane senses, could never have said such things. I give my word that none of my family know where Dorothy is and it is impossible that Griscom could know."

John later told them, "Griscom is lying. His statements to the newspaper men are palpably false and have greatly distressed my father and the rest of us."

The Arnold family attorneys also came out in force to repudiate Junior's statements. Lorenzo D. Armstrong told the press, "I will give you my word of honor that no member of the family nor any of the lawyers in this case, including myself, know where Miss Arnold is."

Keith was dumbfounded by Griscom's statement about his engagement to Dorothy: "If he did say that or anything like it, he is an impertinent liar."

The arrival of Dorothy's mother in New York the following day gave Junior some breathing room. The press flocked to her steamer *Pannonia*. In anticipation, John had already boarded the ship. He met his mother in an empty stateroom and conferred with her before joining reporters in the smoking room.

"There is nothing to tell you, gentlemen. My sister is not on board and that's all there is to it."

Reporters asked after his mother, and John responded, "She is quite well but is naturally very much upset."

Pleasantries aside, reporters proposed a strategy.

"Mr. Arnold, you know that since this matter first became public, statements have been made which proved afterward to be untrue. Frankly, it may not be believed that your mother has said she knows nothing of your sister's whereabouts, unless reporters are permitted to see her and hear it from her firsthand. Would it not be better for her to see one or two reporters, representing all of us, and answer a few questions?"

The assembled journalists wanted to ask Mrs. Arnold if Dorothy was alive and whether she would give her permission for Dorothy to marry Junior.

John told them, "The last question is not proper. I would not consent to its being asked. . . . I might permit you to ask her the first question."

After conferring with his mother and agreeing on the proper format, John allowed one reporter to enter his mother's stateroom and ask two approved questions as long as the press promised to leave her alone as she exited the ship. The reporter asked permission to ask follow-up questions if Mrs. Arnold admitted to knowing her daughter's whereabouts.

John sighed, "If she says 'Yes' to that, you may ask her all the questions you want."

He then ushered the reporter into the stateroom where Mrs. Arnold and two other women were seated. They all wore black and heavy veils. Mrs. Arnold, a stout woman in her late fifties, sat on the far end of a settee.

"Have you received definite information since the disappearance of your daughter that assures you she is alive?"

"None, none," she answered quietly.

"I beg your pardon, but I am not quite sure of your answer."

Mrs. Arnold spoke up: "I have received no word that tells me she is alive or dead."

The reporter continued, "Have you consented to the marriage of Miss Arnold and Mr. George Griscom Jr.?"

Mrs. Arnold spoke with a firm shake of her head, "No, decidedly not."

The questions answered, reporters left so that Mrs. Arnold could join the rest of her family at the pier and travel back to their home in Manhattan.

Reporters asked John some final questions including whether he would continue to search for his sister.

He sighed and answered, "I don't see much use of doing so."

The Griscom family, meanwhile, stopped speaking with reporters. George Griscom Sr. felt that his son had said too much during his last two press conferences. He wrote a letter to Mr. Arnold apologizing for Junior's behavior and promising to keep him in check. Junior became a virtual prisoner in his hotel room, forbidden from leaving without a chaperone or speaking to reporters. His parents hired former Pittsburgh chief of police and then detective Roger O'Mara as a spokesman for the family. The Griscoms, meanwhile, kept a watchful eye on their son.

In his first statement, O'Mara assured reporters that the Griscoms knew nothing about Dorothy Arnold's whereabouts: "I have known Mr. Griscom [Sr.] for fifty years, and I can assure you that he knows just as much about where Dorothy Arnold is as the man in the moon."

The following day, Valentine's Day, the *Boston Globe* broke the story that the Arnolds had been dreading. Through patient sleuthing, they discovered that Junior had booked a room at the Hotel Lenox for Dorothy back in September. The article titled "Griscom and Arnold Girl Meet in Boston" supplied eager readers with a detailed account of the couple's secret six-day getaway.

The Boston story destroyed what little credibility the Arnold family had left. The one bright spot in their day was that reporters had discovered where Dorothy pawned her jewels in Boston, and Mr. Arnold was able to pay for and retrieve them. Keith went before reporters again to defend the family: "Perhaps it is necessary to say again that not one of the family and not one of the family's lawyers and no other person with whom we have communicated in any way knows where Miss Arnold is or has ever found a trace of her movements after December 12. Is that specific enough?"

He continued, "All of us interested directly have been forced to believe that Miss Arnold is dead and probably by her own hand. You cannot get away from the conclusion that if she was alive either she or some other person who was in her confidence would have communicated privately with the family in order to relieve apprehension or avoid unpleasant publicity."

After Keith's forceful statement, newspapers shot back. They published a letter supposedly written by Marjorie Arnold to Dorothy's good friend, Theodora Bates. Theodora and her younger sister, Josephine, were distraught over Dorothy's disappearance. "My dear: Don't worry any more about Dorothy. Don't talk to any reporters whatever, and don't talk to anyone else about Dorothy any more than you have to. Everything is all right, so there is no need for you to worry. How is Josephine? Give her my love and let me know how she is when you write. Marjorie"

Theodora took the letter to heart. While she had spoken to reporters earlier in the case, she and her sister directed all future questions to the Arnold family.

Marjorie had good reason to write this letter to Theodora. The family put out a statement that Dorothy had spent the weekend in Boston with Theodora at the Lenox. They further stated that Junior accompanied her to the theater and dinner a couple of times during her stay, as he happened to be in the area on business.

Meanwhile, Junior was tired of being holed up in an Atlantic City hotel. He longed to escape the hounding of reporters and the daily rumors. Once reporters no longer had access to Junior, they moved on to another story, insinuating that Junior had set Dorothy up with a friend of his, a banker with whom Dorothy eloped.

On the afternoon of February 19, Francis Arnold met with District Attorney Whitman at the Hotel Iroquois regarding two new letters he received about Dorothy's case. After speaking for two hours, Francis exited the meeting and told waiting reporters, "I have stated from the first that I believed my daughter was dead, and I have given the District Attorney all the clues I have. . . . If you were to spend one hour in the midst of my family you could see for yourselves and could reach no other conclusion but that my dear daughter Dorothy is dead. The manner in which she met her death is not known to us, but recent developments which may have a bearing on this point have warranted my visit to the District Attorney and the requesting of his advice and assistance."

The letters suggested that Dorothy Arnold had been kidnapped and taken out of the city. A month after Francis gave his evidence to Whitman, the DA issued subpoenas for four witnesses to testify before the grand jury concerning their sightings of Dorothy Arnold. If nothing else, these subpoenas promised to deter the number of fraudulent sightings with which investigators were dealing.

By March 12, three months after Dorothy's disappearance, her family called off nearly all of the private detectives working on the case. They kept a couple on hand (one slept at the family's home and remained on call twenty-four hours), but for all purposes, the family had given up hope.

Reporters turned their attention back to Junior. The Griscom family spokesman, O'Mara, told reporters that he believed Dorothy was in a sanitarium. Papers reported "sources close to the Griscoms" who stated that Dorothy was healthy and living in Europe, possibly with relatives in Munich (she had an uncle there), and that everyone but the press and public knew about it. Desperate for information about the case, reporters followed Junior when he tried to sneak out of the hotel Chalfonte for a haircut.

By March 22, the Parks Department unsuccessfully dragged three ponds in Central Park for Dorothy's remains. The following day, Keith announced that there was new information in the case and promised to inform the press by midafternoon. At the same time, Junior and his father checked out of the hotel Chalfonte and disappeared. The press was abuzz.

They posed all sorts of wild theories: that the Griscoms were heading to Massachusetts and Dorothy was meeting them in Nantucket, where the family owned a summer residence. Meanwhile, the Woodbury, New Jersey, mayor received a dispatch that Dorothy Arnold and Junior might be in his city. He put out an all-points alert, and the Woodbury Police began searching for the couple.

In actuality, the Arnolds had received a new tip. A man overheard that Dorothy had walked down the stairs below the Bethesda Fountain in Central Park and been attacked on the day she disappeared. The Arnolds paid him a great deal of money for his story, but he could not produce any evidence. Police searched the caverns and vaults under the great stairway that connected the mall and plaza under the fountain, but they did not find any evidence of Dorothy Arnold.

Junior finally returned to his home city of Pittsburgh. He chose to stay with a friend to evade the press, but journalists found and hounded him all the same. Junior actually called the police for assistance.

By April 11, 1911, almost four months to the day of Dorothy's disappearance, the Arnold family officially went into mourning, the women dressed in black clothing and the men wearing black mourning bands. Though they remained open to any clues in the case, they were no longer officially investigating.

With the warm weather in May, two bodies were found in waters near the Arnold residence. John Arnold visited the morgue to view the body of a woman who washed up in the East River. He informed his family that it was not Dorothy, but Mrs. Arnold wanted to know for certain. She accompanied John and their dentist for a second viewing. Although she did not view the body, she inspected the woman's clothing and jewelry. Their dentist brought Dorothy's dental records along for comparison. The woman's corset bore a label, which helped convince Mrs. Arnold that she was not Dorothy, because all of her corsets were made to order. The dental comparisons confirmed John's original suspicions. Shortly thereafter a body was found in the Harlem River, but it was not Dorothy either.

Having officially mourned their daughter, the Arnolds tried to regain some sense of normalcy and move on with their lives. The first real sign of this shift came with the June 11 wedding of their son D. Hinkley to Miss Mildred Culver, a "chum" of Dorothy's.

After the wedding, Mr. and Mrs. Arnold sailed for Germany to stay with relatives and rest. Even then, reporters insisted that the couple had gone to Germany to secretly meet their daughter. When they decided to extend their stay in September, Francis Arnold specifically asked the foreign correspondent to the *New York Times* to relay that they had not found their daughter and had not come to Europe to look for her.

Still, the stories continued: Dorothy was working as a teacher in Geneva; Dorothy had been spotted at John's house; and the family home had been prepared for Dorothy's return (it had been prepared for the Arnolds' return from Europe).

Junior's spokesman, O'Mara, surprised reporters in mid-October with a confident statement that Dorothy would return home within a few days.

"Dorothy Arnold, the missing New York woman, will reappear within a few days, well and happy. . . . It is reported that Miss Arnold has been in Pittsburgh right along."

Dorothy did not surface, however, and O'Mara went silent. The Arnolds returned, dressed in black, from their European trip, preparing to brave the one-year anniversary of their daughter's disappearance.

Unfortunately, at the beginning of 1912, they became the victims of increasingly threatening letters. The *New York Times* and other papers divulged the details of these letters, which threatened harm to members of the Arnold family unless they paid today's equivalent of more than $300,000. People disguised as postal carriers delivered these letters to the home. Other threats were communicated through the newspapers.

Detectives arrested Bessie Greene after she met a messenger boy at an assigned drop-off point specified in the letters. Though she claimed to be another messenger, her handwriting matched the hand-writing in the threatening letters. While she awaited trial in prison, however, Miss Greene also received letters that matched the handwriting of the threatening letters. During her trial, jurors determined that she couldn't send letters to herself and found her innocent.

Happier news came with Marjorie's engagement to George Vaill La Monte at the end of February. In April, Mrs. Arnold left for another European trip. She planned to spend time with family, but her trip raised old suspicions. Journalists questioned whether she was, in fact, visiting her daughter. John told them that his mother had been hassled and simply wanted to get out of New York. Still, papers of the time suggested that Munich authorities were watching her brother-in-law's home. They suspected that Dorothy was living with him, and he refused to allow them to search the premises. Mrs. Arnold arrived home in early June to help her daughter Marjorie prepare for her September nuptials.

Marjorie married Mr. La Monte in a September 10 ceremony at her parents' summer home in Sound Beach, Connecticut. With their children married and settled in the city, the Arnolds attempted to live out their remaining days as peacefully as possible. They still accepted phone calls about Dorothy, but both parents seemed to have accepted the fact of their daughter's death. They battled rumors and accusations right up until the end, even rumors suggesting that their daughter was living with them secretly, some asserting that she was in fact dying in their home. Francis Arnold, too tired and ill to speak with reporters himself, sent messages through his son John and their lawyer, Keith.

They had hired the best detectives, traveled the ocean, opened their private lives, and considered every theory but they were no closer to solving the mystery of their daughter's disappearance.

PRINCIPAL THEORIES

There are so many theories about what happened to Dorothy Arnold that it would take a library of books to accommodate them all, but some of the more popular theories follow.

Dorothy Eloped

One of the first theories considered by Dorothy's parents and often entertained by the media and public is that Dorothy eloped. There is evidence to support this theory. Even though the Arnolds did not approve of Junior as a potential husband, Dorothy encouraged Junior, corresponding with him secretly and spending a clandestine weekend with him in Boston.

Further evidence suggests that Dorothy's parents had already suspected an elopement *before* her disappearance. John's wife, Adelaide, may have unwittingly shared this secret when she swore to the press, "This is the first time that [Dorothy] disappeared."

In fact, Dorothy also may have gone missing a few weeks prior to her famous disappearance. The *Evening World* discovered that Pinkerton agents had searched marriage bureau records for Dorothy Arnold a few days prior to Thanksgiving. Despite the Arnold family's denials or attempts to suggest otherwise, Pinkerton agents did search for marriage records for a "Miss Dorothy Arnold," not a "Miss Arnold." Mr. Edward Hart, the clerk in charge of the bureau, indicated that they did not find a marriage license for 1910. The mere search suggests that the Arnolds were worried that Dorothy had eloped near Thanksgiving, most likely with Junior, of whom they disapproved. In fact, there was a lot of confusion over her Thanksgiving visit to Theodora.

Dorothy supposedly disappeared a few days prior to Thanksgiving. She had plans, of which her parents said they were aware, to visit her friend Theodora the evening before Thanksgiving and remain there through the holiday weekend. According to Theodora, Dorothy arrived as planned but spent Thanksgiving Day in bed because she was ill. Dorothy told Theodora that she was suffering with her period, but Theodora was convinced that Dorothy was saddened about her rejected manuscript. Theodora had received a package for Dorothy on Thanksgiving Day, and she believed that it contained Dorothy's manuscript. Either way, Dorothy left abruptly the next morning, arriving home in New York on Friday afternoon. She spent the remainder of the weekend writing, reading, and resting at home. If she had been missing during the week before she arrived at Theodora's house,

Dorothy's parents dropped the search once they knew their daughter's location.

It is possible that Dorothy went on another trip with Junior and then went to Theodora's house. It is likely that the package contained her rejected manuscript. She did not open it in front of Theodora, but she must have opened it later on Thanksgiving Day. The rejection would certainly explain why she left Theodora's house and returned home. In this scenario, Dorothy simply spent more time away with Junior and then met up with her friend, but her parents, suspecting that she had eloped, began searching for her.

Dorothy Ran Away

A second theory is that Dorothy ran away. Many newspapers of the day subscribed to this theory, wondering how a killer could have possibly concealed her body from the world's greatest investigators. For that same reason, they tended to discount suicide. It was more likely, they argued, that Miss Arnold left home.

Presuming that Dorothy wanted to marry Junior, or some other man of whom her parents disapproved, reporters believed that Dorothy argued with her parents over the relationship. The Arnolds' actions imply that Junior was important enough to Dorothy that they had to keep him close. They asked him to leave Italy so that he could be on hand if Dorothy reappeared, and they also asked Junior to be ready at a moment's notice to return to New York should Dorothy be found. The family clearly recognized Junior's importance in Dorothy's life, even if they publicly denounced him. The question always arises, though: wouldn't she have eventually gotten over her anger and come home? According to statements by the NYPD, that answer is "yes."

Though there were thousands of Dorothy sightings, these are not evidence that she ran away. Further, her family could not conceive that she would watch and allow their suffering. Even if the postcard in her supposed handwriting that read "I am safe" were authentic, why wasn't there any follow up?

Dorothy Committed Suicide

A third theory is that Dorothy committed suicide. At the time, many wondered why a young, pampered, wealthy woman would want to end her life. Today we understand that despite wealth and position, Dorothy Arnold was just as capable of sorrow and depression as anyone else. And she had a few reasons to feel despondent.

First, Dorothy wanted to be a writer. Submitting one's work to publishers is an act of faith. You are putting your dreams in someone else's hands. In response to her first rejection, Dorothy was determined to try again. She received the second rejection around Thanksgiving and told Junior, "Failure stares me in the face. All I can see ahead is a long road with no turning. Mother will always think an accident has happened."

She clearly intimates that she is suicidal over the second rejection. She verbalizes her hopelessness and her intention. Further, she indicates that she would make her death look accidental. These are all serious warning signs.

Dorothy might have been feeling rejected by Junior as well. Investigators considered the idea that Junior had rejected Dorothy or, at the very least, had not written to her as often as she had to him. Investigators believe that she stopped at the general delivery window on December 12, hoping for a letter from Junior that did not arrive.

Others speculate that Dorothy was despondent over her parents' rejection of Junior. Seeing no possible way she could marry him, she chose to end her life. In 1905, Andrew Griscom, Junior's relative, committed suicide under strangely similar circumstances—his family's disapproval of a love match. Dorothy knew Andrew, and his death was said to have made a lasting impression on Dorothy.

People point to the fact that Dorothy appeared cheerful on the day she disappeared; however, many people appear happy prior to taking their own lives. Her jovial demeanor does not negate this theory. Another reason that people eschew this theory is that no one ever found Dorothy's remains, but she may have unwittingly committed the act in such a way that her body was not discovered.

Dorothy Had an Accident

Another theory suggested that Dorothy suffered an accident. The sidewalks on Fifth Avenue were covered with ice. The parkways and the water in Central Park were all covered in layers of ice. Dorothy was wearing low heels on the day of her disappearance. She could have slipped and fallen at any point during her trek.

Mr. Arnold worried that she suffered from amnesia. The *Washington Post* investigated this theory and provided many examples of missing persons who had "suffered a sudden and complete loss of memory." These cases all involved people who were healthy and happy in their lives until one day they disappeared. In each case, these people suddenly remembered who they were after a period of time that lasted months or even years. They fully recovered and usually had no memory of their time away.

If Dorothy had died as the result of a fall, chances are her body would have been recovered. Had she suffered from amnesia, that would explain her disappearance and lack of contact. The family certainly entertained this theory and scoured local hospitals.

Dorothy Died Due to an Illegal Abortion

According to another theory, Dorothy died as a result of an illegal abortion. This theory was bolstered in April 1914 with the dark discovery of female remains in a maternity hospital on the Ohio River dubbed "The House of Mystery." The overseeing physician, Dr. C. C. Meredith, another practitioner, Dr. H. G. Lutz, and two nurses were implicated during a raid of the home where investigators discovered evidence of illegal abortions and female remains. Dr. Lutz told authorities that Dorothy Arnold had sought an abortion at the home. He also insinuated that she died as a result and, like the other women who shared her fate, had been incinerated in the basement furnace. John Keith had already investigated the lead two months after Dorothy's disappearance and did not find Dorothy Arnold on the premises.

Two years later, Octave Charles Glennoris claimed that he helped bury Dorothy Arnold in a New York cellar. The convict, who was serving time in Cranston, Rhode Island, told authorities that he and "Little Louie" went to a New Rochelle home to make some money. A man who looked like Junior loaded an unconscious Dorothy Arnold into a car. A few days later, Glennoris returned to the home and learned that she had died as the result of an abortion. He was supposedly offered $150 to help bury her in an old colonial cellar in West Point. Authorities dug up multiple cellars but never found a body.

Dorothy Was Kidnapped and Murdered

Still another theory suggests that Dorothy was kidnapped and murdered. The Arnold family believed this theory. Dorothy presented herself as a wealthy young woman, and she had cash on her when she disappeared. It seemed entirely feasible to the Arnolds that someone could have kidnapped their daughter. Dorothy's friends did not want to believe it. One anonymous friend told a reporter, "It seems so impossible that a girl of her age could be decoyed away or abducted."

In fact, many women were kidnapped in the city. At first, Dorothy's parents thought she was taken for ransom, but they received no contact until the case went public. More likely, they felt, she had been kidnapped into the growing white slave trade or kidnapped and murdered. The reason they waited six weeks to go public was in the hope that her kidnapper would come forward. After years without clues, Mr. Arnold came to believe she had been murdered in Central Park on December 12.

Dorothy's mother subscribed to the idea that her daughter had been kidnapped. She told reporters, "I think she was kidnapped on that date and is held prisoner in one of the many dens that are allowed to flourish in this city."

Mrs. Arnold was speaking of the "white slavery" problem in the city. Only a month before, General Theodore Bingham, New York commissioner of police, had published his findings on the issue. He explained, "There are in New York . . . regular brokers who maintain in the theater district secret agents employed to secure, for rich clients, any chorus girl whose face and figure strike their fancy."

Such as, for example, the case of Marjorie Graff, who was assaulted at the movie theater in December 1913. A young man sat next to her in the theater and stabbed her in the arm with a hypodermic needle. Miss Graff began to feel drowsy immediately but was able to get away. Although many attackers operated in theaters, they also attacked women on the street in broad daylight. Streets like Fifth Avenue were so busy that it was in fact easy to accost a victim and whisk her away in a waiting car without anyone noticing at all.

Mrs. Arnold knew of the case of a young woman from a prominent family who was kidnapped on Fifth Avenue and taken prisoner. She was found only because a business associate of her father knew the people holding her (they were prominent themselves), and the incident was hushed up when she was returned to her family. Mrs. Arnold was convinced, especially after the family had received letters to that effect, that her daughter had suffered a similar fate.

Many wonder if the family found and hid proof of Dorothy's death from the press. Members of the police and press questioned the family on this point repeatedly. Captain John H. Ayres, head of the Bureau of Missing Persons, announced in a 1921 lecture that the family had solved the case long before, though he later retracted his statement.

EPILOGUE

Francis Arnold died on April 2, 1922. His last will and testament read, "I have made no provisions in this, my will, for my beloved daughter Dorothy Arnold as I am satisfied that she is not alive."

Mary Arnold passed away seven years later, making the same statement in her own will. The Arnold family lived out their final days never knowing what had become of Dorothy. Many believed that one day the woods or water would give up her remains and provide an answer, yet Dorothy Arnold's case remains a mystery.

According to folklore, the day after Dorothy's disappearance, a white swan appeared in Central Park. It was said that the swan had

Dorothy, beloved daughter. *George Grantham Bain Collection, Library of Congress*

never appeared before that day. Many believed that the swan was Dorothy Arnold—the girl who, after a day of shopping, decided to walk through Central Park and never found her way home.

2

ANNA LOCASCIO, 1918

I saw papa with both hands and arms around mamma's neck. —Mary Locascio

MAY 1920: HACKENSACK, NEW JERSEY

On a cool Monday afternoon in late May 1920, eleven-year-old Mary Locascio was led into a New Jersey courthouse. The weather report called for a cloudy, cold, and unsettling day, which surely reflected little Mary's feelings as she entered the imposing building and the awaiting courtroom.

Once inside, she placed her hand on the Bible, swore to tell the truth, and took her place on the witness stand. The prosecutor, Mr. Huckin, asked Mary to tell the court exactly what she remembered about the last night she saw her mother. The courtroom fell silent as Mary recounted that terrible evening. Though two years before, the details remained fresh.

"Mamma put us to bed and she went to bed, too. About midnight we heard awful screams from my mamma and I went to the door of mamma's bedroom to see what was the matter. I saw papa with both hands and arms around mamma's neck. Soon mamma stopped screaming and papa laid her on the bed and straightened out her feet and put the bedclothes over her. Mamma's face was toward the wall.

The next morning when I went to the bedroom, mamma lay in the same place and hadn't moved."

Prosecutor Huckin leaned closer to the child. "Why didn't you speak to your mamma?"

Mary responded, "I was afraid of disturbing her."

THE LOCASCIOS

Mary's parents, Frank and Anna Locascio, were Italian immigrants who arrived in New York City during the first decade of the twentieth century. They were part of the more than two million Italian immigrants who entered the United States during that decade to escape poverty, violence, and social unrest in their home country. Though unlikely to cross paths in their home cities of Naples and Palermo, the young immigrants found each other in the Lower Manhattan section of New York known as Little Italy, where their families settled in hopes of bettering their lives in America.

The young couple was just starting out as the twentieth century dawned. By twenty-two years of age, Frank had already joined the ranks of many young Italian men who worked in trades. As an established tonsorial artist—a term originally attributed to barbers who not only provided haircuts and shaves but also tooth extraction, bloodletting, and occasional surgeries—Frank aspired to own his own shop. He chose to wed fifteen-year-old Antonina from a neighboring family. Though her family was more well-to-do than Frank's family, they must have believed that Frank would be able to provide for their daughter through his growing business.

The couple settled in the city on Eleventh Avenue, where they welcomed their first three children in quick succession: Johanna, known as Jennie, in March 1908; Maria, known as Mary in March 1909; and John in August 1912. After John's birth, the pair moved out of the city a short distance to Ridgefield Park, New Jersey. Though Ridgefield Park was still close to the city, it boasted a small-town feel that was perfect for a growing family and Frank's growing business.

L. C. Wiseman Barber Shop, New York City. *Detroit Publishing Company Collection, Library of Congress*

Frank and Anna weren't the only young couple moving into Ridgefield Park. In the early 1880s, the completion of the West Shore Railroad allowed New Yorkers to travel through Ridgefield Park for the first time. Sixty people lived in the park in those days. Within twenty years of the arrival of the railroad, the population grew to three thousand. An additional fifteen hundred people arrived by 1910. The growing population necessitated various services, barbers included. The opportunity was perfect for Frank, Anna, and their family.

When the Locascios moved to Ridgefield Park, there were already a number of barber shops operating throughout the area, especially on its main street, such as Pete's Barber Shop, Central Barber Shop, Brykczynski's Barber Shop, Court House Barber Shop, and Crown Barber Shop, to name just a sampling. Frank chose to open his business nearby on Paulison Avenue.

There were plenty of barber shop sales and transactions during this period in Ridgefield Park and the surrounding area. One advertisement lists an entire barber shop with all of the equipment for $75,000, today's equivalent of slightly more than $2 million. Others seem more affordable, like the advertisement from a March 1913 edition of the local newspaper, the *Record*: "Barber Shop and fixtures together with cigar counter and lease for three years ... will sell at low figure for cash." Prospective barbers could also purchase supplies at public auctions, such as the auction of the Brykczynski Barber Shop equipment, which took place in January 1913.

Much like the other barbers in town, Frank operated his shop out of a building that served both as his home and his business. It was designed so that half of the bottom floor housed the barber shop and the other half contained the Locascio home. The upstairs bedrooms afforded space for two tenants. Frank ran the shop during the day while Anna managed their home and growing family. Shortly after their move to New Jersey, she gave birth to their fourth and final child, Sadie, in 1914.

The Locascios settled into a seemingly perfect life with their young family. Anna tended to their four children while Frank ran the barber shop. While they worked and lived together in their Paulison Avenue house, life was good for Frank, Anna, and their children. Frank would later testify that he loved his wife "while she was at home."

THE WORLD IS CHANGING

Though Frank's barber shop was not located on the busy main street, he was certainly doing well enough that he needed to hire at least one additional barber. More often than not, barbers worked with relatives but, as evidenced by the journeymen barber's strike in 1913, that was not always the case. According to the 1915 census, twenty-three-year-old Lewis Brescia was working and living in the Paulison home with Frank and Anna that year.

Lewis Brescia was an Italian immigrant who arrived in America when he was fifteen years old, the same year that Frank and Anna married. Like Frank, he made his living as a barber. By 1915, when he began working for Frank, he had been living in the United States for eight years. Frank, who was eight years Lewis's senior, no doubt

The 332nd Infantry arriving in New York City after fighting in World War I.
Library of Congress, Prints and Photographs Division, LC-B2-1234

mentored the young man who lived and worked with his family. Anna, too, would have welcomed and catered to Lewis, as she fixed his meals and his lodgings. She and Lewis were much closer in age, born in the same year. They would have had time to converse during and after meals. With the looming war in Europe, there was certainly much to discuss, especially the fate of their home country, Italy.

Within two years, Lewis left the Locascio household. There are a number of reasons why he may have transitioned from his job in the barber shop. Like many Italians, he could have come to the United States to earn money and then returned to Italy. He could have married, changed occupations, or moved to another state. The most likely scenario, however, is that Lewis was drafted to serve in the war.

A large segment of the Italian population, though not yet naturalized US citizens, volunteered to serve when America entered the war in 1917. Many of them fought in the 332nd Infantry. The only unit to fight on the Italian front, these soldiers fought in their homeland. Though there is no documentation to support this theory, Lewis Brescia could have been drafted overseas.

After Brescia's departure, Frank brought on his brother Salvatore to help him in the barber shop. Salvatore took Lewis's lodgings in the Locascio home. If that had been the only change, perhaps the family would have continued to live in peace on Paulison Avenue. But the world was changing and so was Anna.

THE HOMEFRONT

Whether she was influenced by Lewis is unclear, but Anna was certainly influenced by world events and eager to do her part for the war effort. There were many opportunities for women to support the troops. In fact, American housewives signed pledges to "carry out the directions and advice of the Food Administrator in the conduct of [their] household" (National World War I Museum and Memorial). They canned food, grew victory gardens, and rationed extras like meat. Anna, however, wanted to do more.

The Salvation Army and the Red Cross sought women throughout the United States as volunteer nurses. In fact, the week before Anna's disappearance, an article appeared in the July 3, 1918, edition of the *Record*, the local paper for the Ridgefield Park area, soliciting women to work for the Red Cross. The headline called for twenty thousand student nurses for training, specifically women between the ages of nineteen and thirty-five. Enrollment began on July 29. Training ended in April 1919. With a large majority of trained nurses serving overseas in the war, there was a shortage of nurses at home in America; therefore, the request for women to help the war effort by joining ranks at home. The plea in the article read, "Across the sea from France, with every closing day of the struggle of our fighting men, there comes a more imperative call to the women of America to assume their full share of responsibilities in winning this world war for the right of men, women, and nations to live their own lives and determine their own fortunes."

Anna discussed the opportunity with her mother, who was eager for Anna to come to New York and train for the Red Cross nursing program. It was conceivable that Anna would be able to train during

American Red Cross recruitment poster, "The Spirit of America." *Library of Congress, Prints and Photographs Division, cph.3g09738*

Sewing room view. *Library of Congress, Prints and Photographs Division, LC-DIG-stereo-1s14384*

the day while the children were at school. Her youngest, Sadie, was four years old and no longer a baby, which gave Anna more freedom. In fact, she had recently begun taking the train into the city to work in a shirtwaist factory to bring in extra money for the family. Her aging children and the opportunity to work outside the home afforded Anna a new perspective, and she embraced opportunities to expand her world. Frank, however, later shared that he was not keen on his wife's newfound freedom and longed to keep her within the walls of their barber shop abode.

Frank also admitted that he felt "less than" in the eyes of Anna's family, so he did not voice his concerns to them about the jobs they found for his wife in the city. He may have felt that his protests would only elicit comments about his controlling nature or his inability to provide for their daughter. Instead, Anna took shifts at various factories—Frank didn't even know their names or addresses—where she worked alongside her sister, Katie. These jobs afforded Anna time to herself—away from her responsibilities as wife and mother—and time with her own mother and siblings. Slowly but surely, Anna began to slip from Frank.

JUST A GIRL

When Anna married Frank, she was only fifteen years old. Life with Frank must have seemed exciting. He was an older man who owned his own business and rented his own apartment—not some crowded tenement where she was forced to share a cramped space with her large family. For Anna, marriage to Frank equaled freedom, adulthood, and adventure.

By 1918, Anna was still only twenty-seven years old—a young woman. In addition to her duties as a wife and a mother to four small children, she was also bound to the business that bred her family—for the barber shop was never far from her physical or mental space, which also meant that Frank was never far away, either.

From later statements that Anna made, from Anna's own actions, and from the actions of her family, it is clear that she missed her parents and her siblings who remained in Manhattan. Though the small-town atmosphere was the perfect backdrop for raising children, Anna herself was in many ways still a child who had not had the chance to become an adult before having children herself. The village, complete with the oldest Fourth of July celebrations in the country, was perhaps stifling to a young and beautiful woman who was just coming into her own.

The only freedom Anna enjoyed was through her employment in the city. Since the Locascio home was located near the train station, it was easy for Anna to make the quick walk to the station and be transported to the city to work in various shirtwaist factories alongside her sister, Katie. Because the work was not continual or confined to one factory, Anna's hours varied. This arbitrary schedule allowed Anna even more freedom with her time—freedom with which she may have taken some liberties by early summer 1918.

As a young woman, Anna enjoyed the cabarets—musical and dance numbers performed at area cafes, clubs, and restaurants during which patrons drank alcohol and danced. By July 1, the anti-cabaret ordinance was officially enforced in Atlantic City to deter improper behavior. The mayor intended to discourage fighting and improper behavior among the city's many cafe patrons. Religious leaders felt that, with many young Americans risking their lives overseas, citizens at home should attempt to behave decently as a patriotic duty.

The anti-cabaret ordinance established that "no entertainment, commonly known as cabaret, consisting of vaudeville acts, specialties or special performances of entertainment by one or more persons shall be permitted in any room or place where liquors are sold or served." Though some dancing was still permitted, dances "involving an indiscriminate exchange of partners," such as the Paul Jones, were prohibited.

According to Frank, however, these were just the sort of entertainments that his wife had suddenly taken an interest in secretly attending. The fifteen-year-old girl he married who had moved away from her family, helped him start his new business, and delivered four children in a matter of eight years was starting to enjoy some free time of her own.

INDEPENDENCE DAY

In 1894, Ridgefield Park held its first Fourth of July celebrations. It is one of the oldest Fourth of July parades in the United States and the oldest in New Jersey. Since then, the festivities have expanded to include not only the traditional parades and fireworks, but also bicycle races, home decorating contests, art contests, a reading of the Declaration of Independence, flag-raising ceremonies, baby and youth parades, concerts, and more.

July 4, 1918, was a Thursday. With daily reports of those killed and wounded in action in the war overseas, celebrations at home were particularly poignant and patriotic. On the day before Independence Day, the Red Cross made a call for twenty thousand area nurses. Anna felt compelled to do her part, especially at this time of year, when patriotic feelings and a sense of duty ran high.

She left her house on the morning of Friday, July 5, by foot to catch the train to the city, where she worked for the day in a shirtwaist factory. Frank, too, rose early. He and his brother, Salvatore, opened the barber shop adjoining their home on Paulison Avenue. They readied their tools and chairs, opening the door to welcome the day's customers. The children most likely remained in the home under the watchful eye of ten-year-old Jennie while their parents worked. Frank could easily check on them or tend to them if needed from his adjoining shop.

Normally, Anna returned home by the early evening train in time for dinner. On the evening of July 5, however, the train came and went without Anna. The next train came and went and still no Anna. Frank closed the barber shop and awaited his wife's return. Mrs. Fletcher, the Locascio's upstairs neighbor, alerted Frank to the fact that Anna had been spotted at a local beer saloon.

Armed with this information, Frank investigated. He and a friend went to the beer saloon in question, arriving at about eleven that evening. Frank later testified that he "walked in, opened the door, and saw [his] wife sitting there with a man named Neiding."

According to census information, a Matthew Neiding lived nearby. He was the same age as Anna and single. Frank did not specify who the young man was at the time of the incident. He did say, however, that rather than confronting his wife, he walked around for a while to cool off. He later met his wife near their home in Ridgefield Park. Rather than telling her that he had seen her at the saloon, he casually asked why she was late and where she had been. Anna explained that she had been in Hackensack to see a friend but had missed the last car and had to walk home.

Anna did not report to work the day after this incident. Nor the next day or the day after that. Frank testified that Anna was sick the next day, which is why she did not report to work. She did not report to work again, in fact, until July 9—the last day that anyone saw Anna alive.

One of the Locascio children, their oldest daughter Jennie, also testified to her mother's illness during this time—though she puts the sickness at more like two weeks. She said that on the evening her parents were quarreling, July 9, her father had shut the door to his bedroom, explaining that her mother "was sick." She also testified that her mother had been sick for about two weeks prior to the night she disappeared. Jennie told how her father had taken her mother to a New York hospital in a taxi at one point during those weeks because her mother was so sick, though she did not elaborate on the type or cause of the sickness.

Though, as the county authorities later told reporters, the Locascios had "frequent quarrels" before Anna's disappearance, events were brewing that led up to one final quarrel after which Anna disappeared. That final quarrel centered around Anna's job. Once Frank learned that Anna had been visiting saloons on her way home from work, Frank forbade his wife to return to work. He later admitted to the local chief of police that the argument with his wife on the evening of July 9 began because he told Anna that he did not want her working in New York anymore. His demand and Anna's insistence that she would "do as she pleased" sparked the explosive argument in the Locascio home that evening.

CONSIDERABLE SCREAMING

Anna returned to work on Tuesday, July 9. She met her sister, Katie, in the city and they worked together in the shirtwaist factory to which they had been assigned that day.

According to Frank, he had already closed the barber shop and cooked dinner by the time Anna arrived home from work that evening. He and the children waited at the dinner table for Anna's return. Once she arrived, she sat down with the family, but she did not eat. Frank heard Anna telling the children that it was the last time they would see her.

Sometime between the family dinner on July 9 and the early morning hours of July 10, an alarming argument broke out at the Locascio home—an argument so intense that some neighbors called the police and others knocked on the family's door to check on them.

Certainly, there were issues brewing in Frank and Anna's marriage. Anna wanted to join the Red Cross or attend cabarets, but Frank felt that Anna's place was at home. Anna, according to Frank, demanded more freedom. The couple's arguments had been increasing since the beginning of July and that night, for whatever reason, they came to a head.

Numerous witnesses heard a woman's screams coming from the Locascio residence that evening. Neighbors reported "considerable screaming" to the police. The Locascio's daughter, Mary, described these screams as "awful" in her testimony.

The screams, which according to the children happened in the "middle of the night," were loud enough to rouse the neighbors upstairs, Mr. and Mrs. Fletcher. Apparently, they were not only loud, but alarming enough for Mr. Fletcher to knock on the door and check on the family. Mrs. Fletcher put the time around 2:00 to 3:00 a.m.

A resident of Ficken's Garage, a business across the road, also heard a woman's screams. The neighbor was worried enough to call the police and told officers that the trouble was at the Locascio home. A record of the call was logged with the local police and an officer was dispatched to the scene, though the dispatcher never recorded the name of the caller. Strangely, the only person who claimed that he did not hear Anna's screams was her brother-in-law, Salvatore, who was asleep in the house at the time.

Importantly, witness testimony also corroborates the fact that there was an immediate silence following the woman's screams. In fact, the house remained silent thereafter. In Mary's testimony, she stated that when she entered her parents' bedroom, her mother was still screaming but "soon mamma stopped screaming." Mrs. Fletcher told police that after she heard the screams, "all was quiet." Likewise, the officer dispatched to the scene never approached the residence because "everything was quiet when he arrived there."

In his testimony, Anna's husband Frank admitted that his wife was screaming that evening; however, he told the jury that she screamed at him about wanting to leave the home and later in frustration about not being allowed to leave their bedroom. He relayed that his wife was no longer happy with the home or family and wanted to escape.

The night of July 9, 1918, was the night she had hit her breaking point. He told the jury that Anna rose from bed and screamed at him for more than two hours while he tried to bar her from leaving the bedroom but that finally, in the early morning hours of July 10, he allowed her to go.

Frank told the jury at Anna's murder trial, "I asked her why she wanted to go. Her reply was that it was none of my business why she wanted to go. She had no more love for the home. I told her if she wanted to go to wait until night when the children could not see her. After a while she cooled off. At 10 o'clock she started again about going out, saying, 'I don't know who will hold me tonight; I don't care for nobody.' I told her to keep quiet, as the people might think we were doing something wrong.' About 11:30, she began screaming and shouted, 'I must go. I must go. Don't you understand, I must go.' ... Shortly after midnight my wife jumped out of bed and began to scream, tear at her hair, and rushed the door. It was then that Mrs. Fletcher knocked on the door."

The prosecutor interrupted Frank's testimony to ask exactly how long he had blocked his wife from attempting to leave her own bedroom. "She had been trying to go away for two hours and a half and you stopped her each time?"

Frank responded, "Not steady. She tried about every fifteen minutes." He elaborated, "I would not let her go out. In the struggle at the door, she bit my finger. I did not bother anymore and she went out the door. I told the children to go back to bed. Let her go. God help her."

After Frank's daughter Mary was questioned by the prosecution, the defense cross-examined her. She restated her version of the events during the early morning hours of July 10—her mother's screams; her father's hands around her mother's neck; her mother falling to the floor; her father placing her mother back in the bed; and seeing her mother the next morning in the bed. She insisted that her mother's "posture" was "unchanged." The defense, however, examined Mary closely regarding this second visit. Mary became confused and cried, ultimately contradicting her earlier testimony and stating that maybe her mother was not there when Mary returned to her parents' bedroom in the morning, a crucial point for the defense.

The Locascio's oldest daughter, Jennie, the other witness to the altercation, contradicted her sister's and her father's testimony. Jennie was ten years old on the evening of her mother's disappearance and twelve years old when she took the stand. Still a child, she cried as she was led to the stand to testify and throughout her testimony. Frank also cried during his daughter's testimony. Like her father, Jennie described a struggle between her parents at the door. She also stated that her mother bit her father's finger. Jennie's story differed, however, in that she reported that her mother returned to the bedroom and Jennie (like Mary originally reported) saw her mother in the bedroom the following morning. When asked what her mother was wearing the next morning, the child replied that her mother was wearing the same clothing she had worn to work the day before. Her mother did not move or communicate. Jennie stated, "I saw her in bed after the quarrel. She had the same clothes on as she did when she came home from work that night."

At that point, Frank Locascio stood up in court and accused Mrs. Grace Humiston, a lawyer working with the prosecution, of prompting his daughter. The defense did not cross-examine the witness.

A POORLY TRAINED WIFE

The morning after Frank and Anna's argument, Mrs. Fletcher approached Frank about the cause. He informed her that "what she had expected had come true," seeming to confirm Mrs. Fletcher's suspicions that Anna had been running around with another man and had finally run out on Frank altogether. On that same morning— the morning of July 10—he also repeated the story to his brother, Salvatore, who had slept through the previous evening's altercation. Salvatore testified under oath that he remembered his sister-in-law quarreling with two people in front of the barber shop earlier in the evening but that he was not aware of what happened after he went to bed, for he did not hear any screams or unusual noises during the night. Further, all he knew was what his brother told him the morning after Anna had disappeared.

The purported argument earlier in the evening was between Anna and Mrs. Fletcher. According to Frank, Anna and Mrs. Fletcher fought at about nine o'clock in the evening, when Anna accused Mrs. Fletcher of telling Frank that Anna had been in a saloon. According to Frank, Anna told Mrs. Fletcher that "it was none of her business to tell" and to "let her husband do all that."

During the next three days, Frank told anyone who asked after Anna that she ran away; however, on the fourth day, he reported her missing to the local police. Frank told Chief McElroy another version of the events previously reported, to which McElroy testified during trial.

"His wife had an argument about 11:00 p.m. over her going to New York to work; he didn't want her to go anymore, whereupon she said she would do as she pleased; they then went to bed and later he was aroused by her going to the door; he and the children coaxed her to come back and she did. Shortly after this his daughter came into the bedroom and informed the father that she guessed mamma had gone away. Frank said he found this correct."

Several days after Anna's disappearance, Frank invited her uncle Pasquale to the house and took him into the cellar to tell him about Anna's disappearance. Frank was anxious that the man should know. He also wanted to ask him for a picture of Anna to place in the local newspaper, as Chief McElroy told him it would be helpful to do so, and Frank did not have any pictures of his wife. Frank testified that Pasquale told him that he had better go and take care of his four children unless he wanted trouble.

At about the same time, Frank saw his brother-in-law. According to Frank, the man told him that he had not trained his wife right and that was why she had left him. Frank felt that the trouble was rather that he was "too poor and her people [were] too high."

Certainly, Frank shared the narrative that Anna would do "as she pleased." He further insinuated that she was an uninvolved wife and mother. He testified that she claimed to have "no love for the home." He stated under oath that she told her children that she was going away and that "was the last night they would see their mamma." When he suggested that Anna take the children with her if she were going to

The only known photograph of Anna Locascio. *The (New York) Daily News, May 1920*

leave, he quoted her as telling him, "No. My sister says I must leave the children on your hands."

On the stand, Frank described the patient and understanding attitude with which he approached his wife. While Anna was out working mysterious jobs about which Frank purportedly knew nothing, he remained home running the business, caring for the children, and cooking the meals. When he found his wife carousing at a saloon after hours, he did not confront her. When she arrived home late for dinner and did not eat, he allowed her to sulk while he ate with the children. Later in the evening, she argued publicly with a neighbor while he stood by and said nothing. When she told him that she wanted to leave him, he politely asked her to wait until the children went to bed so that they would not witness her exit. When she woke suddenly and hysterically screamed in an attempt to escape, he barred the door; however, when she bit his finger, he allowed her to leave. He prayed for her after she left him: "Let her go. God help her." Finally, he insinuated that her family threatened him to accept his new situation as a single father. According to Frank, Anna's brother told him that it was Frank's fault that Anna left him; Pasquale purportedly advised him to take care of his children if he didn't want more trouble; and Anna's father told him, "Take good care of the children whether she comes back or not."

In fact, the children were sent away to New York to live in a home for children during the trial. By the 1930 census, Frank's three older children were living with him again. His youngest child, Sadie (also known as Sally) had not yet returned to her father.

THE SEARCH BEGINS

During the trial, much was made of the fact that Frank waited three days before reporting his wife's disappearance. Frank explained that since his wife left him, he did not feel the need to report her missing. Beyond his conversations with his brother, Mrs. Fletcher, and other various neighbors, Frank did not see the need to share his family business. Still, on Saturday, July 13, 1918, he visited the Ridgefield Park chief of police to report Anna's disappearance.

The original investigation into Anna's disappearance was quick and casual. Chief McElroy interviewed Frank, Mrs. Fletcher, and the Locascio children. He suggested that Frank run a photograph of his wife in the local paper, though no photograph appeared. Within a couple of weeks, the case fizzled out. Without any leads or a body, McElroy assumed that Anna left her family, and he dropped the case.

Chief McElroy testified two years later: "I have not a single statement from any person connected with the case."

Prosecutor Huckin pushed him: "Then there is not a scrap of paper in your possession as Chief of Police in regard to this case?"

Chief McElroy responded, "No, sir."

"Then your investigation amounts to this: you asked Frank all he knew?" Huckin asked.

"The case had been taken out of my hands and I did not bother anymore," McElroy explained.

Anna's family, however, would not give up so easily. Her uncle, Pasquale Monfri, became the spokesperson for the family. Indeed, Frank seemed most nervous about informing Pasquale about Anna's disappearance. When asked about his conversation with his father-in-law, Frank actually cried on the stand. The papers reported that throughout his testimony, Frank "showed considerable levity" except when recalling this discussion with his father-in-law. He told the court that Anna's father said to him, "If you don't produce my daughter, dead or alive, I will be one of the men to take your life from you." Upon meeting with his father-in-law again at a later date, Frank detailed a very different conversation. The old man told him, "Never mind, my dear son-in-law, take good care of the children whether she comes back or not. I won't have any disgrace in the family. If I get hold of her, I will do something to her."

Still, Pasquale Monfri felt that his niece's disappearance was suspect from the very beginning. His suspicions were aroused by the sudden and unusual manner in which she disappeared from home. With every passing week and month, he became convinced that Anna had not run away. Pasquale had been searching for her nonstop since her disappearance, and he had yet to find a trace of his niece, even after a year had passed. Other factors bothered him.

If Anna left her husband in order to join the Red Cross, there would have been a record of Anna working with the Red Cross. Frank did not make an effort to find out if Anna had in fact joined the Red Cross after she left him, but her uncle did. Anna had not joined the Red Cross. Furthermore, Frank stated that Anna wanted to work in the city with her sister; however, Anna did not return to any of the factory jobs that she had been working in New York. In fact, according to her sister Katie, there was still money due to Anna at one of those factories, which she never claimed.

Another issue bothered Pasquale, which Frank later divulged on the stand. During direct examination, Frank testified that Anna took all of her clothes with her on the evening she disappeared but later testified that she took only the clothes she was wearing. Where were Anna's clothes? They were not with her family. If she took them all that evening, she could not have gotten very far lugging all of her belongings at 2:00 or 3:00 in the morning when the trolley cars and the trains weren't running. Even without her bags, how would she have gotten far on foot?

A FRESH PATCH OF CEMENT AND A MYSTERIOUS LETTER

There may have been other reasons prompting Frank's visit to the police. It seems that the Locascios' neighbor, Mrs. Fletcher, was concerning herself with Frank's actions as well as Anna's. Since the evening of Anna's disappearance, Mrs. Fletcher noted some suspicious goings-on at the Locascio residence. First, the day after Anna's disappearance, she noticed a new patch of cement and a new trunk in the cellar that she shared with the Locascios. She also detected the odor of chloride, and her husband found the cellar padlocked when he tried to access it four days after Anna's disappearance. In keeping with her character, Mrs. Fletcher may have asked Frank about the reasons for the padlock, new patch of cement, and suspicious odor, thus spooking Frank and initiating his visit to the police.

Strangely, within days of Anna's disappearance, Mrs. Fletcher received a letter from Anna, postmarked from New London, Connecticut. Although we do not know the contents of the letter, we do know that the letter was written in English. Anna's family contended that though Anna spoke both Italian and English, she could write only in Italian. A quick check of the 1915 census supports the family's assertion. The census confirms that Anna spoke both Italian and English, but she wrote only in Italian. She did not write in English, so who wrote the letter? Why did someone pose as Anna? Newspapers of the time called the letter a "canard"—an unfounded rumor or story. Perhaps, though, it was not. Perhaps Mrs. Fletcher did receive a letter purporting to be from Anna for the very reason that she was suspicious about Anna's whereabouts. What better way to assure Mrs. Fletcher that Anna had indeed run away than by sending her a letter written by Anna and postmarked from another state? It would surely not be the first such letter of its kind. Indeed, Chief McElroy testified under oath to seeing the letter.

If the intention was to pacify or quiet Mrs. Fletcher, the ruse did not work. She became even more vocal about her concerns. She wanted to know what became of Anna. She insinuated that Anna had been murdered and buried in the cellar. Very well aware that Frank was friendly with the Ridgefield Park chief of police, Mrs. Fletcher reported her concerns to the Bergenfield marshal, Benjamin Dunn. He in turn reported the matter to Chief of Police F. M. Sandberg, who communicated the information to John A. McElroy, Ridgefield chief of police. Upon hearing of Mrs. Fletcher's accusations, Frank sought an affidavit to bring a slander suit against her. Chief Sandberg recalled in his testimony that "Chief McElroy and Frank Locascio called on me and asked for a retraction of the story. Policeman Dunn submitted a written statement concerning what Mrs. Fletcher had said to him to Chief McElroy and Locascio, which they said would be the basis for a slander suit against Mrs. Fletcher."

Between the time of Anna's disappearance and the time of the murder trial two years later, Mrs. Fletcher moved from the Locascio residence to neighboring Bergen Turnpike. Whatever pressure transpired during those two years must have been great to silence such a strong-willed and vocal woman. When newspapers called on her during the trial to question her about the statement she had given to policeman Dunn, she repeatedly told reporters, "I have nothing to say." She refused to confirm or deny that she heard screams coming from the Locascio residence on the evening of Anna's disappearance. In fact, she never spoke about the case again. Because of Mrs. Fletcher's comments, however, there was much speculation in town about whether the police would dig up the cellar to look for Anna's body. Her uncle Pasquale certainly wondered if his niece had been lying in a grave beneath the home for the intervening years since her disappearance.

DEAD OR ALIVE

Frustrated that the search for his niece had been closed in a matter of weeks in 1918, Pasquale Monfri began looking for help in other places. He did not have to look very far. The year before Anna's disappearance, newspapers ran sensational stories lauding the woman they dubbed America's Mrs. Sherlock Holmes, US Special Assistant District Attorney Grace Humiston. A lawyer and investigator, Humiston had distinguished herself by helping to prosecute the peonage cases in 1906 and 1907, but it was her work on the Ruth Cruger case in 1917 that brought her to national prominence and Pasquale Monfri's attention.

Ruth Cruger was an eighteen-year-old girl who left home the day before Valentine's Day to go ice skating. She stopped to have her skates sharpened at Alfredo Cocci's shop and was never seen again. Police investigated but closed her case in a matter of weeks, believing that she ran off to elope. Her parents knew that their daughter would never leave them and called upon Mrs. Humiston to help investigate. Humiston later found the body of Ruth Cruger in the crawl space beneath Alfredo Cocci's shop. Surely Monfri could not help but see the parallels between this case and his niece Anna's case. Though Anna was almost ten years Ruth's senior and a married woman, she too disappeared out of nowhere and was accused of running off. Her case was closed quickly. Monfri had suspicions that his niece was buried in the cellar, and Ruth was found in a cellar.

Most importantly, it was clear to Pasquale that the Ridgefield Police believed that his niece was guilty of a crime. Chief McElroy painted

Mrs. Grace Humiston. *Private collection of Brad Ricca*

Anna as a disinterested wife and mother—as a woman who had abandoned her family and was therefore not worth their effort to find.

Grace Humiston, however, believed in the goodness of the girls she sought. When the police gave up on them, she believed in them. In fact, newspapers of the time attributed her great success in finding missing girls to her belief in them. The *Knoxville Sentinel* explained her success this way: "Why did Mrs. Grace Humiston ... solve the Ruth Cruger murder mystery when New York's most famous sleuths failed? Because she believed in the innate goodness of girl nature, as opposed to the police theory that most girls who leave home are bad."

Mrs. Humiston's New York law practice, the People's Law Firm, helped to find missing persons and exonerate falsely accused persons. She largely helped immigrant populations. From September to December 1917, Humiston had found 220 missing girls. Of the 383 reports of missing girls she had investigated, only 59 of those had come to her from the police department. They largely came from desperate families like Anna's. By January 1920, eighteen months after his niece's disappearance and desperate for help with her case, Pasquale Monfri sought Humiston's help as well.

Shortly after Monfri retained Humiston's services, he also took his suspicions before Justice Charles T. Mackay. Based on Monfri's complaint and Humiston's initial investigation, Frank and Salvatore Locascio were arrested at 1:00 a.m. on the morning of January 20, 1920, by Detectives Taylor and Allyn. Both Monfri and Humiston believed that Anna had been murdered and then buried in the cellar of the Paulison Avenue residence where Frank ran his barber shop. He and his brother were sent to the county jail without bail.

The local newspapers ran with the question of whether Anna was buried in the cellar and whether the clue was even investigated. On January 21, the day after the brothers' arrest, the local paper, the *Record*, reported that "It is claimed that Pasquale Monfri ... was permitted ... to dig up a part of the cellar and backyard ... but it was understood this search disclosed nothing of an incriminating nature."

The *Daily Record* contradicted this report, stating that the assistant prosecutor in the case, Charles J. McCarthy, ordered the cellar to be dug up early the following week. Three days later the paper reported that Mrs. Humiston had left her New York office for Hackensack to "press for a search of the Locascio premises"; however, a reporter from the *Evening Record* visited the home and communicated that "despite many reports to the contrary, the ground surrounding the Locascio premises had not been dug up."

By March, these cellar search rumors still persisted. The *Record* kept their readers apprised: "It is known that a few nights ago County Detective Hoffman, Chief of Police John A. McElroy, a member of Prosecutor's A. C. Hart's staff and a brother of Mrs. Locascio made a casual investigation of the premises. It is also known that the authorities interested had employed or consulted an expert in concrete work."

The reporter cautioned readers, however, that these rumors had not been confirmed and were circulating only because people had seen four men carrying candles in the cellar before Frank and Salvatore were arrested. According to the same edition of the *Record*, "It was also reported at the time of the arrest that the body ... had been buried on the premises in Ridgefield Park."

For his part, Chief McElroy tried to quash these rumors from the start. He told reporters, "I have no intention of digging up the cellar of his home or of participating in any such search of the premises."

According to Frank's later testimony, Grace Humiston, the prosecutor, and two others came to his house and searched "every inch" of the cellar with flashlights to detect the new patch of cement—which would have been eighteen months old at that point and hardly new anymore. As far as whether anyone actually dug up the cellar, reports seem to indicate that they did not have the funds nor the permission to do so. If Anna is indeed resting beneath the Paulison Avenue residence, her grave has remained undisturbed since her burial.

Prior to her work with Anna's case, Grace Humiston discussed the "mysterious" obstacles she encountered in her investigations at the hands of police. She encountered these same obstructions in Ridgefield Park when she investigated Anna's disappearance. At first Chief McElroy seemed helpful. When they originally discussed the case on the day of Frank's arrest, McElroy told Humiston and Prosecutor Huckin that the case looked rather suspicious. He quickly changed his mind, however, and blasted Humiston in the papers the following day, telling reporters, "It is an outrage if you want my frank opinion, that a woman detective can thus wreck a man's career on charges which she cannot substantiate." He further asserted, "I have known Locascio for five years and his reputation is of the best. I am thoroughly convinced of his innocence."

Further, Humiston asserted that Anna's husband Frank refused to contribute any funds to help look for his wife (not even "one dollar"). She later testified that Frank gave the reason that his wife had run away so why should he pay to look for her. When she asked if he could suggest any place that she might look to find his wife, Frank responded, "Dig in the cellar."

Although Frank acknowledged under oath that he did not provide any financial aid for his wife's search, he testified that the reason was that "he had no money to give."

Humiston attempted to search for Anna outside of the residence; however, there is still debate about how far she was able to search within the Locascio residence, if she was able to do so at all. No doubt Anna's family contacted Humiston because of their suspicion that Frank had buried Anna in the cellar. During three months in 1917 alone, Humiston discovered twenty-two cellars that housed female victims. With Humiston's influence, however, Frank Locascio was arrested on suspicion of murder, and Anna's family was finally able to have their day in court a full eighteen months after Anna's disappearance.

THE MYSTERIOUS TRUNK

In addition to reporting a mysterious chloride smell, Mrs. Fletcher also reported the presence of lime in the cellar she shared with the family. Chief McElroy explained the presence of the lime by telling the jury that Frank kept the lime about the house for use in the cellar: "Frank said it had something to do with rabbits." Mrs. Fletcher also reported a new black trunk in the cellar immediately after Anna's disappearance, implying that Frank had placed his wife's body in the trunk. During the trial, Defense Attorney DeLorenzo offered two trunks into evidence to dispel the rumor that Mr. Locascio had purchased a trunk to hide his wife's body.

Frank explained the strange coincidence in a roundabout fashion. He told the jury that his wife, Anna, had been very "careless" about the way she kept his clothes, so he decided to buy a trunk in order to keep his clothes in an orderly fashion. His friend, Lusitano, had procured a sizable trunk at a reasonable price and offered to get one for Frank. The timing was simply a coincidence.

Another strange coincidence, according to Frank, had to do with his marital mattress and bedsheets. Around the time of his wife's disappearance, Frank got rid of the mattress and all of the bed linens. He explained that they had become infested with bedbugs, and so he "wanted to get rid of them." At the same time, he decided to rent the room to earn extra money. Many times throughout the trial he complained of his poverty and the fact that his wife's family never accepted him because of it. He told the jury, "Because I have no money, I don't count with them."

FRIENDS IN HIGH PLACES

Despite Frank's troubles, he was a popular and well-liked man in Ridgefield Park. The local paper's coverage of the case indicates that the town supported Frank and his brother throughout their trial with few exceptions. After Frank completed his testimony, the local paper, the *Record*, reported, "Frank Locascio . . . concluded his own testimony this morning after denying emphatically the charge of choking her. The general opinion was that he made an excellent witness."

Indeed, from the moment of Frank's arrest the paper reported, "The general inference appears to be that no murder was committed." And in the hours before the jury had even reached a verdict, the public had already made its decision: "The people of Ridgefield Park—that is, the majority of those who attended the trial—seemed to think Frank Locascio innocent."

Throughout the trial it was made clear that Frank was good friends with the chief of police, McElroy. In fact, when Chief McElroy testified concerning the initial call about the screaming at the Locascio home, he indicated nonchalantly, "I never took the trouble to find out who sent in the call nor did I make any notes on it." He seemed almost proud of his apathy toward the case.

When Grace Humiston became involved, however, Chief McElroy made sure his voice was heard. He spoke out in defense of Frank, offering to "bet his house and lot on Frank's innocence."

The Ridgefield paper the *Daily Record* noted that Chief McElroy defended Frank "vigorously."

Apart from knowing one another for five years, what made the barber and the chief of police such good friends?

Two weeks prior to that news article, Prohibition became law in the United States. New Jersey was the last state to ratify the Eighteenth Amendment, and many stills went into operation once the country officially went dry. Frank and his brother Salvatore were known for making wine. During the trial, Chief McElroy was asked if Frank promised him wine, the implication that it would be given in exchange for his support in the case.

Prosecutor Huckin asked Chief McElroy, "Did Frank give you any wine?"

McElroy answered, "Wine was offered me, but I never got it."

Though Chief McElroy did not admit to receiving alcohol, Lawrence Lusitana admitted to receiving wine in exchange for his testimony. Lusitana, a local real estate broker and a former cavalier in the Royal House of Lusitania in Messina, testified to seeing Anna after her disappearance. He described spotting Anna on Canal Street in New York with a man described as six feet with a dark complexion and a small black mustache. Lusitana testified that Anna hid her face when she saw him. He could not recall the color of her hat or her shoes that day. It was later revealed that after Frank had signed an affidavit stating that Anna was missing, he gave Lusitana a gallon of wine in exchange for Lusitana's testimony that he had seen Anna in New York. The story later unraveled, Lusitana admitting that he could not be sure that he had in fact seen Anna at all.

HUNG JURY

The trial lasted six days, concluding on the afternoon of May 26. The jury retired at 4:05 p.m. to deliberate. An hour into their deliberations, they requested to review the Locascio children's testimony. Judge Parker denied their request, stating that it would be irregular. He suggested that the jury rely on their memory of the children's accounts.

The local newspaper, the *Record*, seemed concerned by this decision. "We thought the jurors were entitled to get all the information they needed, in justice to all concerned, and the refusal in this particular seemed a bit strange."

The jurors returned to deliberations without the testimony and remained sequestered for an additional three hours. At eight o'clock that evening they sent another message to Judge Parker. This time, they informed the judge that they could not reach an agreement. Judge Parker summoned the jurors to appear before him, at which time he asked them if they could not agree. Foreman Elliot replied that they had been trying to reach an agreement from the outset but that they had been deadlocked from the start.

Upon hearing this news, Judge Parker excused the jury and entered a verdict of disagreement. Frank Locascio was ordered to appear under a bond of $5,000 (about $75,000 today) and removed to his cell.

Various reports and rumors circulated concerning the jury's deliberations. The exact numbers notwithstanding, most accounts suggested that the majority of jurors voted to acquit, with reports of nine to three, ten to two, and eight to four circulating about town, though no one would confirm or deny these claims. The major issue for the jury was that Anna's body had never been found. They had a difficult time condemning a man based on circumstantial evidence without a body. There simply was no way of knowing whether Anna had run away or been murdered.

With the end of the trial, local reporters voiced the sentiment of the townspeople best: "We had thought a verdict either one way or the other in the Ridgefield Park murder mystery would clear the atmosphere and end all the talk concerning the disappearance of Mrs. Anna Locascio. It is doubtful if [Frank Locascio] will ever face trial again. So the mystery will simply have to die out."

Frank's response on the 1920 census perhaps confuses the matter even more. Eighteen months after his wife's disappearance, Frank listed Anna (giving her name as Antonia, rather than Antonina) as his wife, still living in the home, and provided the census taker with details of her citizenship, education, language, and heritage. Why would Frank report that his wife lived in a home that she had supposedly abandoned a year and a half before? Did he miss her and hope that she would return or were his motives more sinister?

CRIMINAL DEALINGS

Within a few years of the trial, newspapers were reporting Frank's legal troubles again. In March 1923, a seventy-year-old man entered Frank's barber shop for a shave and left with some "hooch." The man partook of a bad batch and ended up sick in his bed. He reported the incident to the police, who set up a secret sting and subsequent raid of Frank's barber shop.

At the time, Frank's brother Salvatore still worked at the shop with him. When the police raided the shop, Frank thought it was a joke. When he realized they were serious, he began speaking in Italian with his brother, but the officer in charge told Frank to speak English or shut up. Police quickly found a still made of a copper boiler concealed in a garbage can. They also found a bottle of red wine and white mule as well as numerous batches at different stages of fermentation.

Officers retrieved a gallon of mash as evidence. When they lit it up, it burned bright blue and the smell was so bad that some of the men became sick. Frank and Salvatore were both taken to the county jail where Frank made $500 bail that day ($7,500 today). Apparently, Prohibition had improved Frank's financial situation.

Chief McElroy was no longer a member of the Ridgefield police force, having been dismissed in March 1921—the year after Frank's trial. John McElroy was accused of various charges ranging from accepting bribes to driving intoxicated but was ultimately dismissed for various charges involving drunken and disorderly conduct while on duty. In light of this information, one wonders about his role in Anna's case and whether a proper investigation would have occurred under the supervision of a different chief. Considering the fact that McElroy was taking bribes and drinking on duty, one wonders if the chief wasn't also taking wine from Frank Locascio in exchange for his silence and support in Anna's case.

Frank's brother, Salvatore, also found himself on the wrong end of the law. Two months prior to the Locascio murder trial in March 1920, Otto Roth sued Salvatore after Roth's wife, Ita, fell to her death when a railing on the deck of their second story apartment gave way. Salvatore owned the apartment building where the Roths lived.

NEVER SEEN OR HEARD FROM SINCE

Though Frank and his brother saw their share of trouble in the small town of Ridgefield Park, life started anew after Anna's murder trial.

After his acquittal, Frank reopened his barber shop on Paulison Avenue. By 1922, providence (perhaps with some help from Prohibition) afforded him the opportunity to buy a plot on Main Street, where he proceeded to erect an impressive brick building. After selling his home on Paulison Avenue, Frank opened his new barber shop in the heart of the business section on Main Street. Frank owned both the property and the business. The Locascio family would remain there for many years to come, Frank's son John taking over the business after his father's retirement.

By 1930, Frank and Anna's three oldest children—Jennie, Mary, and John—had returned from the orphan asylum to live with their father again. Jennie and John worked full time to contribute to the family finances. Whereas Jennie is described as a buyer in a clothing store, John is simply listed as a "wage earner." Their given names— "Johanna," "Maria," and "John"—are provided on the census. Jennie and Mary's ages are off by a couple of years on the 1930 census, which is common in census records. Sadie, Frank and Anna's youngest child, remained at the St. Francis Orphan Asylum in Union City, New Jersey, where she lived with approximately forty-five other children until she was old enough to support herself and return home. Though Frank no longer listed Anna as living with the family in the home, he did indicate that he was still married, perhaps a hopeful man waiting for his wife to return.

For the most part, the people of Ridgefield Park moved on from Anna's story. The local papers ceased to question her whereabouts. The general consensus was that the town's residents simply needed to accept her disappearance, whatever they believed personally. Her husband had been tried for her murder and he could not be tried again. Short of Anna walking back into town, there really wasn't anything for the townspeople to do but whisper their personal beliefs as they passed by the barber shop on 180 Main Street. Even then, what good was the hushed hearsay of passersby?

Anna's family, too, gave up the public face of their cause. There is no record of the family searching the Paulison Avenue cellar, and by 1922 Frank sold the property. Grace Humiston moved on to other cases. Anna's uncle and siblings returned to the city. It is not known whether they fought the return of Anna's children to Frank, but the children were ultimately returned to his care. The only mention we have of their opinion about the case is when Anna's sister, Katie Machello, took the stand. The defense attorney asked her if she was on good terms with Frank prior to her sister's disappearance. Katie answered that they were and that she used to see Anna every other day when Anna worked in the city. The defense attorney continued to question Katie.

"You did not give Frank any pictures of your sister to help him along in his search?"

"No, he had several pictures of her." (Here she contradicted Frank's statement that he had no pictures of Anna to give to the police.)

"How did you know he didn't look for his wife?"

"He should have gone to the State and reported the case right away."

"You are mad at Frank, are you not?"

"No, I am not mad; dogs get mad, not me."

During the same segment of the trial, Anna's uncle Pasquale tells of searching for his niece in morgues. Her sister also speaks of searching for Anna. The family clearly looked for her but eventually had to give up their search. In fact, there is virtually no mention of Anna after the trial until three years later, when Frank was convicted of selling hooch at his barber shop. The paper reminds the townspeople, "Mr. Locascio will be remembered as the man who, with his brother, was on trial for the murder of his wife who disappeared several years ago and has never been seen or heard of since so far as the people in the Park have knowledge."

EPILOGUE

Three days after Anna Locascio went missing, Chief McElroy conducted a quick and superficial investigation into her disappearance, admitting that he did not create even one scrap of paper pertaining to her case. It was only through the efforts of her family that an investigation into her disappearance was reopened. The eventual murder charge against Frank was circumstantial, but the charges against him and his brother were difficult to prove without a body.

It can be argued, however, that Anna was also put on trial during these proceedings—in both the court and the court of public opinion. More often than not, the local paper referred to Anna as a "girl" rather than as a woman or a mother. When she was referred to as a mother, it was to show that she was a bad mother who wanted to leave her family. When she was referred to as a woman, she was a bad or loose woman who frequented cabarets. Frank, in contrast, was described as a "proprietor" who provided financially for his family and a "husband" who cooked and cared for them.

Newspapers blamed Anna for instigating the quarrel that resulted in her disappearance: "She became involved in a quarrel with her husband."

Further, papers cited her beauty as a precipitant to the argument and her vanishing. "She's declared to have been an attractive young woman and possessed of many friends. This may have led to the heated argument which is alleged to have taken place at the Locascio home on July 10, 1918, and which resulted in her disappearance."

Two witnesses testified to seeing Anna with men other than her husband and attempting to conceal her actions when caught. Both men recanted their testimony and admitted to receiving bribes from Frank for their testimony. These attempts were meant to besmirch Anna's reputation and paint her as an unfaithful wife and a dishonest person. Despite the retraction of this testimony, the suggestion of Anna's infidelity had been implanted in the minds of the jury, tarnishing her reputation both inside and outside of the courtroom.

This blaming-the-victim mentality permeated the entire case and was clearly exhibited in Frank's comments prior to his arrest. He told Grace Humiston, "Everyone in Ridgefield Park [is] glad [my] wife went away because she was a bad woman." And perhaps Frank convinced them. The fact remains that after Anna disappeared, Frank went on to enjoy a successful business, to raise his children, and to live a long life. He enjoyed grandchildren and even eighteen great-grandchildren. He died at age eighty-eight after operating his barber shop for sixty-five years.

Anna was not so lucky. Whether you believe she left or she was murdered, the life she had known ended when she was only twenty-seven years old. She never saw the people she loved—her children, her parents, her siblings, or her extended family—again. Her oldest child was only ten and her youngest four when she disappeared. There would be no graduations, no weddings, no grandchildren, no great-grandchildren. Not even an obituary or a resting place.

If she is indeed interred beneath the home on Paulison Avenue, she has remained there for more than a century. Perhaps it is time to find out what truly happened to Anna Locascio—to finally demand answers for a woman who has been silent and hidden for far too long.

3

AGNES TUFVERSON, 1933

I'll never rest until I know what happened to Agnes.—
Sally Tufverson

MARCH 1934: MANHATTAN

Mary Guilfoyle, a secretary for Electric Bond and Share Company, glanced nervously around the office as she threaded a piece of paper through her typewriter. Though she was anxious about writing a personal letter on company time, Mary felt that she couldn't wait any longer. She typed out the address of Miss Olive Tufverson of Detroit, Michigan. After adding a few pleasantries, Mary spilled out the worry that she and everyone else at Electric Bond and Share had been feeling during the previous month: "We have heard nothing from Agnes. And honestly I am almost crazy. People here are driving me stark mad, asking me what I have heard from her. Did you hear anything? If you have, please let me know. It seems very funny that she has written to no one here. As I said before, Agnes was never one for writing, but at the same time, I know she would acknowledge gifts, etc. Several of the men sent her flowers, etc. at the boat, and I suppose they think it rather funny that she did not acknowledge them. I couldn't begin to count the number of telephone calls, too, that have come in from friends outside."

The last time that Mary, or anyone at the company, had seen Agnes was three months before. A lawyer at Electric Bond and Share, Agnes was well-liked and respected. When she embarked on her honeymoon voyage to Europe back in December, her coworkers flooded her with gifts and flowers. Yet in three months, no one had heard one word from Agnes. Though it was true that Agnes no longer worked for the

Agnes Colonia Tufverson. *(Tacoma, Washington) News Tribune,*
March 1940

company—she had given her notice prior to her marriage—Mary knew that Agnes would have acknowledged their generosity. She also knew, in her gut, that something was seriously wrong. Trying desperately to get some kind of information, she reached out to Agnes's sister, Olive. Unsure how to close the letter, Mary urged Olive to contact her with any information about Agnes. "We are busy as the devil, and I have no business writing this during office hours, but am so anxious to hear something about Ag. So let me know please, first chance you get."

Mary sent off the letter, praying for some kind of information about her missing friend. What she did not know was that Olive also had been concerned about Agnes's lack of communication. After her sister had supposedly sailed for Europe in December, Olive and her three other sisters—Sally, Edith, and Amelia—eagerly awaited news about Agnes's honeymoon.

Ten days later, they received a New Year's telegram from Agnes: "Bad crossing. Cannot stand fog. Eyes better. Sailing from India across France. Best love to you all for the coming year."

The strange thing was that the telegram sounded nothing like Agnes. Her family chalked up the unfamiliar tone to Agnes's busy trip and thought no more about it until the weeks continued to pass without word. When Olive received Mary's letter, it validated the family's growing concern.

Everything about Agnes's marriage had been strange and worrisome. She had met her husband, Captain Ivan Poderjay, only about four months prior to their wedding. The whirlwind love affair might have seemed romantic, but the couple spent only a month together after meeting during a European trip that July. They did not meet again until November, when Poderjay came to New York, so their December 4 nuptials seemed rushed. Agnes's own family, with whom she was extremely close, had never even met the man except one brief and bizarre telephone conversation, which, in hindsight, felt quite alarming.

What did they really know about Ivan Poderjay? Only what he told Agnes. He was a retired Yugoslavian military captain living in London who had invented a new lock system that he was currently trying to sell in America and overseas. He didn't need the money, though,

Captain Ivan Poderjay. *Private collection of David and Patricia Rapp*

because Agnes told them he was a millionaire. After their honeymoon trip to India, where his missionary brother lived, they planned to live in London.

Desperate for more information, Olive dialed the London telephone number that Agnes had given her in December. A woman answered the phone, but Olive did not recognize the voice. She asked for Mrs. Ivan Poderjay, only to be told that Mrs. Poderjay was out of the country.

Olive's sister, Amelia, a registered nurse living in Canada, was the first to air her doubts. During their phone conversation with Agnes's new husband, he invited them all to stay in England. She wondered what type of man would pay for his wife's entire family to sail overseas when he had never even met them before. His gesture seemed too eager. Perhaps, her sisters countered, he was simply trying to welcome his new family. Amelia felt otherwise.

MICHIGAN'S MOST INTELLIGENT WOMAN

Agnes Colonia Tufverson was born to Swedish immigrants in Grand Rapids, Michigan, just before Christmas 1891. When Olaf and Augusta Tufverson welcomed their daughter that day, December 11, they considered their toils and travels during recent years. They hoped to provide Agnes, their first child, with an easier life and a successful path. Little did Olaf and Augusta know, as they held their newborn daughter, what tremendous success she would achieve during her short life.

Throughout Agnes's early years, her father worked as the foreman of Grand Rapids Veneer Works while her mother tended to their growing household. Augusta gave birth to two other children after Agnes, but neither of these children survived long enough to receive names. When Agnes was about five years old, however, her mother delivered a second daughter. They called the baby Edith. She was followed by Selma, known as Sally, a few years later. Amelia came along the following year.

Five days after Agnes's eleventh birthday, on December 16, 1902, the family welcomed their first son, Elmer. He, like Agnes before him, was a Christmas baby. Agnes doted on her new brother. Yet by the following Christmas, Elmer would be gone, the victim of whooping cough. His death would be the first to rock the family, but it would not be the last.

Three years later, Agnes's mother gave birth to her final child, Augusta Olive, known as Olive. By 1910, they moved into what was to become the official family home for the remainder of their lives—a spacious two-story house on 869 Tenth Street in Grand Rapids. Built in 1890, the house boasted arched doorways and built-in shelves with roomy bedrooms for the five girls.

As the oldest child, Agnes assumed adult responsibilities from an early age. By the time she was thirteen, she had to drop out of school to work full time as a sewing girl for a private family and at a local carpet and clothing factory to help with family finances. Fiercely loyal by nature—a trait also found in Agnes's younger sisters—she continued to put the needs of her family first. Yet Agnes was an unusually bright young woman and longed to find a career more suited to her intellectual pursuits.

To that end, Agnes enrolled in night school where she studied shorthand and bookkeeping. At age nineteen, she began working as a stenographer for the Grand Rapids Real Estate company Kinsey and Buys. Between working, attending night school, and caring for her family, Agnes barely slept. It seemed nearly impossible for her to add more responsibility to her busy life, yet that is exactly what Agnes had to do.

During the summer of 1912, a change was coming over Augusta Tufverson. Agnes's mother, still young at forty-four years old, did not finish her meals, threw up the little she ate, and suffered terrible stomach pains. By August, she consulted a doctor and remained under his and her family's care. Augusta was suffering from liver cancer, and she would live only another five months—just long enough to see one more Christmas with her family.

On January 2, 1913, as families across the globe rang in the new year, Augusta M. Tufverson passed away. Agnes, now the head of the family alongside her father, informed the authorities. She made plans for the burial, which took place four days later, and she chose the design for her mother's stone. The simple bevel marker includes the loving reference, "Mother."

Agnes, who had just turned twenty-one a few weeks before her mother's death, now fulfilled the role of older sister and mother to her siblings. The youngest, Olive, was only eight years old and still in need of a mother's direction and care. Even the others—aged twelve, thirteen, and seventeen—looked to their older sister for maternal direction. Agnes did not shrink from this role. She doubled down and became a mother, provider, and supporter for her entire family.

Mrs. Kinsey, owner of the real estate company where Agnes worked, recalled Agnes's first days on the job. Though Agnes knew nothing about the details of real estate, she caught on quickly. Mrs. Kinsey remembered Agnes's above-average intelligence, ability, and drive: "The real estate office was located a mile and a half from the Tufverson residence. Agnes would rise early, make breakfast for the family, and send her sisters off to school before walking to work. At noon, she would walk the mile and half home again to make lunch for the family before walking back to work for the afternoon. At the end of the day, she walked home again and resumed her nightly duties of making dinner, helping her sisters with homework, and getting them off to bed before she continued her own studies at night. Everyone admired her."

As her sisters grew into adulthood, she made sure that they, too, received additional schooling to set them up in professional careers. Amelia, Sally, Edith, and Olive all worked as stenographers, and Amelia eventually went to nursing school. During this time, Agnes's sisters claimed that Agnes was voted as "Michigan's Most Intelligent Woman."

A NEW CAREER

When war broke out, Agnes wanted to do her part. She traveled to Washington, DC, and offered her skill set. Once there, Agnes became secretary to Major Parmelee Herrick. Through this connection she met his father, banker Myron C. Herrick. Like Agnes, Herrick came from humble beginnings. Eventually, he established himself as a prominent businessman who served as governor of Ohio (1904–1906) and the US ambassador to France under two administrations. Agnes worked for him in DC and eventually became his secretary in New

A. C. TUFVERSON
ATTORNEY AND COUNSELOR AT LAW
71 BROADWAY
NEW YORK

Agnes's business card. *Private collection of David and Patricia Rapp*

York. She later worked for him in Paris during his second stint as ambassador there.

A much loved and admired political figure, especially by the French people, Herrick mentored Agnes and recognized her potential. He encouraged her to complete high school and study law while she worked for him in New York. Rooming with two other girls in Morning Heights, Agnes attended classes at City College and Columbia University with a focus on utilities. By the time of Herrick's death in 1929, Agnes was working for the Electric Bond and Share Company as a corporation/business lawyer.

Just as she had been recognized for her brilliance back home in Michigan, New Yorkers recognized her talents. In 1930, *McCall's* magazine published an article on Agnes Tufverson titled "Portia Comes East." The writer touted Agnes as "a girl who met toil, hardship, and trouble, and conquered them all single handedly." The *New York Times* described her as a "brilliant corporation lawyer."

Agnes's father, Olaf, was extremely proud of his daughter and marveled at her ambition and drive. Her sisters believed that these natural traits and her affinity for law came from their bloodline. Their grandfather acted as a lawyer back home in Sweden. He advised clients and sometimes represented them in court. It seems he passed his love of law down to his granddaughter. After years of struggle and determination, Agnes had finally earned success and lived more than comfortably. She finally had the opportunity to focus on her own happiness.

Agnes on vacation. *Private collection of David and Patricia Rapp*

Heading into her fortieth year—a prominent and self-made attorney—Agnes must have been pleased with her success. She was, however, beginning to feel her age. Her New York friends later reported that Agnes was plagued by health issues and poor eyesight. By the summer of 1933, Agnes approached her forty-second birthday. The fact that she was nearing the age when her own mother died was certainly not lost on her. Nor was the fact that Agnes was still unmarried.

Although she had no time for any serious romantic involvement, some sources suggest Agnes carried on a five-year affair with a married man who broke off the relationship at the beginning of 1933. In order to forget her heartbreak, friends suggested that Agnes travel abroad. Although there is no evidence to confirm that relationship, records do indicate that Agnes traveled abroad during the summer of 1933. That fateful European tour would change the course of her life forever.

A YUGOSLAVIAN MILLIONAIRE

On the last leg of her vacation, Agnes sailed on the *Ile de France*. The luxurious liner, called one of the most beautiful of the French line, welcomed more first-class passengers in the 1930s than any other liner. Celebrities and royals alike sailed in style in the uniquely decorated first-class cabins like the Fontainebleau (which cost about $54,000 for one week's crossing). The opulent liner contained an indoor swimming pool, a bowling alley, a theater, a chapel, and even a merry-go-round. The likes of Rita Hayworth, Lena Horne, Cary Grant, and Prince Rainier of Monaco regularly crossed on the lavish liner. Though Agnes did not travel first class, her second-class accommodations were still grand. The cabin-class salon featured a sweeping staircase, ornate tapestries, and elegant chandeliers.

The *Ile de France* docked in Plymouth, England, at the end of June 1933. Taken with a bout of seasickness on one particularly warm morning, Agnes sought fresh air on the spacious deck. A man ten years her junior, noticing the tall brunette's distress, came to her aid. He introduced himself as Captain Ivan Poderjay.

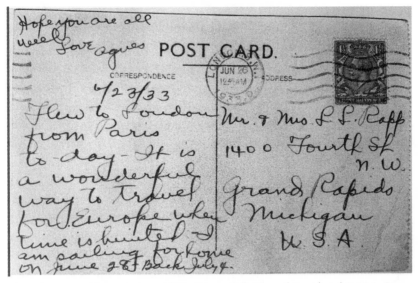

Agnes's postcard home in June 1933. *Private collection of David and Patricia Rapp*

Standing about five feet five inches tall with thick and wavy black hair and piercing gray eyes, the captain cut a dashing figure. With his large smile and friendly manner, he told Agnes that he was a retired Yugoslavian army captain currently residing in England. Regaling her with tales of his many homes, investments, and inventions, the charismatic Captain Poderjay was certainly a panacea for Agnes's ills, and not just her seasickness.

While the ship remained in port, Poderjay took Agnes through London and, in his words, "wined and dined her." Presenting himself as a millionaire, he spent nearly $10,000 in today's money on her before the two returned to the *Ile de France* and set sail for New York on June 28.

During their trip, Agnes spilled her entire life story to Poderjay—her mother's death, her family's struggles, her rise to prominence. A shrewd and knowledgeable lawyer, Agnes trusted her new acquaintance. She took his lavish spending as evidence of his independent means. Agnes admired his intelligence as he explained his new invention—a patent lock—and investment opportunities, both of which they discussed at length. When Poderjay offered to invest some of her savings, she had no reservations about trusting him with her money.

Poderjay, too, shared more of his life. Born to Ivan and Anna Podrzaj, the captain had moved to Belgrade as a youth. He enlisted in the Austrian army at age seventeen and was captured by the Italians a year later. Eventually, he became a captain of gendarmes in Yugoslavia after the war. Resigning that position, he became a personal aide to Queen Marie of Romania. He and the queen, contended Poderjay, were personal friends.

In this stunning man, Agnes found her counterpart, a millionaire with his own business and financial success. More so, she found a companion. An independent woman, Agnes had always taken care of others. For once, she wanted someone to take care of her. From the moment Captain Poderjay offered his aid on the deck of the *Ile de France*, Agnes willingly and happily submitted to him. They spent the entire six-day journey together, arriving in New York on Independence Day.

Yet behind Captain Poderjay's flashy smile was a dangerous man. Agnes, for all of her brilliance, could not see past his cunning disguise.

Ile de France at sea. *Wikimedia Commons, December 28, 2022*

Poderjay hid behind his dashing facade and lay in wait, biding his time and playing his game.

When they docked, Agnes returned to her Manhattan apartment and her Rector Street office at the Electric Bond and Share Company in New York City, but Poderjay consumed her thoughts. She eventually shared the chance meeting with her coworkers and touted Poderjay as a "clever businessman with varied interests," such as the lock he was preparing to put on the market.

During his summer stay in America, Poderjay vigorously marketed his lock invention and vigorously wooed Agnes Tufverson. Staying at the George Washington Hotel, located next to Agnes's apartment building, Poderjay doted on Agnes in a manner in which she was wholly unaccustomed. In turn, she drew up legal contracts for Poderjay's business ventures, specifically his lock invention, which he hoped to sell to a Connecticut firm. She also entrusted Poderjay with the equivalent of $100,000 in today's money to invest, perhaps in the model lock or perhaps other banking investments he touted.

ABBEY ROAD

That August, Poderjay returned to England to make adjustments to his lock, which was deemed faulty. He sought a room in an apartment house on Abbey Road in St. John's Wood. Friendly and charismatic, Poderjay cozied up to the tenants, regaling them with descriptions of his patent lock. He insisted that the lock would make a fortune for those who were wise enough to invest, focusing his attention on a retired businesswoman living in the home. Confiding that he had inside banking information from his brother, Poderjay told her that England was about to inflate its currency, thereby devaluing investments. If she was serious about making money, Poderjay suggested that she invest with him immediately. The woman, who wished to remain unidentified, gave him today's equivalent of £6,000 to help launch the lock invention on the London market.

Claiming that he had been a bank manager in Belgrade, Poderjay assured the woman, "Of course the money will be perfectly safe with me. . . . I understand everything about finance."

Poderjay eventually took over the building lease on Abbey Road and proposed another investment pertaining to Yugoslavian funds, which he claimed he and his banking brother had figured out.

"We can do it," he boasted to his boarders, "although to others it would be impossible."

The retired businesswoman gave Poderjay another £6,000 to invest in Yugoslavian currency. With the woman's government securities and retirement funds depleted, Poderjay turned to a single, middle-aged man who was living in the house. A World War I veteran who had been seriously wounded during the war, he was embarking on a singing career with funds from British war loans. Poderjay persuaded this man to "sell out his stock" to the tune of about £7,000 and invest it in Yugoslavian currency.

After bilking the residents for their worth, Poderjay implored Agnes to send him an additional $100,000. Agnes told her friend Tena Rowat that Poderjay had written asking her for this large sum of money. She also said that he further threatened to sue her for breach of promise or other publicity if she did not marry him. She confided that she was in a tight spot and a little frightened.

Agnes also told her friend Addie Smith about Poderjay's financial demands. Angered by his threats, she swore that she would "show him up." She had prepared a letter in black in white and "had it on him if he tried anything funny." Yet part of Agnes was charmed by the handsome captain.

At the end of September, she wrote to her sisters Sally and Olive. She had told them about the handsome captain when she met him on vacation that summer. She casually mentioned him again at the end of her letter.

"I don't know whether I told you or not but the friend from London went back on the 21st of August, because Yale turned him down on his locks and he had to go back to develop a new theory. He has cabled me five times, and sent me four letters. I send him a night letter. . . .

"I have a cable from him this week in which he thinks he will return in a fortnight. I don't know what to do about him. I may accept him and marry him, which means going to London to live. I don't know what to do, but I'll think some more about it, and do whatever seems best for me to do."

Floundering over her decision, she consulted another friend, Effie Shands. Sharing a picture of Poderjay, she asked Effie if she should marry him. Effie told her that he was very nice looking and she should go ahead. Decided, Agnes informed Poderjay that he would have to return to New York if he wanted additional funds. Poderjay willingly agreed, arriving back in New York at the beginning of November 1933.

POISONOUS REUNION

For all of her talk, Agnes seemed determined to marry the captain when he returned to New York in November. Eager to charm the charismatic bachelor, she embarked on a new beauty routine prior to his arrival. Agnes was known by friends to alter her appearance depending on circumstances. She donned a broadcloth tailored suit and severe felt hat in her business dealings, but she was also known to curl her auburn locks and wear feminine dresses for personal outings. To prepare for Poderjay's return, Agnes tried a new dye—known today as mascara—to darken and enhance her eyelashes. The dye was available at drugstores throughout the city for about $20 and could also be applied at local salons. Agnes's results were disastrous.

During the early 1930s, eyelash dyes were not yet regulated by the Food and Drug Administration. In November 1933, some makeup companies used hair dyes. When used as an eyelash dye, the toxic chemicals seeped into the eyeball causing, in some cases, irreparable damage and even blindness.

Poderjay, who informed his tenants on Abbey Road that he had to attend to business in America, sailed out of Liverpool on the *Britannic*, arriving in the United States on Saturday, November 11. After a nearly three-month separation, Agnes was full of anticipation. No doubt she wore her new eyelash dye as she greeted Poderjay. Within three days of their reunion, however, Agnes—like seventeen other women in the city that month—took to her bed, suffering from crippling headaches and infected eyes. During the two weeks Agnes recuperated from her infection, Poderjay played the dutiful lover. Furnishing a daily supply of flowers and little gifts, he remained at her bedside, further cementing the trust she placed in him.

Agnes's doctor, however, distrusted Poderjay. Dr. Julia Bernat met Poderjay when she attended to Agnes's eye infection. She described him as "demonical," "diabolical," and "capable of hypnotizing." When interviewed later, she reflected that Agnes seemed "giddy" and "euphoric," not her usual self.

While in New York, Poderjay wrote to his London tenants to assure them that the Yugoslavian currency deal had gone through and that he had transferred the funds to an Ohio bank to make even more profit. Still, just to ensure the safety of their investment, Poderjay implored them to send an additional £4,000 to his address in New York.

THE LITTLE CHURCH AROUND THE CORNER

By the time Agnes recovered at the end of November, Poderjay proposed marriage again. This time, Agnes said yes. Poderjay wasted no time and suggested they marry immediately—just the two of them—at the Little Church around the Corner, located just down the street from Agnes's apartment. Agnes allowed herself to be swept up in the romance of it all and agreed. She dreamed of the life she would lead as a wealthy captain's wife and turned over her trust and savings to a virtual stranger.

Marriage was not just a romantic consideration for Agnes, though, it was also an economic one. For a woman who had scraped, from the age of twelve, to support herself and her family, work became an essential part of her life. The fact that she, as a woman in the early part of the twentieth century, had risen to the professional rank she held was a testament to her drive and intelligence.

Still, Agnes considered marrying Poderjay during a time of national crisis. With the Depression in full swing, marriage work bans existed in many states. These longstanding laws barred married women from working. Even in states where these laws did not exist, professional women who worked in cities understood that they were expected to leave their jobs when they married.

Being an attorney was an essential component of Agnes's identity. Her occupation represented more than her income; it represented her persistence in the face of adversity, her devotion to her family, her intellectual needs, and her ability to succeed on her own terms. In leaving her job, Agnes placed her entire future in Poderjay's care. She believed he had the funds to support her, even though she knew that he had failed to sell his latest invention. She quit her job on Friday, December 1.

Poderjay suggested that they wed that Monday, which surprised Agnes, who had always been very close to her family. She couldn't imagine getting married without her father giving her away or without her sisters by her side. She wanted to plan her wedding and to include her friends and coworkers. She wanted everyone to meet this marvelous man. Her trust in him, however, must have been complete. She put away her own dreams and made the uncharacteristically rash decision to marry him within days of his New York arrival. She didn't even tell her family, the people with whom she normally shared everything.

On that rainy Monday, December 4, which should have foretold a long and happy union, Agnes and Poderjay made the one-mile trip to the Church of Transfiguration on East Twenty-Ninth Street, known as the Little Church around the Corner. Nestled between larger structures, the church—a blend of chapels and sanctuaries—sits back from the street and is surrounded by traditional English-style gardens. The gardens must have suggested to Agnes the ivy-covered English mansion where Poderjay described them spending the remainder of their lives.

The couple meandered through the gabled lych-gate and romantic gardens to the main church—also known as the wedding church due to the many couples who marry there each year—where they met with the church clerk, Miss Mary Hanlon.

While Poderjay filled out his portion of the marriage license (occupation: retired army officer and merchant; marriage: first), Agnes

The Little Church around the Corner, New York City. *Detroit Publishing Company, Library of Congress*

and Mary chatted. Once Agnes had filled out her family information and background, Miss Hanlon instructed them to sign the license. Poderjay wrote in large, scrawly, illegible writing above Agnes's neater legible signature.

The ceremony was performed by the rector, Randolph Ray. Miss Hanlon and the church verger, William Beckley, served as the only witnesses to the hastily organized affair. Hanlon later reported that she had never seen a happier couple.

After leaving the church, Poderjay left his lodgings on Lexington Avenue and officially moved into Agnes's apartment on Twenty-Second Street, though he had been unofficially staying there on a regular basis. Agnes's maid, Flora Miller, was wary of the change in the household. He insisted that Flora now call Agnes "Madame," though she had never called her Madame in the three years she had worked for Agnes. Also, Flora had a key with which to let herself into the apartment to clean while Agnes was at work. Poderjay told Flora she now had to ring the bell before entering because they might be "naked" at any time.

Flora later told authorities that Poderjay treated Agnes like a child. He refused to allow her to drink coffee, her daily indulgence, and insisted she drink tea instead. To force this habit, he made her strong coffee that caused her tremendous stomach cramps.

The neighbor in the adjoining apartment could hear the couple through an open window. According to this neighbor, Poderjay's attitude changed after the marriage, and one could hear Agnes respond to him over and over, "Yes, dear." or "No, dear."

While Poderjay asserted his new role, Agnes excitedly planned for the couple's honeymoon—she longed to see India and eventually return to Poderjay's English residence. Before their trip, she tended to her correspondence. That Friday, she declined an invitation to be the director of the Saturday's Children Club, telling Helen Havenor, "I am leaving the latter part of next or the week thereafter for London, England, as I expect to live the rest of my life there." She resigned from her seven-year post as a member of the New York County Lawyers' Association, citing similar reasons. Once she settled her New York affairs, it was time for Agnes to write a more difficult letter.

Part of Poderjay's charm was his total devotion. He became, in Agnes's words, "jealous of anyone close to her." For that reason, Agnes had not told the most important people—her sisters and father—about her marriage. Agnes realized that she had to tell them. After a week of putting off the inevitable, she sat down and wrote a lengthy letter to her father in which she described Poderjay's "glossy wavy hair and gray eyes" and how happy he made her.

Agnes telephoned her sisters to share the exciting news of her marriage and impending honeymoon. Poderjay picked up the receiver and charmed Agnes's sisters with tales of his English estates. He invited them to join the couple in England. When Agnes's sisters pointed out the expense, Poderjay offered to pay. He was a millionaire, after all.

Agnes's sisters laughed at the idea of her drinking tea for breakfast or a "demi-tasse without cream or sugar." They teased her, "Love is a wonderful thing."

It was not until later that Agnes's sisters noted the change in Agnes's demeanor—her dull affect on the phone and her confusing letters. Neither was indicative of her "typical, lucid style." At the time, they chalked up the change to her newfound happiness and excitement. Later, however, they wondered if Poderjay had been drugging her since his arrival in New York.

In fact, Agnes was aware that she did not feel quite right during this time and thought that she might be pregnant—though she didn't think she would feel the effects that quickly. When she and Poderjay visited with her friends, like the Wentzels, they noticed that Poderjay dominated the conversation while Agnes seemed tired. In fact, friends described her eyes as "luminous" during this time. She confided to people at the office and to other women that she felt "queer all over."

Once Poderjay arrived, Agnes acted strangely with her friends. She answered the phone in a weak voice and became indignant when questioned. When Addie Smith offered to call her back, Agnes seemed bewildered. She phoned Tena Rowat and told her she was sorry she had ever discussed Poderjay's threats.

After notifying her associates and family about her new domestic situation, Agnes settled her financial affairs. First, she closed several bank accounts: Seaman's Bank for Savings; Bowery Savings Bank; Chemical Bank; and Chase National Bank. On Friday, December 15, Agnes granted her new husband legal power of attorney and access to her safety deposit boxes. She then honored her earlier promise to Poderjay by cabling a $100,000 check in his name to London from her account at Seaman's Bank for Savings. She never would have given him the funds if she knew what he was going to do with the money. Nor would she have given him the additional $50,000 she gave him later that day.

Little did Agnes know, her perfect new husband was already married. In March 1933, three months before he met Agnes, Captain Poderjay married Suzanne Ferrand—a French medical student he met in London. She was waiting there for him, ready to deposit Agnes's money. Neither would ever divulge the next phase of their scheme.

Back in New York, Agnes and Poderjay enjoyed a Sunday evening with Agnes's friend Julia Tilinghast. As she entertained the newly-weds in her apartment, Julia noted that Agnes was "supremely happy." Little did Julia know that in a few days' time, a horrific tragedy would befall her old friend.

HONEYMOON PREPARATIONS

By all accounts, Agnes was under the impression that Poderjay had booked their honeymoon tickets on the Hamburg-American Line from New York on the afternoon of December 20. Her errands and preparations that day indicate a woman who was leaving the country. That morning, she withdrew $25,000 from her bank accounts, visited the hair salon, mailed a package to her sisters back home in Detroit, and packed her wedding trousseau full of dresses, jewels, and books on the art of love. Later that afternoon, Agnes accompanied her new husband to the Hamburg-American Line pier to embark on their hon-eymoon voyage. So why did the couple return to Agnes's apartment that evening instead of boarding the liner for their honeymoon?

The taxi driver who drove the couple to the pier indicated that the couple argued before returning to the apartment. Authorities later confirmed that Poderjay never booked tickets on the liner. Wedding gifts of fruit baskets and flowers awaited them on the pier. Agnes had already sent thousands of dollars to London. Their trunks were already packed and loaded by the ship. The argument and Agnes's disappointment must have been tremendous.

Agnes indicated to her maid, Flora, and her friend Ruth Farqu-har that they had decided not to sail because Poderjay had business he needed to attend to before they could leave for Europe. Indeed, Poderjay was quite busy purchasing various items on the evening of their December 20 departure date.

Simon Feingold reported that Poderjay entered his drugstore on 365 Second Avenue that evening in a great hurry. He spent $18 (today's equivalent of $350) on razor blades (nearly buying out the entire stock), vanishing cream, and sleeping powders. Poderjay explained to the clerk that he was traveling to Europe where such items could not be so easily procured. The law required that Feingold take down Poderjay's name and address in order to purchase the sleeping powders. Poderjay provided the necessary information and then handed over a $20 bill. Feingold gave Poderjay $4 back by mistake.

After Poderjay left Feingold's drugstore, he proceeded to another drugstore where he unsuccessfully attempted to buy twenty gallons of sulfuric acid. Before returning to the apartment that evening, he also bought large quantities of brown wrapping paper.

Later that evening, Feingold realized that he gave Poderjay the wrong change and stopped by Agnes's apartment after work to retrieve the difference. Poderjay answered the door, but he only opened it an inch or so. Feingold did not see Agnes, as Poderjay blocked any view of the apartment while he returned $2 to the druggist.

Flora Miller, the maid, last saw Agnes at around 11:00 p.m. According to Flora, Agnes was seated in the living room with her hand on her chin. The table had been set for a midnight snack. Before that, Poderjay and Agnes were sorting through papers. Agnes told Flora to come back the following day, but Poderjay told her to come back the day after that. She testified that Poderjay told her, "Flo, we are going away. We won't need you for some time. When we return, I will send for you." Flora looked to Agnes, who didn't seem to understand what Poderjay was saying.

"She just sat there," Flora recalled, "with her legs crossed and her right hand on her chin, as if she didn't know what he was saying. She just stared straight ahead."

After Poderjay closed the door, no one knows what happened in that apartment. What we do know is that after the night of December 20, no one ever saw Agnes Colonia Tufverson again.

The following day, Poderjay asked Sam Lipkin—the elevator man in Agnes's apartment building—where he might purchase a large trunk. Lipkin directed Poderjay to Third Avenue where Poderjay obtained a large brass-bound metal trunk. At 7:00 p.m. that evening, he arrived and insisted on carrying it to the apartment himself, which upset and confused the apartment building staff, both because it was their job to carry such items and because they often received tips for doing so.

At noon on December 22, Flora Miller returned to the apartment to find Poderjay going through Agnes's papers. He told Flora that Agnes had gone to Philadelphia for a day or two on business. He handed over Agnes's papers to the maid and ordered her to burn them in the apartment building incinerator.

Flora noticed Agnes's wedding trunk in the corner, along with Poderjay's trunks, and an unfamiliar trunk. With an eerie feeling, Flora worked quickly and almost tripped over the trunks in an effort to leave the residence. She had been worried about Agnes since Poderjay's arrival. Agnes's lavish spending, which was not characteristic of her thrifty employer, concerned Flora. In fact, in slightly more than a month since Poderjay's arrival, Agnes had cleared today's equivalent of more than $1,000,000 from her bank account (leaving a balance of only about $300).

Flora's gut told her that Agnes had not gone to Philadelphia. She stared at Poderjay as he barreled through Agnes's private belongings. The air in the apartment felt oppressive and stale. Flora could hardly breathe. She knew something terrible had happened. Finishing her work quickly, she hastily left the apartment.

After Flora's departure, Poderjay forwarded all of Agnes's mail to his London address. He also emptied Agnes's safety deposit box and cashed in her bonds, which were worth more than $350,000. Poderjay then hired a truck driver from a warehouse across the street to transport his luggage to the pier for his voyage on *The Olympic*. Explaining Agnes's disappearance, he told the staff that she had gone ahead to Canada and would meet him in England.

Just before he was slated to sail, Poderjay phoned the front desk for assistance in transporting his luggage—four large trunks (one of which was new) and six pieces of hand luggage.

As the building staff loaded up the rental truck and the driver prepared to depart, Poderjay jumped in the passenger seat of the rental truck. The driver looked at him in surprise, but Poderjay just smiled.

"I don't want anything to happen to the luggage," he explained. "It is very important to me."

The driver shrugged and proceeded to the pier, where Poderjay oversaw the lowering of three trunks into *The Olympic*'s storage hold.

He then ordered the new trunk to be delivered to his stateroom, C86. From that point on, he never let the trunk out of his sight.

THE MYSTERIOUS TRUNK

As *The Olympic* set sail at 10:00 p.m. that evening with 273 passengers for its six-day journey to Cherbourg and then Southampton, Poderjay remained in his stateroom, where he had settled himself since he arrived on the liner. His outside cabin on C deck did not have a promenade, which meant that Poderjay's porthole opened directly to the sea. Dressed in his usual dapper manner—a blue striped suit and spats—Poderjay positioned himself next to the trunk and ordered his meals in his room.

The cabin steward, Ernest Churcher, remembered Poderjay and his eccentric manner. He told authorities that "From the time he came aboard, he remained in his cabin, and had his meals there." Churcher also verified that Agnes Tufverson never came aboard the ship.

According to the steward, Poderjay was a chatty and colorful character who had sailed with them before. Whereas some stewards insisted that Poderjay always stayed in his cabin during overseas trips, others testified that it was unusual behavior for the social and charismatic Poderjay. Regardless, he held court from within his stateroom on this trip and regaled the staff with talk of his latest invention—a type of safe that would sell for $1,000,000. He was traveling back to England, he told them, where he hoped to have better luck marketing the product. While drinking double gins, he flashed $10 and $20 bills to show off his wealth and shared details of his romantic life. Poderjay confided to Churcher that he was presently married to two women—a woman in London and another in Czechoslovakia. His Czechoslovakian wife was Seifka Bradaritch. She and Poderjay were married seven years before in Belgrade.

Being married to two women at the same time did not seem to bother Poderjay because, as he told Churcher, neither his British nor his Czechoslovakian marriages were recognized outside of those countries. He failed to share that he had recently married Agnes as well. He simply referred to her as a woman friend he had left behind in New York. He concluded by telling Churcher, "Old chap—you know it's quite odd. I'm married . . . and I haven't got a wife."

Though he appeared relaxed and casual with the crew, they all noticed his strange behavior concerning the black trunk in his stateroom. He was extremely protective of the nearly four-foot-high trunk. The cabin stewards wondered what it contained and surmised that the contents must be extremely special or perhaps illegal.

On the second day of the voyage, Churcher pressed Poderjay to open the trunk. Though he refused to divulge its contents, Poderjay did open the trunk around noon to retrieve a necktie and a drawing to assuage the staff. He remained cheerful and sociable throughout the trip.

When *The Olympic* docked in Southampton on December 28, Poderjay's luggage and trunks would have been searched as he traveled through customs. Steward Churcher remembered a short blonde woman meeting Poderjay at the pier. She was none other than Poderjay's French wife, Suzanne Ferrand. Taking the luggage, they retreated to Poderjay's London address, 31 Westbourne Grove, the address to which Agnes had forwarded most of her money and the one where she had planned to live as Poderjay's wife.

BEST LOVE TO YOU ALL

Prior to her departure, Agnes had phoned her sisters to let them know about her honeymoon plans. According to Agnes, the couple were sailing to Europe and then India. Agnes's sisters assumed that Agnes was on her honeymoon and eagerly awaited word from their newly married sister.

With the arrival of the new year and still no word from Agnes, her family became concerned. Shortly thereafter they received a strange telegram that only heightened their worry, for its short and stilted tone sounded nothing like their Agnes: "Bad crossing. Cannot stand fog. Eyes better. Sailing from India across France. Best love to you all for the coming year."

There were reports of a second telegram, a version of the original telegram, which read, "Cannot stand climate. We are now on our way to India. Will cable and write later. Agnes." Her sisters never confirmed reports of this second telegram.

The original cable, however, raised suspicions. Agnes always wrote long and detailed letters with stories and descriptions of her New York life or her travels. The cable, with its short sentences and formal tone, did not read like anything Agnes had ever sent to them before. As strange as they found Agnes's honeymoon telegram, though, the entire wedding had been bizarre and uncharacteristic. Her sisters decided to wait for more correspondence.

Meanwhile, Poderjay and his "French wife," as he called her, were busy rifling through Agnes's wedding trousseau. They had Agnes's dresses recut for Ferrand, who was significantly shorter than Agnes. They also took one of Agnes's silver candy boxes to a jeweler to remove Agnes's initials and replace them with Suzanne's.

Accosted by his Abbey Road tenants, Poderjay at first assured them that their money was safely housed in a Cleveland bank. Within a week or so, however, he returned to the boardinghouse, claiming that due to unforeseen circumstances, they could lose the whole of their investment if Poderjay did not return to America right away to deal with the bank. He needed £6,000 for travel expenses. So convincing was Poderjay's urgent pleas that the businesswoman borrowed the money from her brother and gave it to Poderjay. For added assurance, Poderjay drew up IOUs and other documents outlining his debts to his tenants before disappearing again.

Poderjay was an expert con man, and the Abbey Road tenants were just one of the many schemes he was working at the time. He had, as he told them, worked as an official in a Serbian bank; however, he was kicked out of that business, just as he had been kicked out of business school. The affable captain also had worked stints as a fortune teller, saloon keeper, and adventurer besides volunteering for the army and serving with the Belgrade police. At the moment, he was posing as a retired military captain and inventor of independent means in order to bilk unsuspecting people out of their hard-earned money.

The next time the tenants heard from Poderjay, he informed them that he had transferred their funds to a bank in Belgrade but that the Belgrade bank refused to release the funds. In May 1934, the victims took their case to Scotland Yard, but by that time Poderjay was long gone. The London paper *John Bull*, reported: "Naturally it was foolish for the retired business woman and the struggling singer to have trusted this foreigner. They realize that themselves now, but they were impressed by the manner of the man, and led astray in their judgement by his falsehoods. It is easy for all of us to be wise after the event."

Perhaps the same can be said for Agnes Tufverson, who was certainly no fool. Yet, in the face of love, she lost more than her savings. Three months had passed since Agnes went missing, but no one realized she was missing. Her family and her office mistakenly thought Agnes was traveling abroad. They would soon realize, however, that Agnes never even made it to her honeymoon.

THE FOUR FURIES

Around this time, Mr. Tufverson had an alarming dream. He was walking through a large green field—a beautiful field. He saw his late wife, and then he saw his oldest daughter, Agnes, standing next to her. The two women beckoned to Olaf, asking him to join them. When he woke, Mr. Tufverson feared the worst for his daughter. He shared the dream with one of his other daughters, Amelia.

Amelia had a psychic experience of her own concerning Agnes. She tried but failed to shake the hollow feeling that something horrible had happened to her sister. When her father shared his dream, she knew that Agnes was gone. She picked up her telephone receiver and began to dial, first Sally and then Olive.

During the three months since they had heard from Agnes, they had written numerous letters to the address Agnes had given them in London, but they had received no replies. That in itself was unusual and cause for alarm. Ever since Agnes had left home for Washington, DC, and later Manhattan, she wrote regularly to her family in detailed and loving letters. Often, she sent little gifts or money. Yet for three long months, they had received no word. When Agnes failed to return to America to handle a transfer of stock for the Electric Bond and Share Company, for which she was counsel, the Tufverson family took Amelia and Mr. Tufverson's premonitions seriously and feared the worst. Amelia learned to trust her psychic intuitions long before.

"I'm psychic," she later explained in an interview. "I have hunches sometimes and they always turn out to be right. I had a hunch something had happened to Agnes. I telephoned Olive and Sally. They laughed at me at first, but it was three months since they had heard from her—and finally they believed me. I couldn't do anything because I just bought a house and we didn't have any money. Sally and Olive, single and working, had more time and money than I did."

Olive cabled the London address Agnes had given her and was told that "Mrs. Poderjay" was in Vienna. The three sisters then agreed that one of them needed to travel to New York to investigate. Olive volunteered.

By the middle of May 1934, the sisters had contacted John H. Ayers, the captain of the New York Police Department's Bureau of Missing Persons to report Agnes's disappearance. Olive learned from the staff in Agnes's building that Agnes never sailed with Poderjay and had, in fact, gone ahead to Canada. She also learned that Poderjay sailed alone for England two days later.

Olive confirmed this information. First, she checked the passenger list on *The Hamburg*—the liner on which Agnes and Poderjay were slated to sail for their honeymoon. Neither Agnes nor Poderjay appeared on the passenger list. She then checked with the White Star Line to see if Poderjay sailed alone to England on another ship. She found that he had indeed sailed alone for England two days later. Next, she checked the White Star Line's passenger lists for Agnes's name. Was it possible she sailed alone as well? She looked at weeks' worth of lists with no luck. Agnes, as far as Olive could tell, had not left New York by boat.

Olive then turned her attention to Agnes's bank accounts and stocks. She knew her sister had depleted her accounts because she transferred her money to England, where she planned to live. At the time, that made perfect sense to her family. If Agnes were not living in England, however, the transactions no longer made sense. Why would Agnes transfer all of her money and stocks to a place she did not intend to go? A darker thought entered Olive's head. What if her sister had intended to go to England but never made it?

Olive shared this information with her sisters. Speaking of these early days in the investigation, Amelia noted, "I was suspicious of Poderjay from the first. I had read about such men, and I did not like him." At first, Olive and Sally did not want to think that the charming captain had done anything to harm their sister; however, as they investigated further into their sister's disappearance, Poderjay's stories did not make sense.

Through Olive's investigation, they learned that Agnes had supposedly gone to Canada. None of them believed that story. Sally later told papers, "If she was going to Canada that day, as he says, do you think she'd have left her fur coat behind? I know she had no other fur coat because she had sent two coats out to us in Detroit. And the 20th of December was a sleety, cold, and miserable day."

Investigators confirmed what Olive had already feared—Agnes never reached the London address where she planned to live with Poderjay. In fact, even if she had gone to Canada as Poderjay said, there were no transatlantic liners leaving Canada at that time. Agnes would not have been able to sail for England from Canada.

If she did not travel to Canada or England and no one had seen Agnes for more than four months, where was she? Where was Poderjay? Her sisters were incredulous that Agnes could have simply

The four furies: Agnes's sisters: Olive, Sally, Amelia, and Edith. *Private collection of David and Patricia Rapp*

disappeared. Edith spoke for the family: "We are afraid for my sister. Living persons do not vanish into the air."

They started running over all of the strange events that they had tried to brush away earlier. They now recalled the horrible stomach cramps Agnes had been suffering from the time of her wedding, which they had thought were caused by the strong coffee or the tea she was drinking at the time. They recalled that Poderjay had administered Agnes's medication after her eyelash dye poisoning, and they wondered if he had been drugging Agnes. If their sister had been doped, it would explain uncharacteristic decisions she had been making during that time period.

Suzanne Ferrand. *Tacoma Daily News Ledger, October 11, 1936*

They thought about the New Year's cable supposedly written by Agnes. The strangely worded cable had concerned them. They were now certain that Captain Poderjay had written the note. Why had he written a note pretending to be Agnes unless Agnes could no longer write a note herself—unless Agnes was seriously injured or, worse, dead?

Realizing that they would have to find Captain Poderjay for more information, New York authorities expanded their search. They enlisted the help of Scotland Yard and other European law enforcement agencies. Due to Poderjay's schemes on Abbey Road, British authorities were already well acquainted with the captain. By the time the New York Police Department sought him in London, however, Poderjay was long gone. So was his "French wife" Suzanne Ferrand.

Eventually, both Sally and Olive left their well-paying jobs to search for their sister full time. Mr. Tufverson gave them the little money he had, and they funded the rest of the expenses themselves. When their money ran out, they borrowed more. Their father helped in the search, but it was the Tufverson sisters who fought with an unrelenting vengeance to find their sister and to make the person responsible pay.

MANY MYSTERIOUS ANGLES

By early June, the case made national headlines. In Detroit, Olive told newspapers, "The police have asked me not to discuss this in any way. I am afraid it is very serious." Olive returned to her job as a secretary for an automobile agency in Detroit. It was Sally's turn to head to New York to continue the investigation, and she left on Thursday, May 30, for the city.

On the evening of Sunday, June 3, Olive received a telegram from Sally regarding the investigation. When pressed by reporters about the contents of the telegram, she sighed, "There is plenty more to say, but I just can't talk in the face of this message. We'll know all about it in a couple of days."

Sally's first stop was her sister's apartment on East Twenty-Second Street. She thought that if she searched hard enough, she might be able to find a document indicating her sister's whereabouts. Agnes kept meticulous records. Sally searched through her desk and her bedroom without any luck. Eventually, she sifted through couch cushions and under rugs. Like Agnes, her papers had disappeared. The only evidence Sally found was a piece of paper bearing the London address where she planned to live. This was not news to Sally, as Agnes had given her and her sisters this same address.

The following day, Monday, June 5, the Tufverson family and the NYPD enlisted the help of the Grand Rapids Police Department in their investigation. Olive and her father, Olaf, met with police and provided them with all of the information they had at the time concerning Agnes's marriage and finances.

Agnes's father Olaf pleaded with the police, "We are anxious, very anxious, for our girl."

Captain John Ayers headed New York's Missing Persons Bureau. He told reporters that the case was "the most perplexing of 350,000 cases on which he had worked." He was aided by numerous detectives, notably Arthur C. Johnson, who had worked on the Lindbergh kidnapping case. In addition to Scotland Yard, New York authorities enlisted the help of Austrian authorities.

The Tufverson sisters also appealed to Agnes's former firm, the Electric Bond and Share Company. A young lawyer there, one of Agnes's friends, agreed to travel to Europe to investigate on their behalf. When pressed by reporters, he told them, "I am not at liberty to discuss the case, because frankly, there are many mysterious angles. We think London will be a good bit interested. Certain things connected with this story couldn't be broadcast."

On the morning of June 7, unbeknown to the Tufverson family or New York detectives working on the case, two young canoeists made a gruesome discovery by the Old Ferry Point rocks in Long Island Sound—the badly beaten and decomposed body of a woman. They reported their discovery, and the body was taken to the Fordham Morgue in the Bronx where Thomas Rogers prepared the unidentified woman's body.

At that point, everyone involved in Agnes's investigation knew that the fastest way to uncover her whereabouts was to find her husband. Having learned in London that Poderjay was in Vienna, authorities sought the help of the police force there. After a week of newspaper headlines featuring titles like "Silence Surrounds Search for Woman," Ivan Poderjay's whereabouts were finally revealed.

HE WILL HAVE A LOT TO ANSWER

On June 12, 1934, authorities located Captain Ivan Poderjay living in a luxurious seventeen-room apartment in Vienna with Marguerite Suzanne Ferrand. When police questioned Poderjay about his wife, he denied that he had ever married Agnes Tufverson. Authorities pressed the captain to explain just what type of relationship he had with the attorney.

Under pressure, Captain Poderjay admitted that he knew Agnes. "I know her, all right. I met her on the boat last year going to America."

He continued to deny, however, that he had married her or that he was ever even engaged to her. Why, questioned authorities, would Agnes think that Poderjay was her husband? She was a smart woman, they reminded him. How could she mistake being married? Captain Poderjay waved his hand in a friendly manner to explain.

"American women always get such ideas in their heads. You know American women."

As he explained the naivete of American women, a French woman sat by his side. Authorities wanted to know who she was and what she was doing in Poderjay's apartment. She was a friend, Poderjay assured them. He was not married to her, either, he explained, nor did she live with him. He actually dared the authorities to prove otherwise.

Taking on that challenge, a representative from the *Daily Herald* in London located the record of Poderjay and Ferrand's March 1933 marriage in the Paddington Register Office. On the certificate, Poderjay is described as "Ivan Poderjay, aged 33, a bachelor, a captain (Jugoslav) retired, and of independent means." Ferrand is given as, "Marguerite Ferrand, a 37-year-old spinster of independent means."

Residents in St. John's Wood also identified Ferrand as Poderjay's wife.

When the Tufverson family received word of Poderjay's statements, Olive made a statement of her own to the press, "His denials are ridiculous. My sister, Sally, in New York, has kept me informed on everything the police there have accomplished and they have made very good progress on the case. He will have a lot to answer."

Indeed, New York authorities easily confirmed Poderjay and Tufverson's marriage at the Little Church around the Corner on December 4, 1933. The church secretary, Miss Hanlon, furnished documentation and described the ceremony to police: "The marriage was absolutely informal. They walked in and asked for two witnesses. I was one. Verger William Beckley the other. The ceremony was performed by Dr. Randolph Ray, rector of the church."

When asked about the couple's honeymoon plans, Hanlon considered and replied, "I believe they left a few days after the marriage, if not the next day. They told me they were going to England, and to Austria to visit his relatives and then to India to see Poderjay's brother who, he said, was a missionary there."

When pressed concerning Agnes's whereabouts, Poderjay offered several possible scenarios: "She may have gone to India or on a world tour. She often told me she was fed up with her family to whom she was giving money monthly. A year ago she had a nervous breakdown. If she had disappeared she probably wanted to get away from worries. Last year everybody in America was worried about what would happen to her money. She is a lawyer and she can take care of herself."

Captain Poderjay, who posed as Agnes's friend, even hinted that, based on what he knew of Agnes, she could have taken her own life. He blamed her family for her troubles.

Agnes's sisters were quick to respond. Her sisters flatly denied the idea that Agnes was suicidal. This time, Edith, now Mrs. Lester R. Rapp of Grand Rapids, came to her sister's defense. "One thing we are certain; that is, Agnes never would take her own life. She was of optimistic disposition, she had won success in life and had everything to live for. Anyway, she is just not the type to commit suicide."

Though the police had considered this theory, Olive refused to buy it and told police that if anything had happened to her sister, it was because of an accident or foul play. She said that Agnes had never even been interested in men until she met Poderjay, and she had always had a happy disposition: "The thought of suicide was never in her makeup. Agnes was the one member of our family always in a cheerful mood. She had everything to live for. She was a success in her profession and had plenty of money."

Suzanne Ferrand, who admitted to meeting Agnes, tried to portray her as a dramatic and nervous type. She told police that "our friend, Miss Tufverson," was "a hysterical type" and "constantly threatening suicide."

When Captain Poderjay was confronted with evidence of his two wives, he admitted to marrying Agnes. He indicated, however, that it was a marriage in name only. Agnes, he said, had begged him to marry her. She was a spinster, he told them, frightened that she would never wed. She wanted to secure her place in society. As a gentleman and friend, he agreed to help her.

So what happened on the evening of December 20, when he was supposed to sail to England with his bride? Poderjay had a ready answer. Agnes wanted to sail as his wife even though she knew he was already married. When he refused, she became hysterical. He decided that he could not sail with her in that state. They eventually decided it was best for him to sail alone.

Sally told newspapers that Poderjay's story about marrying Agnes to save her from spinsterhood was "a damn lie!"

Police questioned Captain Poderjay and Suzanne Ferrand separately, and the two gave contradictory statements from the start. One of the first questions posed by police concerned the lavish apartment in which the couple lived. How did they afford the seventeen-room setup? Ferrand claimed that she furnished the funds with income she earned on properties she owned in France. Captain Poderjay, however, told police that he had used a $600,000 cash gift that Agnes Tufverson had given him before their New York wedding.

Due to Poderjay's many contradictory statements concerning his relationship with Agnes and her whereabouts, Austrian police arrested him in Vienna on June 15 and held him pending the investigation into Agnes's disappearance. Once they had Poderjay in custody, they kept a close watch on Suzanne Ferrand.

Within a couple of days, detectives observed Ferrand leave the flat with a parcel. When they noticed that she was trying to get rid of the parcel, they confronted her. Ferrand became very nervous, and police followed her into the residence. They questioned her about a green trunk in the apartment. Reports began to circulate that there had been small spots of blood found in the lining of the trunk.

In New York, police released Agnes's description: age, forty-three; height, five feet six inches; weight, 135 pounds; hair, dark brown bob; and eyes, dark blue. New York Assistant District Attorney James T. Neary spoke to reporters concerning Captain Poderjay's arrest. He emphasized that they had no evidence that Captain Poderjay had committed a crime.

On Saturday, June 15, Thomas Rogers viewed Agnes Tufverson's picture and story in a New York newspaper. He considered the unidentified woman in his morgue and believed that it might be Agnes. He reported that the woman, whose head had been smashed and badly bruised, was likely murdered and possibly the woman for whom police had been looking. The New York homicide squad alerted Sally Tufverson and asked her to accompany them to the morgue to view the body.

Meanwhile, police in Vienna investigated the contents of the trunk found in Poderjay's apartment. They found a fur coat and a black velvet jacket, dresses, negligees, and jewels (including a striking amber necklace). At first, Ferrand denied any knowledge of the articles, but when pressed she acknowledged that the items belonged to Agnes Tufverson. In fact, while she was being interviewed by police, Suzanne was wearing a red dress that belonged to Agnes.

A further search yielded books inscribed with Agnes's name—one on the art of love and another on birth control. In addition, they found objects like Agnes's typewriters. They learned that Ferrand had been wearing items from Agnes's wedding trousseau, including her negligees. She had even been wearing Agnes's wedding ring. Ferrand tried to convince police that Poderjay told her he had not married Agnes. They were, according to Poderjay, simply good friends. In fact, according to Ferrand, Agnes gave her trunks and belongings to Poder-jay as a gift. Police leaned on Ferrand to divulge Agnes's whereabouts, and she claimed that Poderjay told her Agnes was supposed to be traveling on a world cruise.

Authorities promptly arrested Ferrand. While in prison, Ferrand was made to try on all of the dresses that she originally claimed as her own. Many were found to be too big for her and the ones that did fit her showed evidence of tailoring. Ferrand eventually admitted that Poderjay had married Agnes: "I knew Miss Tufverson. I met her in Jugo-Slavia when she was there last year. She was a charming woman but hysterical and exalted. If women were unhappy, Ivan tried to comfort them. He had some business to settle in New York and that was where our friend, Miss Tufverson, lived. She was looking for a husband and unfortunately, she fell in love with mine."

In England, Scotland Yard detectives investigated the Southamp-ton docks and sought evidence concerning the large black trunk that Poderjay reportedly kept with him on his journey to England. They also searched the Bayswater, London, studio that Agnes gave as her last forwarding address.

AGNES'S BRIEFCASE

In New York, Agnes's sisters learned that her belongings were found in Poderjay's Vienna apartment. Among those belongings was Agnes's briefcase. When they heard about the briefcase, the Tufverson sisters faced the worst day of the search thus far.

To them, the briefcase signaled their sister's death. The briefcase, marked with Agnes's name, was like her talisman. She had purchased it while she was still struggling and continued to use it throughout her professional life. No matter what, Agnes would never have gifted or parted with the briefcase.

Olive told reporters, "The briefcase has never been out of my sis-ter's hands. It was more than just a good luck piece to her. It was a symbol of her success in New York and it meant everything to her. If she were alive, it would be with her."

In a candid moment, Olive admitted, "I know that Agnes is not alive, and I am not afraid of that now. I am more afraid that we will never know; that Captain Poderjay will never talk. I know he can, and so does Sally."

On June 19, Viennese police told newspapers that "Captain Poderjay and Mlle. Ferrand know much more about Miss Tufverson's fate or present whereabouts than they have admitted so far."

A CHAMBER OF HORRORS

With Poderjay and Ferrand behind bars, authorities searched their seventeen-room apartment and found disturbing evidence that added yet another twist to an already perplexing case. Within the apartment, police discovered a secret sadomasochist torture chamber where Ferrand would "chain Poderjay to the floor and abuse him." The room was decorated with erotic images. The police found bludgeons, whips, rods, and tongs, as well as pornographic photographs stored within cabinets. They also found stacks of erotic drawings that Poderjay himself had sketched.

They began to wonder if Miss Tufverson had been fatally injured during some kind of erotic torture session. Had it all been an accident? Had she died in the apartment during some sexual ritual gone wrong? They continued to search through the apartment for clues and evidence.

Three days later, on June 22, they discovered a stash of letters between Suzanne Ferrand and Captain Poderjay. In these letters, Poderjay referred to Suzanne as his "mistress" and signed the letters "slave." Of particular concern to police, though, was one letter that Suzanne wrote to Poderjay while he was in New York with Agnes: "Get money—no matter how—but somehow get lots of money to enable us to live as we may desire."

The contents of the letters revealed a warped and sinister couple who ridiculed the women whom Poderjay seduced and conned. He detailed his love affairs with other women to Ferrand, making fools of the women in his correspondence. He and Ferrand made particularly derogatory references to Agnes. It was reported that Poderjay also created erotic drawings of his sexual relationship with Agnes and sent these to Ferrand.

When Assistant District Attorney Vincent Impelitteri arrived in Vienna with New York detectives, the chief of police let him read some of these letters, warning him, "This man is a sadist and a masochist of the worst kind. I'd like to give you one piece of advice, Mr. District Attorney, whatever you do when you get him back to America, don't give him the third degree. He'd love it."

Police looking into Suzanne Ferrand's background found that before she met Poderjay in England, she had been romantically linked with an Englishman, Captain Frederick Davey. Some reports even suggested that she was married to Davey. At the very least, they lived together. Strangely, Captain Frederick Davey disappeared at the same time that Ferrand started her relationship with Captain Poderjay in 1933. In fact, Davey—like Agnes—was officially listed as a missing person.

Was Poderjay just a sadistic con man or was he also a murderer? If he did murder Agnes or Captain Davey, did Suzanne Ferrand know? Was she part of it? Detectives asked themselves these questions as they tried to piece together Captain Poderjay's disturbing and curious exploits.

Scotland Yard, which continued to work on the case, uncovered more marriages and romantic entanglements. Their dossiers indicated that Captain Poderjay had abandoned two fiancées in Belgrade and one in Nevada.

A CATALOG OF CRIMES

While Poderjay bided his time in prison, authorities continued to uncover his lengthy trail of crime. Numerous countries vied for their turn to try Poderjay. Vienna police wanted to extradite him to Serbia for bilking a Belgrade business house out of nearly $150,000 in today's money. Danish authorities also wanted Poderjay on swindling charges, and Scotland Yard still wanted Poderjay to answer for his criminal activities in St. John's Wood, as well as the disappearance of Captain Davey.

Meanwhile American authorities suspected Poderjay of murdering Agnes Tufverson, but without proof they had no means to extradite him. Vienna police had no concrete reason to hold Poderjay except on bigamy charges. Unless authorities could prove that Captain Poderjay figured in Agnes Tufverson's disappearance, they would have to let him go. Agnes's sisters, who by this time were convinced that Poderjay had murdered their sister or, at the very least, was involved in her disappearance, knew that if Poderjay was released, they would never get answers about or justice for their sister.

Captain Poderjay, an amiable and talkative man, continued to claim innocence and spin explanations. He told police that when he met Agnes, she was suicidal over the end of a love affair. He felt sorry for her and married her to make her happy. As to Agnes's whereabouts, Captain Poderjay provided many possibilities.

At first, Poderjay claimed that Agnes had indeed sailed on *The Hamburg*. When confronted with his lie, Poderjay admitted that she had not sailed. Agnes had in fact traveled to Montreal on business and had planned to meet him in London later, he explained. She had business in Montreal, where she planned to convert her gold into £1 notes. She left on December 20 and promised to contact him when she reached Canada, but he never heard from her. When confronted with the fact that there were no vessels sailing out of Montreal at the time, Poderjay simply shrugged his shoulders.

With time, Poderjay changed this story yet again. He maintained that he and Agnes were married in name only, and then he told authorities that they never argued at the pier. Rather, they parted as friends. In fact, they were such good friends that Agnes gave him all of her belongings—clothes, jewelry, handbags, and so forth. In addition to these, she had also given him one gold and one silver piece by which to remember her. She had also given Poderjay $30,000 ($600,000 today) to invest on her behalf. Poderjay then admitted that he was concerned for her well-being when he last saw her. He told police that she was on the verge of a nervous breakdown.

Even though she showered Poderjay with her money and belongings, he maintained that Agnes had sufficient funds to enable travel, citing two thousand gold pieces and $50,000, which were in her possession when they last met. He insisted that Agnes was alive and would come to his rescue when she learned of his arrest.

As for where she went, he insisted that she traveled to India to escape her troublesome family and poor health. She then planned to travel the world alone and left him with these words, "If you don't hear from me in a month, I'll be dead."

When asked about the cable that Agnes sent to her family on January 1 purporting to be on her honeymoon with Poderjay, he admitted to writing the cable. He insisted that Agnes asked him to write to her family in a month so that they would not worry. He later said that he decided to write the letter: "I admit that I sent that telegram to Agnes' sisters in Detroit. I wanted to give them the impression that nothing had happened to mar the happiness of Agnes' honeymoon."

THE BLACK TRUNK

Sally returned from her visit to the Fordham Morgue convinced that the badly beaten body was not her sister. Her relief must have been great but momentary. Within days another body surfaced, this time in Brighton, England. And this time, police found the body in a trunk.

Ever since hearing of Captain Poderjay's mysterious and obsessive behavior over the trunk he took aboard *The Olympic*, police had been searching for the large black trunk, which was delivered to Southampton. On June 17, a black trunk was found about sixty miles away in the luggage section of the Brighton Railway Station, and the contents proved alarming. Within the trunk, British police found a woman's torso. The body was wrapped in two types of brown paper, presumably like the paper Captain Poderjay purchased on the evening of December 20. There were no wounds on the body, except for those where the head, legs, and arms had been severed with a saw. The legs were later found in London.

Police estimated that the woman was about forty years of age. She was also pregnant. The stillborn body of a baby girl was found nearby in the railway station, but police later revealed that the two bodies were unrelated. Though police at first believed that they had finally found

Agnes, they quickly determined that the torso did not belong to the missing woman. First of all, they estimated the height of the woman in the trunk to be five feet two or three, clearly not near Agnes's five-feet-six height. Also, Agnes underwent an abdominal operation in 1928. Upon autopsy, it was determined that the body showed no evidence of any such operation.

Police continued searching for the fourth trunk, convinced that it contained the answers for which they were searching. Captain John Ayers explained the significance of the trunk to reporters: "We have accounted for three trunks and we are at work now tracing a fourth one. We know that Miss Tufverson had two trunks and that after the wedding at the Little Church around the Corner, Poderjay brought a third trunk to Miss Tufverson's apartment. We know definitely that the truck man carried four trunks to the dock. We have learned where Poderjay bought a fourth trunk, but we have not yet been able to trace that trunk from the purchasing place to the apartment. We are trying to find out, too, from the English customs how many trunks Poderjay had when he arrived there."

Police determined that Captain Poderjay sent a large trunk to his sister, who was living in Yugoslavia. At first, she denied that she had received anything from her brother. On June 23, she admitted that he sent her a trunk full of women's and men's clothing, but she told police that she had donated the items to the needy and no longer had them. Other reports indicated that she sold the items, which included women's dresses. Poderjay's sister showed reporters not a black, but a gray metal trunk purportedly sent to her by her brother during the winter of 1934.

MADAME ZHIVKA AND COMPANY

On June 19, Seifka Bradaritch, Poderjay's first wife, surfaced. Holding a November 1933 divorce record in her hand, Madame Zhivka, as she was then known, described the man she had married in 1926. Obviously still smitten with Captain Poderjay, she asserted that the captain could never seriously harm anyone though she admitted he was unfaithful.

Six months into their marriage, Captain Poderjay left Zhivka for Elli Hansen, the daughter of a general in the Danish army. When Zhivka learned that her husband had proposed to Miss Hansen, she sent Hansen a copy of her marriage certificate. Elli Hansen, however, was not fazed by the fact that her fiancé was already married. She told Madame Zhivka, "I don't care. I want him."

When Captain Poderjay learned that his wife had sent a letter to his fiancée, he told her, "Don't be nervous, darling. Take half the money and furniture and go. A peaceful separation, or divorce, is better than torturing yourself."

When the couple finally divorced in November 1933, Poderjay stole almost $200,000 from Zhivka's safety deposit box. She admitted he was dishonest but maintained that he was harmless. Worried for him, she told police that if Poderjay was in any trouble she had no doubt Suzanne Ferrand was behind it. "He was a good husband. He was easy to get along with. He never abused me and we were very happy until he went away."

Elli Hansen, the woman to whom Poderjay proposed while he was married to Madame Zhivka, claimed that Poderjay married her as well. They lived together for two months before he took off with her dowry and her bank account. She filed bigamy charges in Vienna at the time, but she, too, was still in love with Captain Poderjay. If he would only come back to her, she had told him, she would not press the bigamy charge. He did not, however, return to her. He also denied marrying her, claiming that they had only been engaged.

Ferrand, who by this time had acquired legal representation, was trying to distance herself from Poderjay and his trouble over Agnes Tufverson. She painted herself as a victim, ignorant of her husband's financial and romantic schemes. She denied that she had stolen Agnes's belongings: "I knew the clothes belonged to Miss Tufverson, but I believed Poderjay when he told me she gave them to him. I believe she is on a world cruise. I know nothing of his 'marriage' to Miss Tufverson in New York. He told me of a woman travel acquaintance who proposed a marriage of convenience to him, but he said he did not go through with it."

Still, Ferrand knew more than she pretended. Mary Foley, a London dressmaker, told police that Suzanne Ferrand had come to her shop to have a number of dresses altered. The labels had been cut out of the dresses, but Foley recognized their design as American. Out of curiosity, she asked Ferrand how she came across the dresses, which were all too big for her. Ferrand told the dressmaker that her husband worked in the dress trade and had purchased the dresses for her in America. If Miss Tufverson had simply given Captain Poderjay the dresses, as Ferrand maintained, why had she lied about it to the dressmaker?

Police were finding that Ferrand's affection for and devotion to Poderjay made it very difficult for them to question her, even as she tried to distance herself from him. They played Poderjay and Ferrand against each other and hoped that Ferrand, who admitted the clothing belonged to Tufverson, would eventually crack.

Those who knew Ferrand as Poderjay's wife while she lived in London also began to surface. In addition to the dressmaker who altered Agnes Tufverson's dresses for Ferrand, Ferrand's maid spoke to authorities. She claimed that she was in the apartment one evening when Agnes Tufverson called Captain Poderjay.

According to the maid, Captain Poderjay had asked Miss Tufverson to send money to him. Miss Tufverson purportedly told Captain Poderjay that he would have to travel to New York to get the money. Though Agnes was merely flirting and looking for an excuse to see Captain Poderjay, he did not take this news well. While on the phone with Agnes, he agreed to travel to New York and showed excitement about their reunion. Once he hung up the receiver, however, he flew into a rage and made threats about what he would do to Miss Tufverson when he next saw her. Upon learning of Miss Tufverson's disappearance, Ferrand's maid remembered these threats and reported them to authorities.

Ferrand's lawyer was quick to point out that Madame Zhivka, Captain Poderjay's first wife, was the niece of Punisha Bradic. Bradic, known as "the patriot assassin," had assassinated leaders in the Belgrade Parliament in 1928, thereby enabling a dictatorship in Yugoslavia. This information prompted questions concerning Poderjay's political connections and possible spy ring associations.

Meanwhile, American authorities were investigating yet another woman with whom Poderjay was supposedly linked in New York.

Among the taxi drivers in the area it was understood that Captain Poderjay would leave Agnes's apartment to visit a blonde woman living in the city. After a couple of hours, he would return to Tufverson's residence. Yugoslavian police also wanted to question Poderjay about the disappearance of a woman he had known in 1919.

LIKE A MOTHER TO US

While both Poderjay and Ferrand tried to play victims, the Tufverson family reminded the public who the true victim was in this case. Sally sat down with reporters to share more personal details of her sister's life. She described a vibrant, beautiful, intelligent, and generous woman:

"Her hair was brown with a good deal of red in it and her eyes were very dark blue. Her complexion was like marble. She didn't buy expensive clothes—always felt she couldn't afford them for herself, although she saw to it that Olive and I had the best of everything. But she had lots of clothes, most of them tailored, and she was extremely neat about them.

"I don't remember that she ever had a romance. I never heard her express a wish to be married. She was always too busy. She drove herself. She was always eager to progress further and higher.

"She was intensely interested in her work at the Electric Bond and Share Company . . . and one of her associates said of her that she 'thought like a man, worked like a man and accomplished as much as a man.'

"But she wasn't entirely satisfied with her work as an attorney. She told me once that she would like to be a doctor. She was entirely serious about it. I know that she discussed the possibility with a doctor friend of hers; and she had it in the back of her mind to go out to Leland Stanford some time and get a medical degree. That was characteristic of Agnes.

"I never knew her to have a hobby, except perhaps, driving a car and reading. She read fairly constantly when she wasn't at work, and always works of nonfiction.

"She was devoted to Olive and me—called us her 'kid sisters.' She wrote frequently and telephoned oftener. It isn't true, though, that she sent us money and, as Poderjay said, 'got tired of it.' She sent us many gifts but not money.

"Agnes was the oldest one of our family, and when our mother died she raised us and was as much a mother as a big sister to us.

"I was surprised when she married. I knew that Poderjay was interested in her, though, and when she telephoned us and said they had been married I was very happy for her.

"Poderjay talked to us on the phone that night, too, and he seemed very charming. They said they planned to go to London for a while and then go on to India. After that we heard no more of her, except the cable from London. We could scarcely believe at the time that Agnes had sent it; it was so perfunctory, and she was always so affectionate in her messages to us. We know now, of course, that she didn't send it."

Amelia had a bad feeling about Agnes's marriage from the start. When Captain Poderjay invited his new sisters-in-law to England and offered to pay, Amelia had a hunch that something was very wrong. She shared details of her early hunch with reporters: "The whole thing sounded funny to me. Why should he be so anxious to spend a large sum of money on his wife's relatives whom he did not know?"

Olive agreed that something was not quite right when they spoke to their sister. "There was a strange note in Agnes's voice and conversation. Something she said and an observation on her remark by Poderjay prompted Sally and myself to reprove her over the long-distance wire." Olive would not provide further details about the remark.

After her wedding, Agnes wrote to the family as regularly as she always had, promising them, "My attitude toward the family remains unchanged. My love for you all is greater than ever."

She looked forward to her impending honeymoon and shared her plans with her sisters, "After a short stay in London, I expect to go to India. The captain's brother is a missionary there, and the trip will be grand for me, especially for my eyes."

That trip, the Tufverson sisters knew all too well now, never happened. And they never heard from Agnes again.

WE CAN'T HOLD HIM INDEFINITELY

Austrian police pressed American authorities to charge Poderjay. Though Austrian police held him on a bigamy charge, Poderjay had not committed a crime in Austria and Austrian police could not hold him indefinitely. They awaited word from London or America.

New York Assistant District Attorney Charles G. Garrison investigated Poderjay's correspondence. After learning about the letters he wrote to Ferrand in which he divulged the details of his love affairs, detectives wondered what else he might have divulged. Garrison issued subpoenas to Western Union, Postal Telegraph, and Communication Companies to release any telegrams or radiograms that Poderjay received from July 1933 through January 1934. Detectives hoped that by examining Captain Poderjay's correspondence they might find evidence of what happened to Agnes. They also subpoenaed Tufverson's bank accounts and sought records of all of her purchases.

Meanwhile Viennese criminologists conducted a chemical analysis of spots found on the trunks in Poderjay's residence to determine if they were bloodstains. They employed what was called the "miracle lamp," considered a modern marvel of science at the time, to detect blood.

Sally left her secretarial job to continue searching full time in New York. Olive, who was still working at the company where Sally had been employed, was trying to do her part from Detroit: supporting her family, consulting with Detroit police, and speaking to reporters. Edith and Mr. Tufverson were reported to be "on the verge of collapse."

In a rare interview, Olaf Tufverson showed the suffering he was enduring: "She was a wonderful daughter. No one knows how I loved that girl."

Since the discovery of Agnes's briefcase, the family referred to her in the past tense. They knew she was no longer alive. Their job, now, was to figure out what happened to Agnes. In order to locate her remains, they were certain that they needed Poderjay's cooperation.

On Wednesday, June 20, New York police announced that they expected a major break in the case within twenty-four hours. By this point in time, they had deduced that Agnes never went to Europe. If Poderjay killed her, he did so before he left New York. At this point, they believed that Agnes died in her apartment.

Also at this time, New York dressmaker Miss Susan Sawtell pressed larceny charges against Agnes Tufverson. Sawtell told police that Miss Tufverson and Captain Poderjay had purchased "a large amount of clothing" from her before their honeymoon. Miss Tufverson gave Miss Sawtell her London address and promised to mail a $1,500 check for the purchase. When no check arrived, Miss Sawtell contacted the address Agnes had given her only to find that neither Agnes nor Poderjay resided there. Through Miss Sawtell's larceny charge, New York authorities now hoped to extradite Poderjay.

Police also learned that Poderjay never even made reservations on the Hamburg-American Line for his honeymoon. This fact implied to authorities that Poderjay had never intended to take Agnes to Europe at all. The fact that Agnes told friends and family that they had booked passage meant that Poderjay lied to her. Why? What were his plans?

Also at this time, Agnes's maid surfaced. She testified that she last saw Agnes around eleven o'clock on the evening of December 20. Detectives realized that Flora was probably the last person, other than Poderjay, to see Agnes alive. They pressed her for all of the details she could provide, hoping to piece together Agnes's final hours.

TWO THEORIES

By June 20, police had developed two major theories surrounding the disappearance of Agnes Tufverson. In the first theory, Poderjay murdered Agnes in their New York apartment and then dismembered her body with the help of an accomplice. He then placed her body parts in the trunk—which they believe he bought for that very purpose—and brought the trunk with him on *The Olympic*. He then either disposed of Agnes's body during the Atlantic crossing or once he reached England.

In their second theory, Poderjay also killed Agnes in the apartment. Instead of placing her dismembered body in a trunk, however, he burned the body in the apartment incinerator. Keeping both theories in mind, police were convinced that Poderjay had an accomplice.

On June 19, police returned to Agnes's apartment to investigate the incinerator. They sifted through its contents for traces of blood or human ashes. Captain John G. Stein was frustrated in his efforts as the incinerator had been cleaned and cleared many times over the months since Agnes's disappearance in December. He later told reporters, "That incinerator might have provided a clue if we had been notified soon after the disappearance because I found that it was only 60% effective and that it was necessary at intervals to cart away the residue by truck."

The department's new Technical Research Bureau also searched Agnes's apartment, using the "most modern scientific aids to crime detection," but all they found in addition to Agnes's furniture were her many law and psychology books. The furniture was slated to be sold to pay Agnes's delinquent rent, so police had limited time to search.

Back in Vienna, the miracle lamp did not reveal evidence of blood-stains on Poderjay's trunks, but it did find evidence of "obliterated" labels that bore Agnes's name, thereby proving the trunks belonged to her. One of the three chemists who examined the red stains found on the inside of Agnes's trunk concluded, "They are not blood, that's certain. Just what they are, we still have not discovered, but they are not likely to prove significant."

New York's *Daily News* columnist Danton Walker came up with a gruesome theory based on the items Poderjay purchased the night of Agnes's disappearance. First he used the sedatives to disable Agnes. Then, Danton theorized, Poderjay used vanishing cream in the same manner as a butcher—to protect his skin from Agnes's blood. Having coated his naked body and the bathtub in Agnes's apartment with vanishing cream, Poderjay then "butchered" her in the bathtub and scraped her bones using the many razor blades he purchased. He believed that Poderjay disposed of her flesh in the apartment incinerator and wrapped her bones in the brown paper he purchased. It was her bones, contended Danton, that Poderjay guarded so carefully in his trunk. He proposed that Captain Poderjay slipped the bones out of the porthole during his transatlantic voyage aboard *The Olympic*.

ADVENTURING INTO NEW FIELDS

Toward the end of June, Viennese authorities released new information concerning Captain Poderjay's financial situation at the time of his arrest. For all of his economic scams, Poderjay had no more than $35 at his disposal, about $700 today. Madame Ferrand's financial situation was worse; she had only about $20 left to her name.

That Thursday, June 21, officers turned Ferrand over to the prosecutor in Vienna to determine whether larceny charges would be brought against her. Though she still declared loyalty to Poderjay, her lawyer, Dr. Leopold Bestermann, told the press that she was "just another victim of a clever swindler."

Bestermann further created a sensation by furnishing the possibility that Captain Poderjay was a spy. He told reporters, "I have become increasingly convinced the so-called Poderjay-Tufverson affair is connected with a huge international espionage scheme. It is possible that the 'disappearances' both of Miss Tufverson and Captain Frederick Davey were eyewash to conceal somebody's movements." He implied that Davey was still alive and living in England.

New York authorities, however, dismissed this possibility. An agent in charge of the investigation told reporters, "There are unconfirmed rumors that Poderjay was in the Yugoslav intelligence service but we have found nothing to indicate that he was or is active in such service for any country."

Whether Poderjay's schemes were connected to an international spy ring or not, he was running out of cash at the time of his arrest. In fact, considering Poderjay's financial situation, authorities surmised that he was ready to "adventure into new fields." They discovered a forged passport that they believed Poderjay was using to return to London and scam yet another woman he had met there.

Meanwhile New York detectives were desperately trying to piece together enough evidence to extradite Poderjay before Vienna released him. Police followed up with witnesses regarding an incident that occurred outside of Agnes's apartment three days prior to her disappearance. Poderjay was seen with three men. Witnesses overheard them speaking in German and discussing money.

Authorities also continued to interview Agnes's maid. She told authorities that it was Poderjay who insisted she take December 21 off. He also instructed her "not to talk" about what she saw in the apartment on the evening of December 20, the last time she saw Agnes alive. Flora described Agnes's "dazed" expression that evening. She also explained that when she returned on December 22, Agnes was gone—Poderjay said to Philadelphia on business.

Describing the state of the apartment as "topsy-turvy," Flora recounted the scene when she returned to work on December 22. There were papers belonging to Agnes strewn all over the floor. The captain then proceeded to order Flora to help him burn these papers in the apartment incinerator.

They were still trying to follow the transfer of Agnes's Chase National Bank stock holdings in Philadelphia. On December 15, someone transferred Agnes's funds, but she was supposedly not in Philadelphia that day to approve the transaction. Police were working to identify the person to whom these funds were transferred and to determine whether Tufverson did, in fact, travel to Philadelphia at the time.

The one frustrating and debilitating fact was that without Agnes's body, police had no real case against their main suspect, Captain Poderjay. Considering that Poderjay could have secretly buried Agnes's body anywhere in the city, police looked into all recent and especially unusual New York burials.

Still searching for the fourth trunk that Poderjay checked onto *The Olympic*, detectives also feared that he may have pushed the trunk and its contents through the porthole of his stateroom during the transatlantic voyage. Captain John Ayers interviewed officials of the White Star Line.

"If anything should be put through that porthole, it would be just too bad, wouldn't it?" he asked them.

"There'd be nothing to stop it but the bottom of the sea" was the reply.

Detroit police considered that Captain Poderjay may have committed a similar "trunk" crime in 1920 under the name Eugene Leroy.

Leroy was living in Detroit with Mrs. Katherine Jackson at the time. A day after her disappearance, he left the rooming house where they both lived. Whoever killed Katherine stuffed her body in a trunk and mailed it to New York from Detroit. Police unsuccessfully searched for Leroy throughout 1920. Due to possible similarities in the crimes and the age and appearance of the men, Detroit detectives wondered if Leroy and Poderjay were the same man. They sent Leroy's fingerprints to Vienna for comparison with Poderjay's. The connection was easily dismissed, however, as Captain Poderjay's early life in Ljubljana, Yugoslavia, was well documented.

While the case against Poderjay tightened, the case against Ferrand frayed. Authorities believed that although she certainly profited from Agnes's disappearance, she did not bring about or take part in that disappearance. Her lawyer argued that if Poderjay had not been arrested, Ferrand herself would have been in grave danger. With no relatives and no one to miss her, Ferrand could have disappeared without notice—a fact Poderjay easily could have used to his advantage.

Agnes's maid, Flora Miller, also apprised police of a new detail in Poderjay's romantic life. At the same time that he was living with Agnes, Poderjay was courting a young concert violinist who was living in the city. Helen Vogel, a beautiful and talented musician, spoke hesitantly to papers, concerned that her connection to the case would damage her career. She denied any romantic involvement with Poderjay and any knowledge of Agnes Tufverson's whereabouts.

Vogel met Poderjay through her father, William Vogel, a New York inventor. Poderjay was pitching his patent lock to William Vogel, who was interested in the idea and enjoyed Poderjay's company. Helen Vogel admitted that Poderjay showed interest in her. When he continually asked her out, she declined. Vogel explained that she and her mother had a "feeling" about Poderjay that prevented her from accepting his invitations, even though she found him to be handsome and charming. Though Captain Poderjay eventually discussed marriage with her father, Helen said she never knew the captain except for "casually."

SPECIAL ATTENTION—URGENT

Though police were certain that Agnes Tufverson was dead, without a body they could not dismiss the possibility that she was alive. On June 21, they released a "special attention—urgent" dispatch on the five-state teletype system including Upstate New York, New Jersey, Pennsylvania, Connecticut, and Massachusetts. Citizens were to be on the lookout for and report anyone matching the description of Miss Tufverson.

On the afternoon of June 21, authorities learned that Poderjay purchased "a large quantity" of drugs from a local chemist around the time of Agnes's disappearance. This new finding certainly aided the theory posed by Olive Tufverson: that her sister had been drugged. Police, however, were running out of time. Without more concrete evidence, they could not extradite Poderjay even on a larceny charge. At a press conference on the case, New York Inspector Sullivan explained their position: "The property found on Poderjay is Miss Tufverson's property; there doesn't seem to be any doubt of that. But we can't do anything unless we can build up criminal intent, if any. So far we haven't been able to do that."

Taking this new possibility into account, authorities returned to Agnes's East Twenty-Second Street apartment. This time they literally ripped the place apart. They began by removing all of the plumbing fixtures. The police research lab wanted to examine the pipes for blood. They were also looking for any evidence of acid or chemicals that they believed Poderjay may have used to destroy Agnes's body. After ripping up the rugs and drying out the upholstery looking for similar results, however, they could not find one piece of evidence.

Seeking to learn more about Poderjay and his knowledge, if any, of chemistry, authorities reached out to Captain Poderjay's homeland. They found that Poderjay was born in 1899 in Ljubljana, Austria-Hungary, which later became Yugoslavia. Finishing the equivalent of America's high school education—the sixth-grade gymnasium class—there seemed to be no evidence that Poderjay had studied advanced anatomy or chemistry. England cabled that their searches so far had led them to a string of women duped by Poderjay. They labeled him a "spellbinder with the women."

That day brought bad news. Miss Sawtell's larceny charge—for the wedding trousseau that Agnes and Poderjay purchased—could not be used to extradite Poderjay. Technically, the charges were to be paid by Miss Tufverson and not Captain Poderjay, so he could not be charged in the matter. Though they had also taken a closer look at Agnes's securities, she had signed these over to Poderjay. He could not, therefore, be charged with stealing them. Nor could New York authorities prove that Poderjay had stolen any of Agnes's other belongings.

With no hope of extraditing Poderjay on larceny charges, American authorities considered a new approach and sought perjury charges. Poderjay had certainly perjured himself on his marriage document—stating that he was single and providing a false birthplace—when he wed Agnes Tufverson on December 4 in New York. They were grasping, but it was all they had. They also understood that if they extradited him on perjury charges, they could not prosecute him on any other charge—like murder, for instance. They decided, however, to move forward. On Friday, June 22, District Attorney James T. Neary brought the evidence before the grand jury and everyone held their breath.

Austrian law, however, did not consider Poderjay's crime perjury unless the crime was committed in a court of record. The American treaty with Austria provided that perjury must be a crime in Austria as well as in the United States; therefore, the authorities were unable to extradite Poderjay on perjury.

However, on that same day, Friday, June 22, Bruno Barber, head of the International Police Organization of Vienna, announced that his department had formally charged Captain Poderjay with bigamy and suspicion of murder. The police memorandum read that Poderjay was "suspected of murder and bigamy." This charge, which the Viennese authorities had always informally maintained, allowed them to continue to detain Poderjay and gave American authorities the time they needed to extradite the captain.

The unearthing that day of letters written to Poderjay by Suzanne Ferrand indicates that the couple planned to use Agnes Tufverson for her money and that Ferrand played a much larger role than she had previously testified. In one letter she tells Poderjay, "You marry her. Then if anything wonderful should happen—we have money." They spoke of Agnes as "an old woman" and a "tartuffe," or a hypocrite.

In her early forties, Agnes had not given up hopes of motherhood, work friends told Captain Ayers. She believed that Poderjay's money would allow her to leave her busy work life and begin a family.

That afternoon, six detectives left for Philadelphia to investigate Agnes's Chase National Bank stock transfer from December 1933. Meanwhile, New York police received news that Agnes had been sighted in Boston that very month.

Hans Spring, the officer in charge of the investigation in Vienna, hoped that American authorities would be able to pick up the case. He told reporters, "It is with the greatest reluctance that we cut short our efforts to solve this unusually interesting case. However, we are really up to our necks in urgent business far more important to us than Poderjay."

MYSTERIOUS SIGHTINGS

During his stay in New York, Poderjay had spent time with a blonde woman whom he introduced as his sister-in-law. This woman was known to have visited Agnes Tufverson's apartment on numerous occasions. Surmising that the woman could have been Suzanne Ferrand, police investigated the possibility that the couple worked together to defund—and possibly murder—Agnes. If Ferrand had entered the United States, according to Captain Ayers, she did so under a false name. The police could find no record of Ferrand entering or leaving the country. Detectives continued, unsuccessfully, to look into the identity of the mysterious blonde.

Meanwhile, the first reported sightings of Agnes Tufverson since her December disappearance emerged. After seeing Agnes's picture in a Boston paper, Melrose resident Ruth Hall alerted police that she had seen the missing woman in May and again in June. Miss Hall worked for a city dry cleaner and told police that a woman matching

Agnes's description had dropped off a blue dress to be dry cleaned on May 15. The same woman came into the shop during early June. Though she could not remember the exact name the customer gave, Hall thought the name might have been Codgerson, Todgerson, or possibly Tufverson.

Another woman soon surfaced. She was confused and emaciated. Authorities took her to Bellevue hospital for treatment. She gave her name as Marion Smith but later admitted the name was a false one. Workers believed she looked like the missing Agnes Tufverson. At that same time, detectives received word of a body floating in the Atlantic. The captain of a liner had reported seeing the body of a woman floating on the ocean surface during late December or early January, which fit with the time frame of Agnes's disappearance.

While examining a letter that Poderjay wrote to Suzanne Ferrand, police made a crucial discovery. Poderjay wrote, "A miracle will happen soon, making us both rich." The phrase reminded police of Ferrand's earlier letter to Poderjay in which she told him to propose to Agnes, "and if a miracle should occur, [they] would be wealthy." It seemed clear to police that the "miracle" to which the couple referred was Agnes's demise. If so, the letters clearly showed premeditation. Poderjay referred to Agnes as an "old wagon" in the letter.

I WANTED TO COME

On the evening of June 26, Sally Tufverson, along with sixteen detectives, boarded *The Olympic*. With "elaborate scientific apparatus," they made their way to C86, the cabin in which Captain Poderjay traveled two days after Agnes's disappearance. Sally walked on board the ship and to the stateroom with total composure, but once she entered C86, she broke down. While detectives ripped apart the cabin, searching for blood and evidence, Sally buried her face in her hands and cried. Leaning against the wall of the stateroom and imagining what had happened to her sister, she sobbed uncontrollably and looked as if she might faint.

Taking out a small white handkerchief, she wiped her eyes and told detectives, "I wanted to come, but I should have stayed away. I dreaded seeing this cabin."

Meanwhile, detectives removed the porthole. They attempted to fit one of their own men, who weighed 175 pounds, through the porthole to see if he would fit. Holding him by his heels, they found that he easily would have fit through the porthole, which opened directly to the sea. Captain Ayers established that if Poderjay had in fact pushed Agnes's body through the porthole, the curve of the ship would have hidden the fact. No one would have noticed.

In fact, thirteen years after Agnes's disappearance, a woman was pushed through the porthole of a similar liner during its voyage. Twenty-one-year-old actress Gay Gibson lost her life at the hands of a serial rapist who worked as a steward on the liner *Durban Castle*. The vessel sailed from South Africa to England. In October 1947, Gibson was sailing to Cape Town when she disappeared. Luckily the captain acted quickly and the steward's crime was discovered.

Since Poderjay traveled on the liner in December, the stateroom had been cleaned and occupied many times before the police investigated the room. Had there been any evidence of a crime, it was highly unlikely that any remained. Detectives had better luck speaking to the stewards about Poderjay's general demeanor and the trunk he carried on the ship. Stewards recalled the careful manner in which Poderjay watched over the trunk.

They also provided more information about the woman who greeted Poderjay in Southampton. Poderjay told the steward that the woman was his wife. The blonde good-looking woman who spoke English with a Parisian accent was Suzanne Ferrand. The steward told detectives that she was "all over him," meaning Poderjay.

Their search of cabin C86, like their search of Agnes's apartment, yielded only circumstantial evidence. Poderjay guarded his mysterious trunk, sailed on the liner alone, and could have easily slipped Agnes through the porthole of his stateroom.

WAITING GAME

Though police from two continents had acquired substantial evidence since they opened the case against Poderjay on June 2, the evidence was circumstantial. Still without a body, authorities could not move the case forward. In September, word came that Vienna refused to release Poderjay to the United States on perjury charges. In New York, Sally wrote to Olive to share the disheartening news: "Perjury cannot apply. I don't know what can be done now. . . . It seems so heartless and unfair, but we just have to face it. Don't go haywire over it honey, because it just won't do any good, and we'll have to pull together as best we can until things break."

To make matters worse, Sally could not access Agnes's belongings, which were locked up by the marshal to be auctioned for failure to pay her apartment lease. Luckily, she was able to rent the apartment and apply the rent to the lease payments.

Agnes's sisters continued to push forward, even when others felt they pushed too hard. Sally read an unflattering description of her efforts in an article in *American Detective* that month and told Olive, "I got an idea that [the author] doesn't care much for your sister Sally. Kinda seems like in the article his impress of me is an unreasonable woman when she makes up her mind she wants something. . . . It just handed me a laugh."

In the face of unbelievable despair and pain, Agnes's sisters pulled together and supported each other through the search for Agnes. Sally ended this same letter by telling Olive, "Gosh, can't we find worries, eh. Oh, well, one of these days we won't be all upset Olive, and we will again be eating spinach and beans and a biscuit or two, eh. In the meantime, for heaven's sake if not fer mine take care of yourself, 'cause me mind is on yez always and me love is like eternity so don't you fail me."

Spring turned into summer and summer turned into fall without any further hope of finding Agnes or bringing Captain Poderjay to justice. After four months in New York, Sally returned to Detroit.

Austrian authorities announced that they would release Suzanne Ferrand, as they had no concrete evidence to warrant her continued incarceration. She returned to France, where she quietly slipped into a new life.

In the beginning of November, there was cause for hope. In a joint statement, Sally and Olive Tufverson divulged that they expected Captain Poderjay to be extradited to the United States within a couple of weeks. Sally made arrangements to be there when Poderjay arrived in New York: "I'm going back there to see him brought ashore. He has never seen us, but he will never be able to lie to me. He will have to answer questions, but will he tell what happened to Agnes? He can't just shrug and say he doesn't know anything about Agnes. He can't just shrug away the fact that Agnes's private things were found in her trunks hidden in his flat in Vienna. And he will have to face the maid who saw him ransacking Agnes's apartment in New York after she had disappeared. He'll tell, alright, and I'll see that he does."

After a reflective pause, Sally added, "I'll never rest until I know what happened to Agnes."

She and the other members of the Tufverson family had to rest a little while longer. The search quieted, with the exception of a body that washed on the shore near Cleveland in September. Though the woman was the same size as Agnes and also had undergone an abdominal operation, it was not Agnes.

Though Austrian authorities had refused to release Poderjay on the perjury indictment, they hinted that they would be willing to extradite under a bigamy charge. New York authorities appealed to the US government. They sought and received permission to demand Poderjay's extradition on a bigamy charge.

On November 28, according to the Associated Press, "The United States government made a formal demand upon the Austrian government today for the extradition of Captain Ivan Poderjay on charges of bigamy."

Finally, at the beginning of December, Austrian authorities permitted American authorities to extradite Captain Poderjay. They had longed to release the prisoner, who was not one of their citizens and a drain on their economic and police resources.

Without a body, authorities could not charge Poderjay with Agnes's murder. Captain Ayers, who worked on the case from the beginning once said that he had never worked on such a tough case of proving the "corpus delicti."

Strangely enough, Agnes Tufverson discussed the legality of the corpus delicti at a dinner party only a couple of months prior to her disappearance. She insisted that the law—the idea that a crime must be proved to have occurred before a person can be convicted of committing the crime—was essential to protecting the innocent.

Still, after seven long months of work to extradite Poderjay, this turn of events was cause for celebration and hope. In a perfect twist of fate, Poderjay was informed of the extradition on what would have been his first wedding anniversary to Agnes Tufverson. While American authorities awaited the red tape necessary for the Austrian police to turn Captain Poderjay over to German police, Captain Jacob Von Weisenstein awaited instructions to secure the prisoner.

Von Weisenstein, who had worked on the Tufverson case from the beginning, was consulting with Scotland Yard regarding information he had learned about the case during his time in Vienna. Based on the evidence collected by the German police and Scotland Yard, Von Weisenstein believed that Captain Poderjay placed Agnes's body in a large cabin trunk. Though the world press announced that Scotland Yard would renew and expand their search efforts on December 30, Scotland Yard denied these reports the following day, stating that they had already investigated the case fully.

While Von Weisenstein awaited instructions from New York, Vienna made plans to deliver Poderjay to Austrian detectives and then to German police. Adolf Hitler refused to allow Captain Poderjay to travel through Germany, however, and authorities made an alternative plan with Italian officials. During the week of January 7, authorities arranged for the captain to sail to New York from Genoa aboard the *President Polk* in the custody of Jacob Von Weisenstein.

RETURN TO THE UNITED STATES

Flanked by police, Captain Poderjay boarded a train bound for Genoa on Friday, January 11. By eight o'clock that morning, the prisoner was finally making the first leg of his trip back to the United States, where he would have to answer for the disappearance of Agnes Tufverson. Traveling throughout the weekend, the train arrived in Genoa that Sunday.

As Poderjay stepped from the train that morning, reporters greeted him. Affable and confident as ever, Poderjay told them, "So sure am I of acquittal in the United States that I am now making plans to return to Europe and marry Suzanne Ferrand." When reporters pointed out that the couple were already married, Poderjay admitted that they had been married but it had been revoked for technical reasons, making him a bachelor.

Poderjay planned to join Ferrand in Paris. He beamed as he told reporters of his plans: "This time we shall see to it that all legal formalities are observed. I look forward to a happy future."

Though reporters tried to steer the conversation to Poderjay's bigamous marriages and Agnes Tufverson's disappearance, Captain Poderjay was intent on sharing the details of his patent lock invention and his political beliefs instead.

He finally ended the interview with a note about Agnes: "As far as Miss Tufverson is concerned, I can only say that we parted good friends when I left New York. She agreed to go her way and I my way. I have no idea as to what became of her but I'm certain she is still living."

Surprised by Poderjay's confident announcement, reporters bombarded Captain Jacob Von Weisenstein who assured them, "We've got the goods on him."

That Tuesday, under the guard of Jacob Von Weisenstein, Poderjay boarded the *President Polk*. Housed belowdecks in the ship's brig, Poderjay embarked on a hunger strike to protest his accommodations and menu. He demanded a stateroom. Refusing his breakfast, he yelled out that he was no cannibal and stuck to his strike.

Poderjay, always a dapper dresser, also complained about his wardrobe. Half joking, he grumbled, "Why didn't they tell me I was going to the United States? I've only three shirts with me, which aren't enough for a gentleman."

Though Captain Poderjay refused all food and water during the first twenty-four hours at sea, he remained in the brig. After thirty-six hours without food, Poderjay must have realized that he was not going to win his battle for better accommodations. He relented, ate a dinner of beans and stew, and became a "cheerful" prisoner from that point forward.

The captain brought a significant amount of luggage with him, including Agnes Tufverson's trunks and belongings. Though these items had been confiscated by Austrian authorities, they were returned to Poderjay upon his release from that country. Now New York authorities planned to be on hand to inspect Agnes's baggage when the *President Polk* docked in Jersey City on Tuesday.

This transatlantic voyage was far different than the one on which he sailed to Southampton the year before. He spent his time writing poetry and letters, posting one letter to Paris, presumably to Ferrand, and the other to Vienna. After his initial hunger strike, he enjoyed three meals a day, lots of ice cream, and nightly Manhattans until the last leg of the voyage when he became seasick.

THE GIRLS MUST THINK I'M NICE

His mood changed significantly by the time he docked in New York. The captain was all smiles and poses, waving his hat in the air and joking with reporters. Though the ship landed at 9:30 a.m., Poderjay was not taken from the vessel until 11:15. At that time, he posed on the rail of the ship for photographers, obviously enjoying the attention he was receiving. Smiling from ear to ear and looking dapper in a camel hair coat, he joked with reporters, "I must look good if you want to take my picture. The girls must think I am nice."

The clicks of sound reels and a flurry of questions surrounded Poderjay's arrival. When asked if he was Ivan Poderjay, the captain replied, "Yes, I am. Be sure to save a picture of me."

He told reporters that he ought to be paid for posing. When asked if he thought Agnes Tufverson was dead, he shook his head and scowled, "Baw, rubbish!"

"When did you last hear of Agnes Tufverson?" someone yelled from the crowd.

"I don't remember," returned Poderjay wisely.

"Are you as happy as you look?"

"I'm alright."

Poderjay continued to joke with reporters about his free first-class travel to the United States. He also informed them that he would act as his own lawyer in the case against him, even though he did not understand American law. Had he done something wrong, he would be willing to pay for it, but he had done nothing, he said, maintaining his innocence. He even told immigration authorities that he believed in polygamy, though he recanted this statement the following day, saying he misunderstood the question.

Admirers wired money to the captain, though he did not receive it. From the docks, authorities escorted Poderjay to police headquarters in Jersey City and then to the Elizabeth Street Station in Manhattan, where they booked him on a bigamy charge. As the police car started to move from the pier, Olive Tufverson jumped on the back running board to get a look at the man who she knew in her heart had killed her sister.

Then the questioning began. For three hours Poderjay sat with authorities. When asked if he married Agnes Tufverson, he freely admitted to having wed the attorney. He told authorities that Agnes had acted as his lawyer, informing him that his marriage to Ferrand was not legal; therefore, he was free to marry Agnes and could not be prosecuted. He continued to make a lengthy statement concerning Agnes, but he denied murdering her or knowing her whereabouts. He continued to insist that Agnes was alive. As for the last time he saw her, that was on December 21, he said, when she boarded a train for Montreal. According to his testimony, he left for Europe the following day because he preferred to sail alone.

Lyon Boston, one of the assistant district attorneys assigned to the Tufverson case, translated 1,200 letters written by Captain Poderjay. He questioned the captain, "This case seems to follow a pattern. One you probably read in a book. What's the book?"

"Sonya," Poderjay responded without pausing.

Boston, along with an officer, checked through numerous books without any luck. Though a Milwaukee resident wrote to Lyon saying he had a copy of the book, nothing ever came of the lead, and no one ever located such a book.

After questioning, police fingerprinted and photographed Poderjay. Upon meeting with Assistant District Attorney Harold Hastings, Poderjay attempted to make a deal. If the United States would drop the bigamy charge, Poderjay would produce Agnes Tufverson alive. When asked how he could be so sure that Agnes was alive, Poderjay told DA Hastings that Agnes had written to him over the summer in Vienna.

"She told me she was alright and said for me not to worry. I did not show the letter over there because judges there and here might differ on it."

Though he admitted he did not know Agnes's exact whereabouts, he insisted he could put police on her trail if they were clever enough to find her. He further told police that Agnes had never intended on staying with him and only married him to secure her social standing, since she had "become too friendly with a married man."

In a final statement to the press that evening as he was escorted to prison, Poderjay assured reporters, "Agnes is all right. I know the whole story. If police are clever enough, they will find her."

PLEADING GUILTY

The following day, Captain Poderjay found himself before Justice George L. Donnellan. Olive Tufverson sat in the back of the courtroom, unbeknownst to Captain Poderjay.

Referring to the charge of bigamy, Justice Donnellan asked the captain, "How do you plead to this charge?"

"I guess I better plead guilty," admitted Poderjay. "If I am guilty under the American law I am willing to pay the penalty, but I didn't know I was guilty."

"So you will not be under any misapprehension," returned Justice Donnellan, "I will refuse to accept your plea and will assign counsel."

Poderjay, who had planned to represent himself, refused. "If I am guilty, I don't see what good a lawyer will do me. I don't want any lawyer."

"I think under the circumstances," advised the judge, "you had better have a lawyer."

After Justice Donnellan appointed Clyde Dart as Poderjay's counsel, he released the prisoner back to the Tombs, where he was incarcerated while awaiting trial. Assistant District Attorney Harold W. Hastings told the press that Poderjay was suspected of murder and the state would deny any request for bail. The captain, however, did not attempt bail and willingly conferred with his new counsel before he cheerfully returned to his cell. Even there, the flirtatious captain could not help sweet-talking a young, attractive female scribe.

Explaining himself, the captain shrugged, "I like women. I always have. They are a bright spot on life's pathway."

And that, he asserted, was why he would not betray Agnes Tufverson. According to Poderjay, his wife was alive and well. She was afraid, however, of being implicated in the bigamy charges he was facing. Should those charges escalate, however, Poderjay was certain that Agnes would come to his rescue.

"What I am keeping back from the public, I wouldn't tell my own mother. According to my code, if I were to reveal anything against a lady's honor I would lose my rank as an officer. Miss Tufverson would come forward the minute anything in the way of a charge more serious than bigamy was placed against me. She is not worried because she knows they will never find another charge. As sure as I see you here now, I know she is alive and happy. She's as free as the air and is absolutely not hiding. I have no desire to find her until the bigamy charge against me is dropped."

On Friday, February 1, against the advice of counsel, Poderjay repeated his guilty plea before general sessions. Olive Tufverson, who reiterated her belief that her sister was dead, was also seated in court again that day. She made no comment, however, concerning Captain Poderjay. After his court appearance, Poderjay was returned to the Tombs once more. His hearing was set for two weeks, which was appropriately Valentine's Day. While jailed, Poderjay regaled his fellow cellmates with stories of his many romantic encounters with various women.

After the court sessions, Olive joined Captain Stein and officers of the Missing Persons Bureau to look through Agnes's luggage and point out her belongings. In all, she identified two trunks full of personal belongings—a typewriter, three handbags of clothing, and Agnes's treasured briefcase. As she was shown each item, she repeated, "This is Agnes." She also found twenty-five letters that Agnes had written to Captain Poderjay, as well as another unidentified packet of letters. Police hoped that this correspondence might yield more clues than Poderjay was willing to provide.

As she held her sister's dresses in her hands, Olive could not help but think about the other woman who had dared to wear her sister's personal items. To her shock, however, she was informed that Suzanne Ferrand was not the only person who had worn Agnes's dresses. Captain Poderjay, she was told, had also donned her sister's clothing. The captain, authorities discovered, enjoyed wearing women's apparel. They even found a closet full of gentleman's clothing lined with lace in his apartment.

SIGNED BY PODERJAY

Sally planned to return to New York the following week with the telegram Poderjay had sent to them in Agnes's name. Their family was convinced that Captain Poderjay had murdered Agnes, and they wanted to hand over any evidence that might help authorities build a case.

The captain, dubbed a "gigolo" among other monikers by the press, seemed committed to serving a bigamy sentence. He would not, however, admit to murder. He spoke freely about his belief that Agnes was alive and that he was still on good terms with her.

He seemed more concerned with his appearance during court proceedings and his reputation with the ladies than he did with his wife's disappearance. Indeed, he flirted with many women throughout his first week back in the United States as if driven by an uncontrollable weakness for them. Canadian papers commented on Poderjay's charm: "He's an alert lad; he knows his America. With his white, wide-spread teeth and his dry, black hair, he's another daring young man on the front page trapeze."

Other papers mused that Poderjay would rather plead guilty to bigamy and face prison than face any one of his wives. One could see why Agnes had fallen for the man. Though newspapers poked fun of the captain's weight and dubbed him "pudgy," even they were taken by his good looks, dapper outfits, and evident charm. Agnes's great intellect was seemingly no match for the captivating captain. He was good looking, bright, charismatic, funny, and romantic. He spoke several languages and wrote romantic poetry. On the whole, he was also a rather witty, cheerful, and agreeable man. One can only imagine the love letters he wrote to her, the gifts with which he showered her, and the attention he paid to her.

LET YOUR GIRLS MARRY YOUNG

Police intended to issue a valentine in the form of a jail sentence to Captain Poderjay on Friday, February 14. The District Attorney's office, however, requested an adjournment to March 7 to give them time to collect more evidence against him. Although they had more than enough evidence to press the bigamy charge, they actually planned to try Poderjay on murder charges. The trouble was that they did not have enough evidence to bring these charges forward. By holding off on the bigamy charge, the court provided an opening for the police to investigate the murder charge.

New York authorities felt that once they had Poderjay in their possession, they could warrant a confession or at least evidence from the man. By February 14, however, they had done neither. During this time, newspaper coverage of the story also changed. Though they still covered the photo-loving Poderjay, some writers warned older women about the dangers of marriage. Most covered the mysterious angles of Agnes's disappearance. The country could not get enough of the mystery, which read better than any fiction of the time.

On March 6, the day before Poderjay's sentencing, Judge Donnellan signed an order for Poderjay to have a psychiatric evaluation at Bellevue Hospital. The ten-day observation gave authorities more time and renewed hope that they might glean something from Poderjay's evaluation. The psychiatrist concluded, however, that Captain Poderjay, despite "a penchant for wearing women's clothing and being thoroughly egocentric" was "perfectly sane."

Upon Poderjay's release from Bellevue, Judge Donnellan signed yet another postponement, setting the new sentencing date for Thursday, March 21. If the police had learned any new information regarding Agnes Tufverson's whereabouts, they remained tight-lipped.

GREAT AMERICAN JUSTICE

On that cloudy and cold March day, Poderjay remained hopeful as he entered the court. His carefree demeanor implied that he thought he would receive a light sentence or no sentence at all. During the proceedings, chief probation officer Irving W. Halpern presented his report. Though the prisoner insisted that Miss Tufverson was still alive, Halpern's information concluded otherwise.

He highlighted Poderjay's sudden financial gain after his wife's disappearance and outlined how Agnes transferred her funds to Poderjay during the last two weeks of her life. Halpern concluded in his report, which was read before the court: "The disappearance of Miss Tufverson was not voluntary but was directly caused by the defendant, who had no affection for her and who could profit financially by her wealth."

Prior to sentencing Poderjay, Judge Donnellan made his belief clear, "In my opinion, you should have been brought to this court on another charge."

With the bigamy charge before him, Justice Donnellan asked the prisoner to rise. He sentenced the captain to two and a half to five years in Sing Sing. Upon hearing the sentence, Captain Poderjay gulped audibly, his eyes filled, and he appeared shaken. Obviously shocked, he managed to nod his head to indicate that he understood. For once, the captain remained quiet and attentive.

He wasn't the only one who was shocked. Assistant District Attorney Harold W. Hastings beamed, "Well, they thought we couldn't do it, but I guess we showed them we could." Thanks to the efforts of Agnes Tufverson's sisters to reach out on her behalf, many people had worked to bring Poderjay to some semblance of justice that day, though as Judge Donnellan pointed out, it should have been on a murder charge.

Regardless, as Captain Ayers came to realize, as much as Poderjay liked to play off his sentence, he loathed prison.

Ayers wrote to Olive, "The more I think of it, the more I believe that imprisonment for him is the worst sort of punishment he could receive. You know what he is—I mean the type of animal—and being shut away . . . must be just plain hell for him."

The following day, the captain was back to his usual witty self, albeit obviously angered by the previous day's verdict. Clearly not a fan of the American justice system, he told reporters while he was being fingerprinted and photographed for his transfer to Sing Sing, "This is the third act in a great American comedy. The first act was my being returned to this country. The second act was yesterday in court. The third act is my going to Sing Sing prison today. But, the play is not over yet."

Poderjay complained about the proceedings that led to his sentence: "Yesterday I was presented with a wonderful courtroom exhibition of your great American justice. They sent me to jail without asking me a single question. The judge listened to others and acted in accordance with letters he received. This country may laugh at me now, but I will have the laugh on 125,000,000 American people when Miss Tufverson returns to clear up this matter. I cannot fight 125,000,000 people single handed."

EVERYTHING IS BRIGHT AND SUNNY

When Poderjay arrived at Sing Sing, he refused to give the press any satisfaction. Outside the gates of the prison, he gave a last goodbye to the press. When asked with whom he would correspond while in prison, Poderjay replied that he planned to write to his wife, Suzanne Ferrand. Refusing to name Agnes, he indicated that he would not be writing to the missing attorney.

"Everything is bright and sunny here," he quipped, as he turned over the $18.14 in his pocket (about $350 today).

He enjoyed a hearty breakfast of corned beef hash, bread, and coffee. For lunch, he consumed frankfurters, sauerkraut, boiled potato, bread, and more coffee. In between meals he joked with the prison officers. When told that his sentence had been prorated fifty days for time served, Poderjay smiled, "It's nice to get this discount so soon."

GHOST IN THE SUNNIEST DAY

After his meal, Poderjay was taken from his cell and led to a small office for an impromptu grilling by the Tufverson sisters' lawyer (though even they were unaware of this encounter until after the fact).

In the presence of other officers, the lawyer leaned in, faced the prisoner, and began. "I not only represent Agnes's sisters, but I know them and many of Agnes's friends personally. My wife and Agnes were sorority sisters in college. For all of these reasons, I have the utmost personal interest in learning her fate."

The prisoner shifted uneasily, while the lawyer continued. "Do you have any message that I can give to Agnes's family and her friends?"

Poderjay dodged the question, and so the lawyer attacked him on his correspondence with Suzanne Ferrand and the "miracle" they hoped to achieve. Poderjay, though, argued that they were simply conversing about the money they hoped to gain from his lock invention and Agnes's help with converting Yugoslavian dinars into American money. When the lawyer saw that this line of questioning was equally useless, he changed tactics.

"Can you sleep nights, Mr. Poderjay?"

Poderjay answered that, of course, he slept and wanted to know why the lawyer asked him such a question.

"Agnes Tufverson does not come to bother you in your dreams?"

The prisoner did not respond.

"If she has not already come, she surely will be there every night from now on as long as you live. I wonder if you realize that you would be convicted of murder if this were France or Austria instead of the United States. In those countries a defendant must prove himself innocent instead of the State proving him guilty of the crime."

The lawyer then recited the evidence against Poderjay and asked him if he would find himself guilty if he were a member of the jury.

Poderjay lifted up his foot and said, "If I were not in this position, I would shove my foot into your face."

When they led him away, Poderjay broke down and immediately wrote a letter to Olive proclaiming his innocence. He told her that her lawyer saw ghosts in the sunniest days. He begged: "Do you have a heart, a sister's heart? If you do, so I cannot understand, how you could allow a mad man to influence you so much, as to persecute your own sister!!?? Why did you not come to see me, why did you not try to get in touch with me, in Vienna? You could have done it. . . . You do not know how Agnes is feeling all about, you probably will never know it. . . . But you have done her wrong, terribly wrong! You are doing me wrong, but I am excusing you because I had a talk with your lawyer, who has to be blamed for everything."

Poderjay then wrote a fourteen-page statement concerning the disappearance of Agnes Tufverson, which Captain Ayers called "a lot of cockeyed lies." In addition to his insistence that he married Agnes to "save" her, the prisoner then added a more detailed account of why she needed saving. According to Poderjay, Agnes was pregnant with a married man's child. Poderjay confronted the wealthy man from Greenwich Village and called him a scoundrel. He asserted that Agnes planned to go to Europe to have the man's baby. She asked that Poderjay marry her to save her reputation. Rather than fighting on the pier the evening Agnes disappeared, Poderjay swore that they had just decided to go to Europe separately so that the father of the baby could take Agnes to Montreal.

Clearly rattled by the lawyer's grilling, Poderjay told his stories to anyone who would listen: inmates, guards, and reporters alike. Agnes, he exclaimed, was more alive than he was! She had sent him notes and roses while he was imprisoned in Vienna. When asked where these notes were, he admitted to destroying them. When asked why, he said it was because she hadn't signed them and no one would believe him. No one did believe him.

Having spread his tales to everyone within the prison walls, Poderjay settled into prison life and hoped that he could serve his time without having to answer any more questions about Agnes Tufverson. He requested a job as a linguist within the prison walls since he spoke eight languages, but prison authorities assigned him to the mop and broom crew instead.

"It's humiliating," he admitted, "but nothing matters now."

Captain Ayers told Sally and Olive that he had the opportunity to spend three hours with "the brute" and if he had any doubt at all, he was then "convinced that he [was] responsible, wholly and entirely, for what we have always believed him to be."

He also explained the almost magnetic hold "the devil" Poderjay must have had over Agnes. "I can well understand how he could intrigue any woman. If a woman had eyes such as his, they would be described as melting. Add to that a very pleasant smile, a beautifully modulated voice, a great facility in the selection of his words, and the suavity of bearing that results from mixing with all sorts of suave and polished people, and one has a man who can easily make an impression on a woman."

Poderjay hoped for an eventual transfer and relished the quiet of his prison cell where nobody bothered him and he could work on his inventions.

Within a matter of weeks, however, Poderjay was transferred to Auburn Prison. Despite his protests, he and thirty-six other prisoners made the switch. Shackled with handcuffs and leg irons, Poderjay was escorted to his new home on the evening of Monday, May 13. Within a few weeks he received more bad news. Yugoslavia, his home country, stripped Captain Poderjay of his military rank. And finally, Sally Tufverson wrote to the district attorney of New York and met personally with the Auburn Prison warden to express the importance of keeping Poderjay in prison as long as possible. Because of her actions, Poderjay, who was slated to be paroled after two and a half years due to good behavior, would serve the full five-year prison term with the possibility of only thirty days per year off his sentence for good behavior.

What Sally really wanted to do was to confront Poderjay. According to Amelia, Sally wanted to look Poderjay in the eye and ask him, "What have you done with my sister?" The police, however, advised her against it. Captain Poderjay was so cunning that it would not be wise for her to speak to him alone.

THE AVENGING FURY

A little more than a year into Poderjay's sentence, Sally contacted New York assistant district attorney, Harold Hastings, to request that he try Poderjay on a perjury charge—citing a case in which a criminal had been tried on a second charge while in prison. Agnes's sisters realized that after Poderjay served the five-year bigamy charge, he would go home to Yugoslavia and disappear. He would never be held responsible for his crimes against Agnes. Furthermore, he had no reason to speak about how he disposed of Agnes and every reason to remain quiet while in prison if he wanted to ensure his release and his ticket out of the United States.

If the district attorney could try Poderjay on another charge and extend his prison sentence, Agnes's sisters planned to dash Poderjay's hope of escaping the United States and break his spirit so that he would eventually talk. They came to believe that he had disposed of their sister so thoroughly that he was the only person who could tell them what happened to her or where to find her. For that reason, they planned to keep him in prison on whatever charges they could until they could break him down.

In order to pursue the charge, the Department of State in Washington, DC, would need to obtain permission from the Austrian government. Hastings made the request to the Department of State at the end of June 1936, but Secretary of State Cordell Hull denied the request in July 1936 since the Austrian government had declined to extradite Poderjay on the perjury charge in the first place.

Undeterred, Sally wrote Carrol Sweet, a contact in Michigan who knew the secretary of state and President Roosevelt. In a three-page letter, she impressed upon him that she could not give up until she had done everything possible to clear up the mystery of her sister's disappearance. Though Mr. Sweet attempted to intervene through the secretary of commerce, chief justice of the Court of Special Sessions, and the secretary of state, he was not successful.

The Tufversons' lawyer, Detective Ayers, and everyone who encountered Agnes's sisters on this case marveled at their tenacity, gumption, and grit. Detective Ayers, whose relationship with the family was formal when they first opened the case, came to love the sisters. His later letters are friendly and informal: "I want to say, right here and now, that I have never met two such swell kids as Sally and you [i.e., Olive]. . . . Seriously, girls, you are just awfully worthwhile, and I admire you a whole lot. My dears, you can rely on my being with you all the way in anything that may be done to pin the goods on the devil."

By October 1936, newspapers across the country ran a story about the Tufverson sisters' fight to keep Poderjay behind bars. Titled "The Avenging Fury of the Tufverson Sisters," the article applauded the tenacity of Agnes's dedicated sisters.

Amelia Tufverson told reporters, "That's all we want to do now—keep him in prison. When he has served this term we will try to place another charge against him."

Mr. Tufverson was an old man by that point and knew he would not live much longer. He refused visitors and no longer spoke.

Amelia, who lived with her husband and children only a few blocks from her father, begged reporters to leave him alone. "Don't disturb him. He is an old man. Before this happened, he seemed young. He mustn't be disturbed now."

When asked why her sister Agnes would have given Captain Poderjay all of her money, Amelia considered, "Well, Poderjay must have fooled Agnes completely. She was always so honest and straightforward. I guess she thought everyone was like that."

The Tufverson sisters eventually realized that Poderjay might never divulge what happened to Agnes, and they might have to be satisfied with keeping him in prison. They wanted "an eye for an eye," they said, "if they could not have a life for a life."

Little did they know how prophetic that phrase would turn out to be.

Three and a half years into his five-year sentence, Poderjay got into a fistfight with another inmate. It was a hot day in the middle of June when Poderjay and twenty-four-year-old prisoner Frank Rawlings came to blows. Rawlings was uninjured but Poderjay lost his right eye and several teeth in the brawl. The fight with Rawlings, who was imprisoned for theft, ended quickly. By the time the guards arrived to break it up, however, Poderjay's right eye was already gouged out. They could not save it.

He was taken immediately to the prison hospital, where he remained for more than a month. News of the fight was not made public until Poderjay was released from the hospital on July 19, 1938. The Tufverson sisters must have mused that one of their wishes literally came true.

During his time in prison, Poderjay was considered a fine prisoner. Though he did not get along with other prisoners, as evidenced by the fight, he did get along with the guards. For the most part, he kept to himself, and he never had a visitor in all of his five years.

GOD BLESS AMERICA

On February 1, 1940, Poderjay was released from Auburn Prison and turned over to immigration authorities. Flanked on either side by officers and dressed in dapper fashion, he held up his manacled hands for photographer's cameras as he was led to Cayuga County Jail to await deportation.

He wore a scarf and socks that he said his wife knit for him. Newspapers joked, "Which one?"

Angry that he had been released from one prison only to be transported to another, Poderjay griped, "So this is America. This is civilization. God bless America. This is just another form of kidnapping. How long am I going to stay here?"

Poderjay remained in holding for four days before officials moved him to Ellis Island on February 5. Surrounded by reporters, he maintained that Agnes Tufverson was still alive and that she had often contacted him while he was in prison. He regaled reporters with stories

Poderjay about to be released from prison. *Pittsburgh Post-Gazette, February 3, 1940*

of how Agnes, who he said was in hiding, had secretly communicated with him through coded newspaper advertisements and flowers. In fact, he told the press that he had heard from Agnes seven months before, when she told him he should "stick it out until the end." He blamed the police for her continued absence: "The police could find her, but they don't want to spend the money. Some day they will pay me a lot of money to bring her back to life."

Police Commissioner Lewis Valentine responded to this comment, assuring the press that he had not closed the investigation into Agnes Tufverson's disappearance and that she was still considered a missing person. The department, he told them, was "still making every effort to find her."

Poderjay then proposed a deal to the press, the same deal he had tried to make with the police and with Agnes's sisters: "I will produce Miss Tufverson in 60 days if your government will guarantee that neither she nor I will be prosecuted. Certain people are forcing her to be in hiding."

When asked about the possibility that he had murdered Agnes Tufverson, Poderjay smirked, "I had to laugh when they accused me of her murder. I had talked to her the day before I was arrested yet they said she had been dead for six months."

Poderjay also stuck to the story that his London marriage to Suzanne Ferrand was never legal because she was French and not a British citizen. Therefore, he informed reporters, he intended to marry her "properly" when he reunited with her. Poderjay claimed to have a little money from inventions he sold while he was in prison. He planned to travel somewhere, perhaps India, where his brother was a missionary, to live quietly with Suzanne.

On Saturday, February 10, Ivan Poderjay boarded the liner *Washington* for his return trip to Yugoslavia. As he stepped aboard, the press bombarded him with their final question: "How did you kill Miss Tufverson?"

"I didn't kill her," Poderjay replied. "She is still alive. I was just a knight riding to her rescue. You Americans don't give a nickel for a woman's honor. We do."

With a final wave, he took a parting shot at the country that had imprisoned him for the past five years: "I am glad to get away from America. The United States authorities have something to answer for in the way they treated me. And the newspapers were most unfair and unkind."

With that statement, Poderjay boarded the *Washington*. He balked at his third-class accommodations as he began the transatlantic sail for his home country of Yugoslavia. While England urged American authorities to apprise them of Poderjay's release, Scotland Yard no longer wanted him in connection with Ferrand's missing lover, Captain Frederick Davey. Scotland Yard had determined that Davey had good reasons of his own to disappear. Nor were they willing to try Poderjay on swindling charges; they simply wanted assurance that he would never set foot in England again. And though he was also wanted on charges in other countries, they no longer wanted him, either. With war raging in Europe, they had far more urgent business at hand.

When he stepped off the *Washington*, Ivan Poderjay slipped into oblivion. The man who said he would devote his life to finding Agnes Tufverson simply disappeared. The last authorities knew of Captain Poderjay, he was living with Suzanne Ferrand in Belgrade. Perhaps he remarried Ferrand, as he planned to do. Perhaps they moved after the bombing of Belgrade in 1941. Regardless, both Poderjay and Ferrand stayed out of the public eye.

Ferrand eventually returned to Paris, dying there in June 1975 at age seventy-nine. Although the Podrzaj family is buried in Ivan's native Slovenia, formerly part of Yugoslavia, Ivan Poderjay is not buried with them. Nor are there any records to indicate that he died in France. Though he may have returned to Slovenia, what became of Ivan Poderjay and when and where he died remains a mystery.

EPILOGUE

The more important mystery is what happened to Agnes Tufverson. After all of these years, no one has found a trace of the missing attorney.

When Poderjay left the United States for the last time, Agnes's sisters gave up their search.

On the day before Poderjay's release, Sally explained the family's position to reporters. "Yes, they will have to let him go. He has served his maximum sentence. There is nothing more that we can do and there is nothing more that we can say about it. We feel now that the less said the better. We have done all we can."

Amelia added, "If we did not try to forget, we would go mad."

Authorities and experts have weighed in on the case. In 1945, Captain John G. Stein reflected on the possibilities: "Did he murder Agnes Tufverson? Well, now that ten years have passed since she disappeared, it's a good bet that he did. He could have drugged her first. You will remember that when Flora Miller walked in on the night of December 20, Miss Tufverson appeared dazed, and the drug could have been taking effect right then."

At the Little Church around the Corner, someone made a notation on Captain Poderjay's portion of the marriage license. The note at the bottom of the page, which was written in 1935, reads, "Bigamist. Arrested in Vienna." The writer details Poderjay's sentence in Sing Sing and then concludes on the side, "Bride disappeared."

The last entry into Agnes Tufverson's missing persons case file was made on February 10, 1940—the day on which Poderjay was deported. It simply provides the date and details about Poderjay's release. As the Tufverson sisters feared, Ivan Poderjay most likely took the secrets of Agnes's disappearance with him. Her family was left to guess Agnes's fate. Sally shared her fears with reporters, "I think my sister lies at the bottom of the Atlantic. I think she was drugged and doped and thrown out of that porthole of *The Olympic.*" If Sally was right, we may never recover Agnes Tufverson.

We can, however, marvel at four strong young women who put aside their professional and personal lives to seek justice for their older sister. Their actions are a testament to the love that binds families together and to the will to press forward even in our darkest hours. Although one man likely ripped Agnes from this world, she was a brilliant, successful, generous, and loving woman who had already created a legacy that he could never destroy.

4

JEAN SPANGLER, 1949

OCTOBER 1949: LOS ANGELES, CALIFORNIA

As she gathered her luggage, Florence Spangler looked over at her twenty-seven-year-old daughter, Jean.

"I shouldn't go."

"Now, mother," Jean began.

"I had a premonition that something is going to happen if I leave."

Jean soothed Florence. "I'm a big girl now and I can take care of myself."

HOW DO I LOOK?

At about 5:00 p.m. on Friday, October 7, 1949, twenty-seven-year-old dancer and bit actress Jean Spangler hurried down the stairs of the apartment she shared with her mother and her five-year-old daughter, Christine. The striking brunette wore a pair of dark green slacks, a wool blouse, and a white sports jacket. Jean planned to meet her ex-husband, Dexter Benner, to discuss an increase in child support payments as well as overdue payments before heading off to the movie set where she worked as an extra. Or at least that was what she told her sister-in-law Sophie.

Jean Spangler. *Los Angeles Evening Citizen News, October 1949*

Jean found her sister-in-law sitting in the living room. Sophie, who had been visiting for the past six weeks with her five-year-old daughter (also named Jean), often watched Christine while Jean worked. Since Jean worked as an extra on film and television sets and as a dancer at local nightclubs, it was not uncommon for her to work until the early morning hours.

On this particular evening, Jean was worried about Christine, whom she affectionately called Christy. The little girl had a cold, but Jean could not delay her plans and she knew her sister-in-law would take good care of her little girl.

"How do I look?" Jean asked Sophie before giving Christy an affectionate kiss.

"Where are you going?" Christy asked her mother.

"To work," Jean replied. She then looked at Sophie, smiled, and winked.

Jean typically worked eight-hour shifts at the studio. Sometimes her takes were done in a couple of hours and sometimes she had to work the whole shift. She told Sophie that she was meeting with Dexter, her ex-husband, to collect a child support check before work. She promised to call Sophie when she arrived at the studio. Jean always called to give Sophie a number where she could be located in case there was any trouble with Christine.

With a mischievous smile, Jean told Sophie to "wish her luck." Then, after kissing her daughter and her niece, Jean waved goodbye.

Jean headed toward the marketplace on West Third Street and Fairfax Avenue. She first chatted with Ray Miller, the owner of a key shop. They discussed her plans to buy a pocketbook for her daughter Christine. Miller put this encounter at about 5:30 or so. He reported that Jean was "cheerful" and "in good spirits."

At about 6:00 p.m., cashier Lillian Marks saw Jean enter another area of the market. Marks recognized Jean, who was sometimes a customer. Jean seemed to be waiting for someone, but Marks never saw anyone with Jean at this time.

Also at around 6:00 p.m., Jean called Sophie from a pay phone at the Town and Country Marketplace in order to check on Christine. She informed Sophie that she had to work until the early morning hours and urged her not to wait up. By the urgency in Jean's voice, Sophie could tell that Jean was in a hurry to get off of the phone. Sophie assumed that Jean was waiting for someone to pick her up and had spotted her ride. The call ended. That was the last time Sophie ever spoke to Jean.

I WAITED AS LONG AS I COULD STAND

The following morning, a Saturday, Sophie woke to find that Jean had never come home. She was a little concerned, but she knew that Jean worked odd hours and figured that maybe her schedule had changed. Expecting Jean that morning, Sophie prepared breakfast for the girls and went about her daily routine. Dexter Benner, Jean's ex-husband, arrived later that morning to pick up Christine for his weekend visitation. Strangely, however, he did not come to the door to collect his daughter as usual. Instead, he waited on the sidewalk and Christine ran out to meet him.

Morning turned into afternoon and still there was no sign of Jean. Sophie became worried. It was unlike Jean not to call if she was going to be late. She tried to busy herself with her daughter and household chores, but she could hardly contain herself. Sophie fielded the first of many phone calls from writer Peter Brooks, who may have been a love interest of Jean's at the time. Brooks was looking for Jean and was also uneasy about her absence. He urged Sophie to go to the police. As evening approached, Sophie's worry turned to alarm. Where was Jean?

By 10:30 p.m., she was convinced that something was terribly wrong and could wait no longer. She arrived at the Wilshire Police Station at 10:50 p.m. and filled out a missing person report on Jean. Though the police officers were kind, they did not seem concerned. Jean was an adult and could do as she pleased. With her job and social scene, authorities figured that Jean had just gone off somewhere without calling. Sophie knew better. If Jean were okay, she would have called. She always called. She checked on Christine religiously. She never stayed away from home this long. Sophie returned home in a state of panic.

Almost eight hours later, at 6:00 a.m. on Sunday morning, Henry Anger was beginning his day as a foreman of Griffith Park. Near the Fern Dell entrance, he spotted a dark object about ten feet from the road. Investigating further, he found a black purse. As he picked up the pocketbook, Anger noted that the left strap had been broken and the cloth had been practically ripped from the purse's frame. Upon opening the purse, he found various forms of identification—a driver's license, a Screen Actors Guild card, a Screen Extras Guild card, and other forms of identification all belonging to a Jean Spangler. Not wanting to rifle through the other items, Anger used the information on Jean's identification to find her phone number and call her home.

Jean and Sophie. *Private collection of Gayland Isley*

At 6:30 a.m., Sophie hastily answered the call hoping for news of Jean's whereabouts. Instead, she received the ominous news that Jean's purse had been found, torn and abandoned, in the park. Henry Anger hung up with Sophie and immediately called the police.

Officers quickly arrived at Griffith Park that morning to investigate. Upon inspecting the purse, police noted its torn strap and the various forms of identification inside. They also found a silver dollar—which Sophie later told them that Jean kept in her purse for luck—and a mysterious note. The note read: "Dear Kirk: Can't wait any longer. Going to see Dr. Scott. Will work best this way while mother is away."

Police took the purse to headquarters, where Sophie identified it as Jean's purse, though she could not identify the "Kirk" to whom the note inside was written. Authorities believed that Jean had written the note. On closer inspection, they found that the note ended with a comma, as if the writer was interrupted. Fearing foul play, they began an immediate investigation and issued an all-points bulletin, asking help from other area police departments in the hunt for Jean Spangler that evening.

Jean's disappearance sparked an exhaustive search, a Hollywood scandal, and a mystery that has yet to be solved.

DESTINED FOR STARDOM

Elizabeth Jean Spangler was born on September 2, 1923, in Seattle, Washington, to Cecil "Martin" and Florence (Morris) Spangler. The youngest of four siblings, Jean had two brothers, Richard and Edward, and a sister, Betsy. The family eventually moved to Los Angeles. Jean attended and graduated from Franklin High School, where she was a member of the ice-skating club, served as a school senator, and performed in the Senior Class Day.

As a teenager, Jean began dancing at local clubs like Slapsy Maxie's as part of the chorus line. Her big break, however, came when she was eighteen and landed two important dancing jobs—one at the Earl Carroll Theater and the other at the Florentine Gardens.

The Earl Carroll Dinner Theater, located on Sunset Boulevard, was known for its lavish shows and scantily clad performers. Their beauty was advertised not only in print media but above the very entrance of the establishment. An electric sign with a woman's head greeted customers and read, "Through these portals pass the most beautiful girls in the world." Jean was proud and excited to be one of those girls. The Florentine Gardens was a dinner theater that served Italian food and burlesque entertainment. The enormous space could seat more than a thousand customers for dinner. Jean grabbed as many shifts as she could at these establishments and hoped to make the right connections to advance her Hollywood career.

It was at the Earl Carroll Dinner Theater that Jean met plastics manufacturer Dexter Benner. A native of Los Angeles and a recent graduate of University of Southern California, Benner frequented the club. Though he and Jean were not compatible by any account—she was sociable and sought stardom whereas he was conservative and sought family life—the two began dating and married soon thereafter on July 1, 1942.

At nineteen years old, Jean quickly realized she had made a mistake. Her job at the theater meant that she worked long hours, often well into the night and the early morning. Benner, who had been a regular at the club, knew that his wife had to pay extra attention to the male guests and wear skimpy costumes. He hated the idea and spent hours at home imagining what Jean was doing at the club. Upon marrying Jean, he assumed that she would give up her job and become a housewife, but Jean had dreams of stardom, and she never intended to give them up. Within six months, their marriage was over. Jean filed for divorce, citing Benner's "mental cruelty."

For some reason, however, she soon dropped the charges, and she and Benner remained married. Even though they remained married, their relationship has been described as "on-again, off-again" over the next few years. During this tumultuous period in their relationship, however, Jean gave birth to their daughter Christine in April 1944.

Benner enlisted during the war and was called to service in September of that year. While Benner was overseas, Jean supposedly conducted a number of affairs. According to her lawyer at the time, one of these affairs was with an air force lieutenant named Scotty. Scotty allegedly became abusive, and Jean often would show up to work with bruises. When Scotty wrecked her car and threatened to kill her, Jean officially ended the relationship. She figured that she had told enough people about his threats that he knew he would be the first person suspected if anything happened to her. Apparently, her plan worked, and she never saw Scotty again. Dexter returned from the war in 1945 to find that his wife had wrecked their car, spent all of their money, and been unfaithful. Dexter sued for divorce in 1946.

By all accounts, the divorce was ugly. Even though Jean was not a Hollywood figure yet and Benner was in the plastics business, their divorce made newspaper headlines because of the intense courtroom drama it entailed. The couple's battle was fought largely over custody of their daughter, Christine. Benner purported that Jean was not a serious mother. Instead, she was a philandering, party-girl wife who could not handle finances or their small child. The judge agreed and awarded custody of Christine to Dexter Benner in 1946. Devastated, Jean moved in with her mother in the Park Le Brea apartment complex on 6216 Colgate Avenue.

PARTY-GIRL PRIORITIES

Though her ex-husband had painted Jean as a party girl who favored the nightlife over motherhood, Jean spent every moment after she lost custody of her daughter fighting to regain custody. She was especially motivated because Benner, in direct defiance of their court order, had denied Jean access to Christine on no less than twenty-three occasions since the decree. According to Jean, he also threatened that "he would make it so she would never see Christine again." Jean was finally granted a new hearing in 1948, which turned out to be further fodder for newspaper headlines. Benner continued his character assassination of Jean, telling the presiding judge, Albert F. Rose, that his ex-wife was a "glamor girl mother" and accused her of caring more about Hollywood than their four-year-old daughter. This time, however, Benner could not convince the judge. The fact that he had

Jean and her daughter Christine. *Los Angeles Times, August 1949*

denied Jean visitation rights in defiance of the original court order, along with the fact that the judge believed the child belonged with her mother, helped Jean win the case. The judge also disagreed with Benner's portrayal of Jean as an unfit mother because she worked in the club/film industry.

Judge Rose explained his decision: "Many actresses, models and dancers—professional glamor girls—are known to be excellent mothers."

The bitter custody battle ended in the judge finding them both fit parents but awarding custody to Jean, stating that "a girl belonged with her mother."

Jean with her siblings (from left to right: Richard, Jean, Edward, and Betsy). *Private collection of Gayland Isley*

He awarded Jean physical custody and Benner visitation rights on alternate weekends. Christine moved in with her mother and grandmother in their Park Le Brea apartment. The year 1948 was proving to be a promising year for Jean. Not only did she regain custody of her daughter, but she also began to earn small dancing roles in film and television. Though uncredited, she appeared in three movies that year: *Mummy's Dummies* (a Three Stooges short); *Miracle of the Bells*, starring Fred MacMurray and Frank Sinatra; and *When My Baby Smiles at Me*, starring Betty Grable.

Her newfound success continued into 1949, during which time she was cast in three additional films: *Chicken Every Sunday*, starring Celeste Holm and Natalie Wood; *Young Man with a Horn*, starring Kirk Douglas; and *The Pretty Girl*, starring Robert Cummings. She played a chorus girl in one of her final roles, the Fred Astaire picture *Let's Dance*, which was released after Jean's disappearance in November 1950.

Certainly, Jean felt that life was looking up after the bitter war years during which she had lost so much. In addition to her marriage and her daughter, Jean had also lost her brother, Edward. With only two years between them, Jean had always been close to her older brother. In fact, he named his own daughter (who was the same age as Christine) after Jean. Edward was killed in action on June 1, 1945. Serving as a technical sergeant and a right gunner on B-29 *Poison—Second Dose*, Edward and his entire eleven-man crew were killed in an accidental collision with another B-29 bomber during an attack on Osaka, Japan. His body was unrecoverable. He was twenty-three years old, and he left behind his wife of three years, Sophie, and their one-year-old daughter, Jean.

A HAPPY HOUSEHOLD

Sophie, who had been living and working as a saleswoman in a department store back in St. Louis, Missouri, had recently traveled to California with little Jean to visit. They had been staying at the Park Le Brea apartment for the past six weeks. Sophie and Jean got along like sisters, and Sophie often watched Christine while Jean worked. Soon, the Spangler family would be expanding again. Jean's brother, Richard, and his wife were expecting a baby at any time. Jean's mother, Florence, had recently traveled to Lexington, Kentucky, to be there for the birth.

In addition to the happiness in her family and professional life, Jean also had found happiness in the romance department. A week before her disappearance, Jean was working on the film *Pretty Girl*, starring actor Robert Cummings. Jean was playing a society woman in a night-club scene in the picture. Cummings would later report to police a conversation that he had with Jean in the studio lot.

One day, as he was sitting on the steps outside of his trailer at Columbia Studios, Jean passed by. She was whistling, and Robert teased her about how happy she sounded. She confided in him that she had a new romance. When she told him it wasn't serious, she smiled mischievously and added that she "was having the time of her life." However, she did not divulge the name of her new love interest to coworkers or to her family.

For all of these reasons, Jean seemed perfectly happy when she left for work on the evening of Friday, October 7. Her sister-in-law Sophie informed police that Jean had been in good health and good spirits in the weeks leading up to and on the evening of her disappearance.

Jean's attorney, S. S. Hahn, knew—almost better than anyone else—how happy Jean was with her daughter and her career. He had represented Jean during the contentious custody battle with her ex-husband, and he spoke with Jean often. For these and other reasons, he was convinced that foul play was involved in Jean's disappearance.

"She was very happy with her baby and had no reason to run away," he told detectives.

In fact, the day before Jean disappeared, she had been given a bit part in a motion picture. According to the Allied Artists Agency, Jean was very excited about the role and was supposed to start work at Big Bear Studio on Monday. She did not, however, report to the studio.

Hahn reread the note found in Jean's purse and took off on his own to find the mysterious "Kirk" and "Dr. Scott." After the discovery of

Jean's purse, homicide detectives M. E. Tullock and William Brennan joined the investigation into the missing starlet.

PERFECTLY NORMAL

On Monday, detectives Tullock and Brennan visited Griffith Park. They spent the morning searching the area near the Fern Dell entrance where Jean's purse had been discovered. They, along with park employees, sifted through the undergrowth for clues. The shady canyon area was covered in many different varieties of dense fern plants. About fifty yards from that location, they found a makeshift bed of two blankets and a "soiled" pillow. Someone, they surmised, had been sleeping in the area recently, which was hidden from the road by various shrubs. They collected hair and fingernail samples from the bedding.

Detectives had to consider the case of Mimi Boomhower, a widow who disappeared that August. Her ripped white purse was discovered at a market about a week after her disappearance. Written on the purse was the message, "We found this at the beach Thursday night." Tullock and Brennan wondered if they were dealing with a killer who had a fetish for women's purses or clothing. Could they tie the disappearances of these two women?

Police also had to consider the possibility that Jean could have been the victim of the Black Dahlia murderer. Although police suspected the unidentified killer in nine deaths, most of them took place in 1947 in quick succession. The mutilated bodies of a series of women were found in various locations. Elizabeth Short, known as the Black Dahlia, was a twenty-two-year-old starlet when she was killed, mutilated, and bisected in January 1947. Most importantly, a purse played a key role in her case. An anonymous person mailed Short's purse to the police during the investigation into her murder. The killer posed Short's body, however, in a manner that suggested she was meant to be found. The same cannot be said in Spangler's case.

Police divulged the contents of Miss Spangler's purse to reporters. They even shared images of the purse and its contents. The usual assorted items such as makeup, identification, hairpins, and an address book filled the black cloth pocketbook. The note within Jean Spangler's purse provided detectives with their first tangible clue. They concentrated on finding the identity of the doctor mentioned in the letter, as well as the identity of "Kirk," to whom the note was addressed. Jean's sister-in-law had never heard of either man, but she told authorities that she was not well acquainted with Jean's personal life. Detectives wondered if Jean had arranged to meet "Kirk" at the park after work.

Back at police headquarters, Captain Harry Didion continued to field calls from people who reported seeing the missing woman since

Dexter and Lynn Benner. *Los Angeles Mirror, April 1953*

her disappearance. These clues kept officers busy throughout the beginning of the week.

Later in the day, detectives visited the home of Jean's ex-husband, Dexter Benner. Considering the couple's contentious divorce and the fact that Jean planned to meet with her husband on the evening of her disappearance to discuss his overdue child support ($500 in today's economy) as well as a possible increase, detectives were quite eager to speak to Benner. Detectives Tullock and Brennan later reported, however, that Dexter Benner was "unable to shed any light on his ex-wife's disappearance." He denied that he had met with Jean on Friday night and told detectives that he had not seen his ex-wife in several months. Dexter's new wife, Lynn, backed up her husband's claim, stating that Dexter had been with her the entire evening and that they had not seen Jean at any time. Interestingly, Lynn's first husband, mobster Eli Lasky, was also friends with Jean.

Jean's attorney, S. S. Hahn, asked Superior Court Judge Thomas Cunningham to award temporary custody of Jean's daughter to Jean's mother. Hahn also told reporters that under the custody settlement, Jean was not allowed to leave the state without her lawyer's permission. Sometimes her work took her away from her child, and she had always notified him when this was the case. Hahn explained that they spoke frequently and he had talked to Jean only a few days prior to her disappearance, at which time she sounded "perfectly normal." He further told reporters, "I am sure Jean has met with violence."

Detectives also checked local television stations and movie studios for any information about Jean's activities on Friday night. These inquiries, however, failed to yield any more clues in the case.

WE HAVE BEEN EXPECTING A CALL

Mrs. Florence Spangler, Jean's mother, was still visiting her son Richard in Louisville, Kentucky, when she received word of her daughter's disappearance. On Monday, Richard told reporters that he and his mother were waiting for word from their lawyer.

"We have been expecting a call," he told reporters. Other than that, he informed them that he and his mother knew nothing about his sister's disappearance.

In an attempt to retrace Jean's footsteps, detectives interviewed Sophie Spangler again. Had Jean walked to work that evening? Sophie wasn't sure. She was watching the children, so she did not pay attention to her sister-in-law's movements after she exited the house. Sometimes, Sophie told the police, Jean took a cab to work. Other times she took a bus. Friends had given her a ride to work in the past. Jean also had been known to walk if the studio was close by.

It was important for police to find the studio at which Jean had worked that evening. Again, as much as she tried, Sophie was not much help. Jean worked at any number of television and movie studios—wherever she could get work. Detectives spoke with the Central Casting Corporation and the Screen Extras Guild in an effort to find Jean's whereabouts on the evening she disappeared, only to learn that Jean had not been booked for any work that evening. Further, none of the studios were even open that night. At that point, detectives realized that Jean lied about her whereabouts on the evening she disappeared. Now they needed to figure out why. What was she trying to hide? And did it have anything to do with her mysterious disappearance?

When pressed further about her last exchange with Jean before she left the house, Sophie told police that Jean's daughter had asked where her mother was going.

"Going to work," Jean answered her daughter.

As she responded, however, Sophie remembered that Jean winked at Sophie. In hindsight, thought Sophie, perhaps that wink was a signal that Jean was not going to work. Maybe, thought detectives, Jean was really going to see "Kirk," to whom she addressed the mysterious letter in her purse.

They read through Jean's address book in an effort to find out Kirk's identity. They also searched for evidence of the "Doctor Scott" referenced in the note. After finding no clues in Jean's address book, they searched telephone number pads at the house, but these did not turn up any clues either. None of Jean's family members had heard of Kirk or Doctor Scott. Scott was not the family physician.

Spangler's lawyer also met with detectives. He shared the conversation he had with Jean three days before her disappearance.

"She expressed her usual affection for the child and her happiness in living with her daughter," he told police. He had not noticed anything concerning in her tone or demeanor. The conversation, he reiterated, had been normal.

Hahn also notified police that he had wired Jean's mother in Kentucky to inform her that he planned to ask the judge to give her temporary custody of Christine.

TUESDAY

The LAPD organized another hunt of Griffith Park for late Tuesday or early Wednesday morning. This time, they called up two hundred reservists to comb through every inch of the four-thousand-plus acre park, which included canyons and mountainous terrain. By that point, detectives were convinced of Spangler's death and were looking for her body. After meeting with detectives for more than an hour, department chief Thad Brown told the press as much when he stated that "death by violence was indicated in the girl's mysterious disappearance."

Detectives suspected that the mysterious "Kirk" played some role in the mystery. Since he had not come forward, they suspected he was hiding something from the police. They also interviewed various "Dr. Scotts" in the area; however, they focused on one particular Dr. Scott who was reported to use offices on the Sunset Strip. Based on Spangler's note, detectives suspected that Jean might be pregnant and planning to undergo an abortion. Her sister-in-law, Sophie, denied this theory, stating that Jean was not in need of any medical treatment. She did, however, tell authorities that Jean was currently suffering from "an ailment common to her sex" though she did not supply specifics. Jean's friends came forward to tell police that Jean had confided in them that she was indeed three months pregnant, though this was never confirmed.

On Tuesday evening, a group of police officials met to discuss the case before proceeding. Department Chief Thad Brown and

Detectives Tullock and Brennan met with Inspector Hugh Farnum, Captain Harry Elliott of the Central Homicide Squad, and Detective Lieutenant Harry Didion. Chief Brown reported after the conference that they had discovered a "Scotty" who was part of Jean Spangler's crowd. Spangler met with Scotty and other friends during evenings out at the nightclubs. The police did not, however, know Scotty's whereabouts.

HOLLYWOOD'S YOUNG LEADING MEN

Actor Robert Cummings already had come forward to describe his interaction with Jean at the beginning of the previous week, in which she described a new and secret romance she was having, when leading man Kirk Douglas phoned detectives concerning the case. Vacationing in Palm Springs at the time, Douglas called authorities before they even had a chance to consider his connection to the case.

Douglas informed Chief Brown that Jean worked as an extra on a picture in which he starred called *Young Man with a Horn*. He told police that even though they had worked on the same film, he did not know Spangler nor had he ever gone out with Spangler, though he may have run into her on the set.

Shortly thereafter, Douglas called authorities again. This time, he told them that he remembered Jean because friends with whom he worked on the film pointed out that Jean was the tall girl who wore the green dress. He wanted to change his previous statement to let authorities know that he did remember Jean Spangler and had "kidded around" with her on the set, but he maintained that he had not dated her. He eventually released the following statement through his attorney:

"Mr. Douglas didn't even remember the girl but when he talked with people who worked with him on the picture, *Young Man with a Horn*, they recalled to him that she was a woman who wore a certain type of dress. Then he remembered her and the fact that he had kidded around with her a little on the set as he had done with numerous other extras. However, he didn't even know the girl's name and never went out with her or saw her except on the set."

In her syndicated Hollywood gossip column, "The Voice of Broadway," Dorothy Kilgallen also added her two cents concerning Kirk Douglas's relationship with Jean Spangler. "His story is that on two of the occasions she told people she had been out with him, he can prove he was elsewhere; once home in bed (to which his housekeeper will testify), the other time at a party with his two children."

It is not clear whether Jean told people she had been out with Kirk Douglas, but her mother and sister-in-law did later remember that a man named Kirk had picked Jean up on two occasions. He remained in the car, however, and never came to the door, so they did not see his face. These may have been the two occasions to which Kilgallen referred in her statement.

Up-and-comer Mike Howard was also questioned in Spangler's disappearance. Before he met with police, he admitted to reporters, "Sure I knew her. Everybody along Sunset Strip knew her. But I was never out with her and what the hell is this all about anyhow? Everybody knew the girl."

In fact, many prominent male actors were noted in Jean's address book. Detectives could not distinguish the professional from the romantic contacts, however, without interviewing every contact they found in the book. To make matters more confusing, they concluded that Jean had struck up a new romance within that last week or so of her life, but there was no way to determine if the Kirk addressed in the note was the new man she had been seeing.

EARLY SIGHTINGS

On Tuesday morning, one of Jean's male friends visited the police station. Asking to remain unidentified, he reported that he saw Jean Spangler in front of a Vine Street market at about 10:30 p.m. on Friday night. Other papers reported that the man said he had seen Jean on Saturday night, a full twenty-four hours after she had reportedly disappeared. He informed police that she was eating hotdogs with a "clean-cut young man." The informant approached Spangler, who introduced him to her companion, though he could not remember the young man's name. Under police questioning, however, the informant admitted that it may have been on Thursday evening, not Friday or Saturday evening, that he had seen Jean.

Another informant, Art Rodgers, reported that a young woman entered a filling station near Sunset Strip at 3:00 a.m. on Saturday, October 8. The woman was riding with a man in a blue-gray sedan convertible. The man, who ordered gas, told the attendant that they were traveling to Fresno. Rodgers reported that the female passenger shrunk down in the passenger seat. She was crying and asked the attendant to have the police follow their car. She yelled out as they were leaving, "Call the police and get our license number." As the car sped off, Rodgers called police, but they were unable to locate the car. Upon seeing Jean's picture in the papers, Rodgers believed the woman was Jean.

Still other informants claimed to have seen Jean with the same "clean-cut young man" on early Saturday morning as well. Just an hour before the Rodgers sighting, guests reported seeing Jean in the Hollywood Cafe called the Cheesebox. They speculated that the man was between thirty and thirty-five years of age, and they identified Jean Spangler in police photos.

A popular Sunset Strip disc jockey, Al "The Sheik" Laazar, also reported seeing Jean Spangler at the same cafe about 2:30 a.m. Saturday morning. According to Laazar, who did tableside radio interviews, Jean Spangler was arguing with two gentlemen. When he approached their table for an interview, the men shooed him away.

The owner of the cafe, Terry Taylor, reported that Jean Spangler was at his establishment that evening, seated at a front table with a "clean-cut fellow." A newsboy also reported seeing Spangler outside this cafe. These sightings are significant because they are her last known sightings, placing Jean Spangler at the Cheesebox during the early morning hours of Saturday, October 8. Authorities believed that the young man with whom she was seen might have been the Kirk or Scott referenced in her note.

By the middle of the week, Jack J. Williams, a man from Stockton, told authorities he had seen a woman on Tuesday morning at the Greyhound bus station who matched Jean Spangler's description.

Williams noted the woman in question when she lost her key to a locker containing her suitcase and had to sign for a new one.

Meanwhile, a pretty, unemployed waitress, aptly named Bonita Jane Walter, was looking for a job. Focusing on the classifieds rather than the front-page news, she was unaware of Jean Spangler's disappearance. When she left her apartment, however, she noticed that people were giving her strange looks and staring at her. One man even followed Bonita home.

When Bonita answered her door, the man asked if she was Jean Spangler. "No," the dumbfounded Bonita replied. Once she realized that people had been mistaking her for a missing actress, she notified papers to dispel the rumors. "Now, at least, I know why everybody was giving me that fishy eye. I was beginning to wonder if I had two heads—or something," the pretty waitress told reporters.

WEDNESDAY

The search of Griffith Park, which had been scaled down since Tuesday, took place on Wednesday morning and failed to produce any signs of a struggle. Police believed that whoever killed Jean Spangler threw her purse near the entrance of the park to throw police off the scent.

Detectives finally had the chance to question park foreman Henry Anger, who had been off work since finding Jean's purse. He informed them that the purse he found on Sunday morning had not been there as of 7:30 Saturday evening, further prompting police to believe that someone tossed the purse into that area.

They questioned Jean's ex-husband, Dexter Benner, again on Wednesday. He had never heard of Scotty, Dr. Scott, or Kirk; however, he told detectives that when he came back from serving in the war, he found clothes belonging to an army officer named "Scott" in his wife's closet. Jean's mother, Florence Spangler, returned to Los Angeles on Wednesday. She told police that the Scott in question, an army lieutenant, had figured in her daughter's divorce. Police doubted that he was the Scott mentioned in the note. Benner informed police that before their divorce was finalized in 1946, Jean had married another man in Las Vegas. After a year, the marriage was annulled.

Mrs. Spangler told police that she was sure her daughter had been murdered. Further, she gave police the name of the man whom she thought was responsible.

"I am sure this man hired somebody to do away with my daughter," she told them.

Though police would not release the name to reporters, they assured the press that they had already spoken to the man in question at great length.

Meeting with reporters for the first time since her daughter's disappearance, Florence Spangler sobbed, "I can't imagine what's happened to Jeannie. I have never heard of this 'Dr. Scott' or Kirk. Something terrible must have happened to my little girl."

She added, "She was a good girl and wouldn't stay out at night."

This statement notwithstanding, Mrs. Spangler told police that Kirk was an acquaintance of Jean's through her studio work. In an effort to clarify, she told reporters, "You know how it is. I heard her talk about a 'Kirk' she knew over on the sets. But she was at first one studio and then another. I simply can't remember."

ARRESTS

High-profile and wealthy Las Vegas gambler Tom E. Evans was jailed in connection with Spangler's case. Previously jailed on suspicion in the disappearance of widow Mimi Boomhower, police wanted to take another look at the former smuggler and bodyguard for the mob. They arrested him on a suspicion of robbery but planned to question him in the Spangler case. From his jail cell, the forty-nine-year-old suspect vented his frustration to local papers.

"I never met either Mimi Boomhower or Jean Spangler. I don't want to meet them. I don't know what happened to them. I don't want to know. Despite my age, police evidently think I'm a Casanova. What would a good-looking young actress like Miss Spangler be doing with me?"

"Vegas Tom," as he was known, was eventually released when police realized he had no connection to Spangler's disappearance.

IN SERIOUS CONDITION

After two hours of questioning, on Thursday, October 13, Jean's fifty-six-year-old mother collapsed. Doctors determined her condition to be serious. Police were hoping to elicit some type of clue from the starlet's mother to help with the case. Mrs. Spangler suffered from a heart ailment, which had been exacerbated by her sudden return trip home, the shock over her daughter's disappearance, and the stress of the police interview. Mrs. Spangler was by that time convinced that her daughter had been murdered, and the stress of that knowledge was simply too much to bear.

Despite the beliefs of police and Mrs. Spangler that Jean was dead, reported sightings continued to trickle in to the police station. Detectives had to investigate each and every one of these sightings, especially those that seemed credible. On Friday morning, October 14, Shirley Ann Morse made her report to police. The thirteen-year-old schoolgirl was a friend of Jean Spangler. As Shirley's school bus traveled through the North Hollywood district on Thursday morning, she looked out the window and thought she saw Jean in a large Buick that drove beside the school bus. According to Shirley, Jean was wearing the same white jacket she had been wearing when she was last seen the previous Friday. An elderly man was driving the car.

Shirley told police, "I could see Jean plainly inside, and I recognized her positively. She was nervous, and frightened looking. The man driving the car seemed to be older."

Shirley's mother, who accompanied her to the police station, was certain that her daughter had seen the actress, telling police that Shirley was a "level-headed girl" who had "known Jean for a long time."

A less credible account was given by three waitresses at a carhop in Northern California who swore that Jean had lunch there with a large man the previous Tuesday. They reported that the couple headed for San Francisco in a green Lincoln Continental. When asked why they thought the woman was Jean Spangler, the waitresses replied that the woman looked like an actress and resembled Jean's images in the newspapers. Police received many other sightings like these every day following Jean's disappearance. Still, Jean's friends and family assured police that if Jean were alive, she would have come forward by now. She would not want them, especially her mother, to worry. Most importantly, she would never leave Christine. They believed that Jean was either dead or in great danger.

FIFTY MEN IN THREE MONTHS

Meanwhile, unverifiable reports of Jean Spangler's romantic liaisons prompted media questions. Albert Pearson, an attorney for whom Jean had worked as a secretary, told reporters, "A million and one things could have happened to her."

He rattled off various clubs where Jean performed as a dancer while she tried to break into motion pictures, and he insinuated that she had most likely dated at least fifty men in a three-month span. He seemed to imply that her job as a dancer was linked to her numerous dates. Jean's friends also seemed to verify this statement when they described Jean to the press as a "loveable screwball who particularly likes men."

On Friday, October 14, Dexter Benner, Jean's ex-husband who had already been questioned multiple times in her disappearance, filed a petition seeking custody of their five-year-old daughter. He had been taking care of their daughter, Christine, since his wife's disappearance and asked for custody until his ex-wife could be found. The hearing was set for October 26.

On Saturday, October 15, detectives questioned the actress's friends—both male and female—in an attempt to learn more information about the missing starlet. They also interviewed dozens of movie and television actors and actresses acquainted with the actress. Jean's friends described her as "strong as an ox." They had trouble imagining the type of man who could overtake their friend. They also recalled her keen sense of character and told police that Jean "could spot a phony a block away." Despite hours of investigation, however, police learned nothing new or substantial from these interviews.

FRAGILE CLUES

A full week after Jean's disappearance, detectives were no closer to finding the missing actress. Frustrated by what they deemed "fragile clues," detectives planned to enlist the help of mounted reservists. These were members of a reserve squad formed during the war and stationed in the San Fernando Valley. Police organized a search to commence at nine o'clock Sunday morning. Sixty mounted reservists—male and female—would ride their horses through the trails, terrain, and woods of Griffith Park. Though detectives originally had given up the idea that Jean's body was located in the park—at first thinking her purse had been planted there—they were now convinced that they could find clues there. They set up a command post at the entrance of the park where Jean's purse was originally located.

There was one significant lead, however, that detectives were working. They were fairly certain that they had finally figured out Kirk's identity. Though they shared with reporters that the man was a former Hollywood promoter, they would not release any other details. They also started to zero in on a young, former medical school student who went by the name of Scott, frequented the Sunset Strip clubs, and posed as a licensed medical physician.

Detectives investigated the idea that Jean could have taken off on a yacht. Her friends described her as a yachting enthusiast and explained that she often went on extended sea cruises. Investigators also continued and expanded their search of North Hollywood hotels. The expansive search now encompassed both land and sea. And, as is often the case, Jean was not the only missing person for whom detectives were searching. There were so many missing people in Los Angeles at the time, in fact, that newspapers ran stories with headings like, "Where, Oh Where, Have They Gone in Los Angeles" and "LA Police Baffled by Missing Persons." One article ended with the question, "Who's Next?"

On Saturday evening, two gentlemen were visiting friends on Colgate Avenue, a couple of houses down from Jean Spangler's home. When the men, Sidney Cassyd and Frank Orvy, left the residence, they noted a heavyset man lurking in the bushes of Jean's home. They called out to the man, who turned to them and immediately fled on foot down an alley. They gave chase but lost him.

Strangely, their story sounded very much like the story Robert Stack had told police almost immediately after Jean's disappearance. Stack, who would later achieve fame as the host of *Unsolved Mysteries*, was Jean's friend. The night before her disappearance, Stack was walking by Jean's Colgate Avenue apartment when he spotted a shadowy figure lurking by the windows. It was too dark to make out whether it was a man or a woman. The figure was gone before he could discern its identity or purpose, so Stack determined to tell Jean about what he saw the next day—only he never saw Jean again. Instead, he told authorities.

YOU AREN'T JUST LOOKING FOR A BODY

On that Sunday, more than two hundred police reservists met at the Fern Dell entrance to Griffith Park. Thirty-five were mounted on horses, some were accompanied by dogs, and some were volunteers who joined the reservists. Flanked by a variety of exotic and native species of ferns, the well-maintained walking path greets visitors to this Griffith Park entrance. Wooden railings frame the trail as you venture into what feels like another world. It was in this setting that Lieutenant George Banta directed his posse of reservist volunteers. The group, dressed in cowboy boots, hats, and jeans, awaited instructions.

"You aren't just looking for a body," he reminded his charges. "I want you to turn in anything you find."

After their initial meeting at Fern Dell, the police posse spread throughout the park and searched the thick foliage, uneven terrain, and large forests for clues. By the end of the day, they had found a few items: a pair of women's underwear, an LA County jail uniform, and some tools wrapped in an old rag, among other small items. They did not, however, find any items linked to Jean's case.

Rather than feeling frustrated by the lack of evidence found during the dusk-till-dawn search, Lieutenant Banta was encouraged. He felt the lack of evidence pointed to the possibility that Jean Spangler might be alive. Mrs. Spangler was equally hopeful. She appealed to the public the following day, urging them to report any sightings or clues concerning her daughter. Despite their renewed hope, some newspapers reported that detectives had put the Spangler case on the inactive list, as they had exhausted all avenues of inquiry in the case.

NOW WE'LL GET IN SOME REAL WORK

Two weeks into Jean Spangler's disappearance, media coverage waned, and police welcomed the quiet. Big media stories covering disappearances, especially those of celebrities, hindered investigations.

Head of the police's homicide division, Captain Harry Elliott told reporters, "Cranks give us the most trouble. That's why we welcome the day when newspapers stop printing stories about famous missing persons."

Elliott felt that, especially in the Jean Spangler case, more authentic leads would follow once the media coverage died down.

He concluded, "Now we'll get in some real work." He also promised that none of the missing persons cases would be closed until the missing persons were found. Police issued Jean's name, image, and description over the police bulletin that week, but they did not release this information to newspapers.

Indeed, Jean Spangler's name all but disappeared from newspapers in California and throughout the country until October 26, the day of the custody hearing concerning her child. Christine Louise, or Christy, as she was known to her family, had been living with her father, Dexter Benner, since Jean's disappearance. The hearing was held in domestic relations court. Superior Judge Thomas J. Cunningham heard arguments.

Though the couple had fought a bitter custody battle, Dexter Benner swore that he would not take advantage of the tragic circumstances surrounding his ex-wife's disappearance. He told their daughter that Jean was working, so Christy was having a vacation at her father's house. He shielded his daughter from any news or information concerning her mother's disappearance.

Jean's mother also filed for custody. During the hearing on October 26, her lawyers petitioned that there was still a possibility that Jean would be found. Therefore, they argued, she should not be put through the further trauma of trying to regain custody of her child. Mrs. Spangler's attorneys further stated that an abrupt change in custody "would be unseemly and grossly harsh." Mrs. Spangler appealed to the judge, stating that Jean had been "deeply and strongly devoted to the child, who should be permitted to return to the home she has loved."

The final judgment allowed Benner custody until Jean was found or declared dead. Mrs. Spangler asked the judge that she be allowed visitation. Before he left the courtroom, Benner arranged for Christine to visit her grandmother "as often as possible." He reiterated his stance that he was not trying to take the child away.

The arrangement, however, did not remain civil for long. Mrs. Spangler, who suspected that Benner might have had something to do with her daughter's disappearance, did not trust him or his wife with her granddaughter. In fact, Lynn Benner had lost custody of her own two children to her ex-husband, Eli Lasky. He asserted that she had neglected her children while carrying on an affair. Lasky signed an affidavit to the effect and on December 12, Mrs. Spangler filed for custody on the grounds that Lynn Benner was an unfit caretaker. She also asserted that her ex-son-in-law "associated with people of questionable moral character in front of the child" and was also unfit.

Held a week later and presided over by Judge Mildred Lillie, the ensuing court battle was fraught with accusations from both sides. Mrs. Spangler accused Lynn Benner of striking her ex-husband, carrying on extramarital affairs, and rarely visiting her own children. Dexter Benner accused Mrs. Spangler of planning to run away with Christine. Mrs. Spangler accused Benner of denying her court-ordered visitation. Benner's lawyers countered that Mrs. Spangler was a "legal stranger" to the child. The result was that Benner retained custody of his child, and Mrs. Spangler was granted visitation twice a month.

MISSING OF HER OWN VOLITION

In a strange twist of events, that Tuesday the LAPD released a statement contrary to their initial investigation. They told reporters that "Jean had suffered a slight illness but would return shortly as soon as she felt better." They clarified that Jean was alive and missing "of her own volition." They concluded that Spangler was suffering from an illness that she wanted to keep secret. Though the police did not supply any details, they implied that they had information that led them to believe that the young actress would return on her own. They also felt safe in the assumption that Jean would be recovered enough to return by the end of that week. If she did not, only then would police assume she was dead.

The source of this theory has never been divulged nor credited, though her sister-in-law Sophie was purported to have alluded to an illness from which Jean suffered. Conversely, she also told police that Jean had been in good health and good spirits at the time of her disappearance. Regardless, Jean did not return and Sophie's statement was forgotten.

At the same time, detectives checked out a lead from a woman who reported that she saw what looked like a body about a mile from Sheep Hole Pass, which was four hours away from Griffith Park. The body, she said, appeared to have been wrapped in canvas. Local authorities investigated the clue only to find a burlap bag filled with dozens of tin cans.

When Mrs. June Davis of Sacramento opened her door to a magazine saleswoman who identified herself as Jean Spangler, Mrs. Davis promptly called the police, who investigated. This Jean Spangler, however, had been working with the magazine company for the past three years and was not the missing actress.

During Thanksgiving—a time when Americans join together with family—Jean's family could not celebrate. The holiday only reinforced

Jean's absence. Had she been ill, they were certain she would have returned to be with her family for the holiday. Perhaps that is why Mrs. Spangler acted a week later. She issued a $1,000 reward ($10,000 today) for any information leading to the arrest or conviction of Jean's murderer—no paltry sum for the family to raise. With little progress and no new leads in the case, the Spanglers were desperate.

"No Dr. Scott has ever been found," explained Mrs. Spangler, "and I do not believe Jean would bring sorrow to me and her little daughter, Christine, by remaining away for so long without even a word to us. I am sure she was kidnapped and murdered."

Her words, a near copy of Francis Arnold's spoken decades before, illustrate the unspoken knowledge that parents of missing persons share.

Curiously, the arrest of a Los Angeles cook, not the offer of the large reward, provided the next potential clue in the case. Los Angeles police arrested the cook, William Leonard Burbank, and transferred him to San Diego, where he was promptly searched on Friday, December 9. Folded within Mr. Burbank's wallet, they found a newspaper picture of Jean Spangler.

Police questioned Burbank about the picture.

"Who is in the picture?" they asked.

"Oh, that's a murdered girl," he replied.

"Why do you keep her picture inside your wallet?"

"I kept her picture because it looked a lot like a girl I used to go with."

Upon further questioning, Burbank denied knowing Spangler. He told authorities that he had seen her picture in the paper and heard of her disappearance, but that was all. And just like that, another lead fizzled. The investigation stalled for months.

WE ARE STILL DOING WHAT WE CAN

As 1950 rolled into view, Mrs. Spangler continued her search. That February, she wrote to her daughter-in-law Sophie, "We still are doing what we can to find Jean, and that is always the paramount thing in my mind. All else is minor."

She urged Sophie to run over the events surrounding Jean's last days and weeks to see if they might come up with an overlooked clue.

By this time, police had established that the new romance Jean was carrying on just before her disappearance was not connected to the Kirk in her note. They identified Jean's boyfriend as Peter Brooks, a fellow bit actor on the movie set where she had been working. They also crossed him off as a suspect in her disappearance. Another bit player on the set, Evelyn Ceder, pointed out that something must have happened to her friend Jean. "It isn't like Jean to drop out of sight without telling anyone. She was devoted to her daughter, Christine."

Jean's sister-in-law Sophie agreed: "She worshiped the child. After all the trouble, the distasteful court battle, she went through to gain custody, I know she wouldn't just walk off. It meant too much to her."

The "distasteful" custody battle, it seemed, was doomed to continue even after Jean's disappearance. Though Mrs. Spangler was not awarded custody of Christine, she was allowed to visit her granddaughter twice a month: once at Benner's house and once at her own home. Dexter Benner, however, was becoming increasingly concerned that Mrs. Spangler was telling the girl that her mother was still alive. Viewing this behavior as psychologically damaging to his daughter, Benner petitioned the court in March 1950 to revoke Mrs. Spangler's visitation rights altogether.

Meanwhile, police continued to field Jean Spangler sightings. They also began to investigate Jean's connection to "Little Davy" Ogul, a missing mobster, and her relationship with multimillionaire Tommy Lee, a radio station owner who committed suicide in January 1950. Rumors began to surface indicating that Spangler was hiding out somewhere near the Texas–Mexico border with Ogul and fellow mobster Frank Niccoli. They could not find Ogul nor could they make a definitive connection between Spangler and these men. Mrs. Spangler lashed out at such rumors: "Jean was not the kind of a girl to get mixed up with people like that." These reports and other gossip hurt their family.

However, detectives had reason to follow up on Jean's mobster connections. Little Davy Ogul and Frank Niccoli both worked for mobster boss Mickey Cohen. Cohen owned one of the clubs where Jean danced. As such, many underworld figures frequented the establishment, and Jean would almost certainly have associated with them. Further linking Jean to Ogul and Niccoli is the fact that both of these mobsters disappeared around the same time as Jean, Ogul only two days after Jean. Additionally, witnesses placed them together well after their disappearances.

Still, the "gossip," as Mrs. Spangler viewed it, certainly hurt her family in unimaginable ways. When Dexter Benner had his day in court regarding Mrs. Spangler's visitation rights, he cited the news stories, saying that his ex-wife was running around with mobsters. He also yelled out that she "had the address of Mike Howards" in her purse. Mike Howards, along with Ogul and Niccoli, worked for mobster Mickey Cohen, who himself had worked under Bugsy Siegel. Cohen's subordinates were known as "Mickey's Seven Dwarfs," and two of those dwarfs were missing. Benner contended that his wife was running around with "Cohen's Seven Dwarfs" shortly before her disappearance. He countered that he had even been questioned by police about his ex-wife's connection to these mobsters.

Superior Court Judge Elmer D. Doyle looked into Benner's claim that Mrs. Spangler was mentally harming his daughter by telling her granddaughter that Jean was alive. Benner further asserted that by reminding the child that Jean was her "real" mother, she was confusing the child. Christine began asking her father if he was her "real daddy."

Benner cited what he felt were two disturbing incidents before the court. At Christmas, Mrs. Spangler gave Christine a doll. Christine named the doll Jean Elizabeth, after her mother, and thought of her mother whenever she held the doll. Benner accused Florence Spangler of initiating the name and symbolism. He further asserted that Florence Spangler had his daughter create a valentine card for her mother. Mrs. Spangler denied these allegations. She admitted to making valentines with Christine, but said they never made a valentine for Jean. When asked by the judge where her daughter was, Florence Spangler simply replied, "God, I wish I knew, Judge Doyle."

Mrs. Spangler's daughter, Betsy, defended her mother, saying she "would lean over backwards to avoid upsetting her granddaughter" with talk of Jean.

After Mrs. Spangler accused Lynn Benner of teaching Christine an improper way of kissing, Judge Doyle ordered a recess until the following morning. He also ordered that Christine, who was to turn six years old in a few weeks, come to the court. He wanted to speak to the child himself.

The following day, Christine entered the court in a frilly short-sleeved white dress with matching gloves and hair bow. Looking angelic with her wavy blonde curls and blue eyes, she stood by her father. Judge Doyle approached the child and handed her a candy bar and then led Christine to his chambers so they could talk. He was immediately impressed with the little girl's manner.

"She's one of the smartest children of her age I've ever seen," he remarked as the two came out of his chambers after their talk, and Christine ran over to her father. Clearly smitten with the child, he added, "I'd like to have that baby myself."

During his talk with Christine, the judge concluded that her step-mother was treating her well and that the "bad ideas" referenced in court had come from the little girl's playmates and not her caretakers. He also referenced the toll that the divorce and her mother's disappearance had had on Christine. In the end, he felt that the two parties loved the child and could come to an agreement amicably and without lawyers. He ordered Dexter Benner and Florence Spangler to return to his chambers the following morning at 9:00 a.m.

After his meeting with the two parties, Judge Doyle took a few days to think over his decision. A week later, he released his ruling, allowing Florence Spangler to continue her visits with her granddaughter. Explaining his ruling, Judge Doyle stated: "It would be grossly harsh and inequitable to deprive Mrs. Florence Spangler of the right to visit the child of her missing daughter. It is natural for a child to inquire about her mother, after the mother's strange disappearance, and it is natural for the grandmother to try to explain this to the child."

Judge Doyle further found that Jean had treated her daughter very well and that there was no evidence to show that she had willingly left the child. At the same time, he felt that Christine was also well cared for by her father. He upheld Mrs. Spangler's rights to visit her granddaughter once a month at Benner's home and to take the child once a month to her home.

Despite the court order, Benner allowed Mrs. Spangler to visit Christine only a handful of times during 1950. In December, he found himself in contempt of court and was sentenced to five days in jail. The sentence was suspended, however, and he did not see a day behind bars.

Within months, Dexter Benner was back in court. His wife, Lynn, wanted to legally adopt Christine. Again, Dexter Benner hurled damaging rumors about his ex-wife's disappearance, citing her "mobster" connections. He also stated that Jean had abandoned Christine and therefore Lynn should be her legal mother.

On the day in question, Dexter Benner brought Christine to court. She waited outside during the proceedings. Florence Spangler appeared with her attorney to defend her daughter. She asserted that there was no proof that Jean had abandoned her daughter. Superior Judge Georgia Bullock presided.

Benner's lawyer remarked during the proceedings that Jean had gone "away with a gangster and abandoned her child." When he tried to introduce this line of questioning, Florence's lawyer objected, and the judge sustained the objection. In the end, Judge Bullock denied Benner's petition.

"This is not my idea of abandonment," the judge decided. "Since the petitioner has failed to prove abandonment by the mother, we will not proceed with the adoption."

Benner's lawyer sarcastically admonished the judge, claiming he had looked everywhere for Jean Spangler and there was no other conclusion to make except for the fact that she had abandoned her child. He questioned the judge as to what more he could have done to prove it, asking, "How have I been derelict in my duty to my client, Judge?"

The papers followed the salacious details the following day, but one reporter spoke out against the rumor, smear tactics, and animosity that was leveled at Jean Spangler and her family. In her column, "Florabel Muir Reporting," Muir did not hold back her contempt for the way the police had been handling the case: "So far the police had turned up no clues to indicate what has happened to this poor, unfortunate girl, but with an almost malicious intent some of them have allowed her to be smeared with all sorts of half-veiled innuendos about an illegal operation, association with gangsters, and charges that she was a 'Hollywood Party Girl' although there is nothing in their investigation as far as I can learn that will substantiate any such insinuations."

Muir had even more to say about Jean's ex-husband and his continued efforts to remove Jean's family and her memory from his daughter's life. "As for her ex-husband, why does he keep reiterating vicious charges against the mother of the little girl he says he loves? . . . Also, why doesn't he leave Mrs. Spangler the few crumbs of comfort she can find visiting with her little granddaughter? Whatever hatred he had in his heart for his wife who left him should have faded by now since he has a new life with another woman."

Florabel Muir actually knew Jean when Jean was working at Slapsy Maxie's. Muir paints a very different picture of Jean Spangler, one that's Jean's family had been trying to present to the media since the actress's disappearance. To set the record straight, she includes the picture of a hard-working and determined young woman: "I never saw her hanging around the place after she had finished her work. She always seemed to be a hard-working girl interested in getting ahead through her own efforts. I saw Davy Ogul with many girls, but never with Jean. There is no evidence that the disappearance of Jean Spangler had anything to do with Mickey Cohen and why this rumor keeps being circulated is difficult for me to understand."

She concluded that the public should stop smearing Jean's name, if not out of respect to her, then at least out of respect for her mother and the trauma she had suffered. She used some choice words to end the article: "I would suggest to the cops who are so busy trying to prove that Jean was a bad girl that they get off the lard and try to find out what happened to her."

Florence Spangler told Judge Bullock that Dexter Benner "never once said anything to [her] or offered any sort of condolence" at the time of her daughter's disappearance or in the months since. Further, Florabel Muir reminded her readers that Jean planned to meet

Jean Spangler. *Los Angeles Times, December 1949*

with her ex-husband on the night of her disappearance. Benner, who worked until eight o'clock that evening, denied that Jean came to visit him. There is no doubt, though, that he carried an immense amount of hatred toward his ex-wife and was bitter that she had taken custody of their daughter away from him. So bitter, in fact, that he continued to petition the courts to remove all traces of Jean Spangler from his daughter's life. Since he worked so tirelessly to erase her in the months following her disappearance, it's entirely possible he was willing to make her disappear permanently.

A HEARTBROKEN MOTHER

Two days before Halloween 1951, the body of a nude woman was found stuffed in a trunk in Los Angeles. Authorities sent the body for autopsy to determine if it might be Jean Spangler or any of the many missing women from the area. The medical examiner performed a three-hour postmortem but failed to identify the victim or the cause of death.

The examination determined that though the body shared many similarities with Jean Spangler—the woman in the trunk was a brunette in her late twenties and about five feet seven inches tall—it was not Jean. Defeated, Jean's mother sent a letter to La Reina Rule's syndicated question-and-answer column the following year.

"Dear Miss Rule: On October 7, 1949 about 5:30 pm, my daughter Jean Spangler went to keep an appointment with her ex-husband to get the check for the support of her five-year-old daughter. He always sent the check in the mail but failed to do so this time. Jean mentioned to four or five of her friends that she would be meeting her former husband that evening.

"When she left the house, she went over to the Town & Country market and it was from there she disappeared and has never been seen or heard of since. She was dressed in slacks and not for the street and had no money.

"There were many rumors in the papers and by radio about her, all of a smear nature, but the police in checking out all these rumors have never come up with any proof that they were true. I checked with one columnist and several city desks and found that the rumors had been phoned in by an anonymous person. There never have been any facts found to substantiate the rumors that she had run away with someone.

"Do you feel that a devoted mother could go away of her own free will and leave her child and never contact her or her family again? I am a broken-hearted mother, and the terrible suspense of not finding my daughter is killing me.

"Her dear little child is looking to me for answers as to why her mother doesn't come home. I have prayed for help in finding my daughter and the whole truth about her disappearance.

"Jean and I were very close and I felt before her disappearance that she was in danger and since then I have felt in my heart that she is dead, but why, and if I only knew where. This isn't imaginary with me but a firm conviction which refuses to be shaken. As long as I have a breath of life in my body, I shall strive to find the truth about her disappearance. I have promised myself that Jean's little daughter shall not grow up believing that her mother ran away because she didn't love her or didn't want her. Can you please help me?"

The letter was signed "Mrs. S." In her response, Miss Rule shared her sympathies and assured Mrs. Spangler on a few points. The fact that Jean left home without dressing up or taking money indicated that she had not left of her own volition. Second, even if Jean were overwhelmed with caring for her daughter or had met a man with whom she ran away, she would have checked in on her daughter by this point. And Miss Rule said that it was not possible for a mother who loved and was devoted to her child to suddenly abandon that child forever. Miss Rule concluded her response by inviting readers to weigh in and help the brokenhearted Mrs. Spangler.

Dexter Benner, however, was not sympathetic to Mrs. Spangler's plight. Whether he read her letter or not, he petitioned the court yet again that September to terminate Florence's visitations with her granddaughter. He stated that Florence assured his child that her mother would return someday and spoke of the mother, which was upsetting to the child. It was not his first time back in court since his failed adoption petition. It seems Benner, despite a court order, refused to allow Mrs. Spangler to visit with her granddaughter. He found himself in contempt of court repeatedly. His petition, just another means to deny Mrs. Spangler access to her granddaughter, failed. In early October, the District Court of Appeals denied Benner's plea and upheld the original ruling. The decision came down almost three years to the date of Jean Spangler's disappearance.

Still, despite the new court hearing, Benner refused to allow Christine to visit Mrs. Spangler at her home on at least twenty-five occasions since the original court order. Considering that the order gave Mrs. Spangler one day a month on which her granddaughter could visit and stay overnight, twenty-five times is significant.

On January 14, 1953, Mrs. Spangler sought to have Benner fined and jailed for breaking their court order. Superior Judge Philbrook McCoy presided over the hearing in April 1952 and admonished both parties before issuing his decision. He told Benner, his wife, and Mrs. Spangler that they were all acting like children. He further stated: "You have both used the child, Christine, as a weapon to fight each other. Did you ever stop to think of the nervous havoc you may have caused this nine-year-old girl?"

He then spoke to Dexter Benner directly before sentencing him to fifteen days in prison, telling him, "I am utterly appalled by your conduct." The judge gave Benner a five-day stay of execution to file an appeal. In all, Benner won fourteen continuances in the case before his appeal was rejected by the California Supreme Court in July 1953.

By early December of that year, Benner had failed to appear in court for sentencing and on December 9, 1953, a bench warrant was issued for Benner's arrest. But Benner, like Jean Spangler, had disappeared. He, his new wife, and Christine were simply gone.

UNSOLVED CASE

In June 1958, E. W. Scott wrote to the editor of the *Los Angeles Mirror*. After cleaning out a closet, he found an old edition of the newspaper dated October 11, 1949. Scott had saved the paper because it was the first anniversary edition. When reviewing the paper almost a decade later, Scott began to wonder about the headline: "100 Comb Park for Actress." He wondered what had happened to the actress and if she had ever been found. The editor's response encapsulates the case even today. He told Mr. E. W. Scott: "No trace of Jean Spangler has ever been found, although the police never officially close an unsolved case."

More than sixty years after that response and seventy years after Jean Spangler's disappearance, her case remains open and the question remains the same: What happened to Jean Spangler? Was she murdered or did she willingly disappear? Over the years, authorities have posed many theories.

THEORY 1: DEXTER BENNER MURDERED JEAN SPANGLER

Every homicide detective will tell you that the spouse is the first suspect when foul play is involved. If Jean was murdered, her ex-husband certainly had motive. During their volatile divorce proceedings three years prior to Jean's disappearance, Benner painted Jean as an unfit and irresponsible mother. He also made clear that he had no respect for her profession. Initially, Benner triumphed and won custody of his daughter. With a new wife on the horizon, Benner seemed to have everything he wanted. Yet Benner refused to allow the court-ordered visitations that Jean had been legally granted. As stated previously, he refused to let Jean see Christine on at least twenty-three occasions. Based on the evidence, Benner wanted sole custody of his daughter so that he could begin a new life with his new wife, as if Jean had never existed. In fact, he told Jean that he would make it so that she would never see her daughter again.

Jean fought to regain custody and won her daughter back in 1948. Benner retained visitation rights and was ordered to pay Jean child support, but he had been negligent in his payments. Jean disappeared only a year after she gained custody of her daughter. The very day after her disappearance, Benner picked up his daughter. Within another day, he petitioned the judge for temporary custody. Slightly more than two weeks after Jean's disappearance, Benner petitioned for permanent custody. Though he won custody of his daughter, Jean's mother was awarded visitation rights. Like he had done with Jean, Benner barred Florence from visiting with Christine on numerous occasions and took her to court to terminate all visitation rights. Further, his wife attempted to legally adopt Christine. By all appearances, Benner wanted to build a new family and remove all traces of Jean and her family. Did he take it to the next step and literally remove all traces of Jean?

Evidence from police interviews indicates that Benner had scratches on his face the day after Jean's disappearance. Benner told police that he had dropped a case of glasses inches from his face while at work. The glasses cut his face, which is why he appeared to have scratches on his face. He insisted that he had not seen Jean for weeks, and his wife verified that at the time of Jean's disappearance Benner had spent the entire evening with her. As the only proof of Benner's whereabouts, his wife's word is not exactly airtight. In fact, according to Kyle J. Wood's research, the LAPD had documentation that Benner had taken his boat out on the night Jean disappeared. Detectives did search his garage, but there is no evidence that they searched any other areas of his home or his boat.

After a lengthy battle with Mrs. Spangler over custody of Christine, Benner was sentenced to serve jail time due to denying her visitation rights. Rather than serve time, however, Benner appealed all the way to the state supreme court. When he lost, Benner left the state rather than comply with the law. The evidence shows that when it came to his daughter, Benner was willing to break the law on multiple occasions to retain custody. The question is, how far was he willing to go to create his new family? Jean's mother went to her death believing that Dexter was willing to murder and that he had, in fact, killed Jean.

THEORY 2: JEAN SPANGLER DIED DURING AN ILLEGAL ABORTION

Based on the note left in Jean's purse and later admissions by Jean's friends that she was three months pregnant at the time of her disappearance, detectives investigated the possibility that Jean may have sought an abortion on the evening of her disappearance. This theory posits that Jean died during the abortion. Since abortions were illegal, supporters of this theory believe that the doctor who performed the operation would have hidden Jean's body to cover up the illegal procedure.

In their quest to investigate this angle, detectives searched for the "Dr. Scott" mentioned in Jean's letter. According to multiple sources, police eventually learned of a former medical student who was performing illegal abortions along the strip who went by "Doc" or "Scott." He supposedly frequented the spots where Jean worked and hung out. Detectives never found this "Doctor Scott."

There are a few problems with this theory. Podcaster Robin Warder says the biggest hole in this theory is that if Jean was the victim of a botched abortion, why would the people who worked so hard to cover it up leave the note in her purse that named the doctor?

Podcasters for "Gone" bring up the fact that the abortion theory is problematic when considering the timeline. Surely Jean, last spotted at the Cheesebox around 2:30 a.m., did not have an appointment for an abortion after 2:30 in the morning. They contend that she could have planned to go for the abortion but had not been able to find Dr. Scott. But why would she disappear?

Entangled in this theory is the man to whom the note was addressed: Kirk. Though at first Jean's mother and sister-in-law denied knowing any "Kirk," they later admitted that a man named Kirk had picked Jean up on two occasions—though he always waited in the car and never came to the front door. Jean had recently worked on a film with Kirk Douglas, who became tied to the mystery.

Before police even had the chance to contact him, actor Kirk Douglas inserted himself into the investigation and went as far as holding a formal press conference to deny involvement in Jean's disappearance. He also phoned authorities while on vacation in Palm Springs to tell them that he never knew Jean.

People who believe that Kirk Douglas may have had something to do with Jean Spangler's disappearance cite then-sixteen-year-old Natalie Wood's accusations against the actor. Others assert that Jean planned to abort his child while Douglas was away in Palm Springs (hence the note—she couldn't "wait any longer" and wanted to take care of it while her "mother was away"). Others believe she went to Palm Springs with Douglas.

There are many questions associated with this theory. Why would Jean's purse be deposited back in Los Angeles? Further, why would the note be left inside? Is it possible that Jean was pregnant with Douglas's child but that Douglas had absolutely nothing to do with her disappearance? The only facts we know for sure are that Jean addressed her letter to a man named Kirk and that Kirk Douglas was not a suspect in the original investigation.

THEORY 3: AN EX-LOVER MURDERED JEAN SPANGLER

Some people believe that "Dr. Scott" is the air force lieutenant "Scotty" with whom Jean carried on an affair while her husband was stationed in the South Pacific. Though by all accounts Jean had not seen Scotty since 1945, he had been abusive while they were together. According to Jean's former lawyer, he spent all of her money and wrecked her car while Dexter was away at war. Jean often showed up to work with bruises. Scotty eventually threatened to kill her if she ever left him. His threat was the catalyst that prompted Jean to finally leave Scotty for good. She had told enough people about his threats that she felt she could safely end the relationship. And according to Jean's lawyer, she did. After 1945, the couple never saw one another again. Or did they?

THEORY 4: JEAN DISAPPEARED WITH OR WAS KILLED BY THE MAFIA

Jean made many connections while she danced at the various clubs along the Sunset Strip, and many of those connections were mob related. Though her family and friends insisted that Jean was not involved with the Mafia, there is evidence to suggest that Jean not only knew important Mafia figures of the day, but that she may have been meeting with one on the night she disappeared. These connections simply could be due to proximity—Jean worked at clubs these figures frequented—without anything nefarious transpiring.

A few days before her disappearance, Jean was seen with Davy Ogul—Little Davy—in Palm Springs. In the months before her disappearance, she was also spotted with Frank Niccoli. Both Ogul and Niccoli worked for Mickey Cohen. Cohen, who had worked under Bugsy Siegel, ran clubs and betting operations along the Sunset Strip.

On the evening of Jean's disappearance, multiple witnesses placed her at the Cheesebox with two men, one of whom fit Ogul's description. A witness claimed to have seen Jean arguing with them. Detectives were particularly interested in this angle, because two days after Jean's disappearance, Davy Ogul disappeared as well. Also, Jean had been spotted on numerous occasions with Ogul, who was under indictment for conspiracy, and his name showed up in her address book. Niccoli had disappeared about a month prior to Jean.

Though detectives originally believed that Jean was murdered, they increasingly began to believe that perhaps she ran away with Ogul instead. Detectives traveled to Palm Springs to investigate the sighting of the pair the previous week. During the weeks and months following Jean's disappearance, there were other sightings that linked Jean to the two mobsters.

In fact, four months after her disappearance, US customs agents in El Paso followed a woman whom they thought was Jean. A hotel worker identified Jean based on newspaper images. Police believed that Jean, Niccoli, and Ogul had left El Paso for Las Vegas. As with the other theories, however, there are problems with the idea that Jean ran away with Ogul and Niccoli.

First of all, family and friends discount the notion that Jean would have left her family and never communicated with them again. Considering the long battle for custody of her daughter and the close relationship she had always had with her family, they believe it is impossible that Jean would have left of her own volition. They believe the sightings, especially by people who did not know Jean, were simply errors. There were certainly many other mistaken sightings throughout California and Mexico City.

Second, even though there were sightings of these men and Jean in the days prior to and after her disappearance, many believe Niccoli and Ogul were killed when they disappeared. In her podcast,

The Trail Went Cold, Robin Warder contends that the sightings were false information spread by Mickey Cohen's rivals, intended to cause financial difficulty for the mobster. Cohen had paid $75,000 to bail Ogul and Niccoli out of jail and would be reimbursed only if there was conclusive proof that they were dead. Without that proof, Cohen had to forfeit the money, which caused him serious financial problems. Within a couple years, he went to prison for tax evasion.

Niccoli's disappearance remained a mystery for thirty years until Jimmy Fratianno turned government witness and detailed Niccoli's final hours. On the day of his disappearance, Frank Niccoli visited the home of another mob associate, Joseph Dippolito, where he was supposedly strangled and later buried in a lime pit in Cucamonga on the Dippolito property.

An associate of Fratianno, Salvatore Piscopo, became an FBI informant in the 1960s, more than a decade after Ogul's disappearance. He told police that Ogul was beaten to death by Harold "Happy" Meltzer and his body was buried in a remote mountain spot in northern Los Angeles. Fratianno also later confessed to Ogul's murder, saying he strangled him and put him in a lime pit.

Even though it seems unlikely that Jean disappeared with Ogul, if she were with Ogul when he was murdered, it is possible that Jean was murdered as well. Though it took decades, people came forward concerning the disappearances of Niccoli and Ogul. Perhaps one day the same will happen for Jean Spangler.

THEORY 5: JEAN WAS MURDERED BY A SERIAL KILLER

Jean's purse was found about a quarter of a mile from Dr. George Hodel's home, known as the Sowen House, in Los Angeles. Dr. Hodel was a prominent neurosurgeon who performed abortions for the wealthy, as well as for the girlfriends of local officers and politicians. He was part of an abortion ring that operated in the city. According to Dr. Hodel's son, ex-LAPD homicide detective Steve Hodel, his father began dating Jean Spangler in late September or early October 1949.

Jean Spangler, studio photograph. *Sterling Trevor Photography, Tessa Digital Collections, Los Angeles Public Library*

Steve Hodel further contends that his father was the mystery man seated with Jean at the Cheesebox on the night she disappeared. He believes that the gas station attendant, Art Rodgers, did see Jean Spangler. He also believes that the man driving the car was his father. Though it was not "blue-gray," his black 1936 Packard matched the model that the attendant described. Further, he hypothesizes that the

"Dr. Scott" to whom Jean refers could have been one of the doctors in the abortion ring with his father.

Hodel's most significant claim is that his father was the Black Dahlia murderer. In fact, authorities suspected Hodel in the murders of Elizabeth Short, Spangler, and a string of other women during this time. They surveilled the Sowen House, and Hodel fled for Asia in 1950 to evade authorities. Steve Hodel outlines his fascinating theory and his father's criminal life in the updated version of his book *Black Dahlia Avenger*. If there is a break in Jean's case, it will probably be largely due to the current efforts by Steve Hodel.

EPILOGUE

Jean Spangler's case has never been officially closed. Shrouded in Hollywood hype, her story contains the makings of the movies she longed to break into—courtroom battles, secret notes, mobsters, nightclubs, and parties. The real story, though, is about a young woman who worked tirelessly to achieve two dreams—motherhood and stardom. These dreams did not come easily, and it would have been far simpler to give up. Jean, however, persevered in the face of a system that took away her child, an ex-husband who denied her rights, and a society that told her she could not be a mother while having a career. Jean's story is the story of a young and vibrant woman who was taken from her mother and her child. It is the story of a rising starlet whose career was cut short before it ever really began. Until we find Jean, her story will never have an ending, which she so truly deserves.

5

SIMONE RIDINGER, 1977

No one deserves that—just to be lost.—Sergeant James
Godinho, Sherborn Police Department

SEPTEMBER 1977: NATICK, MASSACHUSETTS

Simone, a free-spirited seventeen-year-old, had just finished her
waitressing shift at the Rainbow Restaurant—a popular breakfast and
lunch spot in downtown Natick, Massachusetts. With her warm and
friendly personality and long, flowing strawberry-blonde hair, the
teenager was popular with customers and workers alike. She loved her
job, but she hated the scratchy polyester uniform she and the other
waitresses wore.

After her shift, Simone grabbed her gray duffel bag and headed for
the cafe bathroom. None of the girls liked their waitressing outfit—a
dark blue skirt and vest—so they brought clothes to change into at the
end of their shifts. Simone always chose the same outfit: a pair of blue
jeans and a white T-shirt. She placed her polyester work uniform back
in her duffel bag when she was through, exited the bathroom, and
waved goodbye to the other waitresses.

It was a Saturday, Labor Day weekend, and Simone had plans to
meet her mother on Martha's Vineyard—an island off the coast of Cape
Cod where Simone and her family had spent many happy summers.

Simone Ridinger, 1977. *Private collection of Betsy Bailey*

Just the thought of their home on the bluff brought back memories of eating picnic lunches on the beach, clamming at low tide with her sister, and sailing summer waters on their Sunfish. These were happy times of games, puzzles, swimming, cousins, and independence.

Sometimes on sunny days, Simone's mother, Jane, would send the kids out on a special mission known as "shell of the day." Simone and her sister, Betsy (who was two years older than Simone), would head out first thing in the morning and begin hunting for whatever shell their mother chose—razor clams, quarterdecks, mussels—and then search the entire day for the perfect version of that particular shell. At the end of the quest, they would bring their treasures back to their

Simone (left) with her sister, Betsy, at their Vineyard cottage during the late 1960s.
Private collection of Betsy Bailey

mother who would choose the best one. If the winner was really spectacular, the girls would paint it with clear nail polish to bring out the shell's colors.

Though the sisters were older in 1977 and Betsy could not join Simone for that Vineyard trip, she did stop at the restaurant on Friday to offer Simone a ride to the bus. Simone, who did not have a car, would need to travel about seventy miles to the Woods Hole ferry on the Cape and then sail to the Vineyard from there. Simone thanked her sister for the offer but assured her that she was all set. Betsy assumed that Simone arranged a ride with a friend.

Simone later told the other waitresses that she planned to hitch to the Cape. The problem was that though Simone hitched on a regular basis—to and from work and pretty much everywhere she wanted to go—she had never hitched such a long distance before. The other waitresses voiced their concern, but Simone did not relent. Even though she was only five feet two and petite, she was fiercely independent and had already set her mind on hitching to the Cape. Her friendliness never wavered, but she forged her own path. Pushing through the double doors, she stepped down onto the wide sidewalk that hugged the restaurant. Extending her arm and raising her thumb, Simone made her way along Main Street. When her friends looked out the window, she was already gone—a shadow heading south on Route 27.

BLENDED FAMILY

Simone Stephanie Ridinger was born on January 5, 1960, to George Harry Boltz and Jane Gregg Barrett. The young family settled in Pittsburgh, Pennsylvania. Simone's father was a German immigrant and an award-winning photographer. He unfortunately passed away just before Simone's fifth birthday in November 1964 when he was only thirty-four years old.

Simone's mother was devastated. The young widow gathered her daughter and returned to her parents' home in Chappaqua, New York, where she attempted to rebuild her life. Meanwhile, a neighboring family was about to encounter a tragedy of their own. John S. Ridinger Jr. had just transferred through his job to Chappaqua from Pittsburgh with his wife, Shirley Ann, and their seven-year-old daughter, Betsy. Since John couldn't take a vacation with his new job, Shirley and Betsy took long weekends at the beach. One weekend just before Betsy entered third grade, she and Shirley were spending time at Jones Beach. While wading in the water, Shirley suffered a cerebral hemorrhage and passed away. She was only thirty-nine years old.

Both recovering from the tragic loss of their young spouses, John Ridinger and Jane Barrett became sources of comfort and solace for one another. Soon, they began dating and eventually married. Jane adopted Betsy, and John adopted Simone. The newlyweds blended their family under the Ridinger name and life became brighter for the girls and their parents.

Five-year-old Simone and seven-year-old Betsy could not have been more different. In fact, Betsy wonders if they would have known one another if their parents hadn't married. They looked nothing alike, and they had different interests. However, when their family blended, they became sisters and friends.

CHILDHOOD

Simone was a bright child with many interests. Nearly a half century after Dorothy Arnold attended Mademoiselle Veltin's immersive French kindergarten class, Simone Ridinger also attended a French-immersion kindergarten in New York. In fact, she became fluent in the language by the time she was seven years old. Simone also excelled in music. Betsy studied piano for years before Simone, but Simone was a natural. Betsy later joked that because Simone played by ear, she first played all of Betsy's mistakes until their piano teacher figured out how to work with Simone. Since she didn't take to the piano, Betsy tried the guitar instead. After that didn't work out, Simone picked up the guitar as well.

Betsy believes that Simone inherited her musical talents from their mother, Jane, who studied at Oberlin College and performed

Simone playing ukulele. *Private collection of Betsy Bailey*

in Gilbert and Sullivan shows. She took the girls to the opera and even brought them to see Pete Seger on the Hudson River. Whereas Betsy appreciated and dabbled in music, Simone was a natural. She loved it.

When they lived in New York, there were plenty of fun activities to keep the sisters busy. They enjoyed ice skating and sledding in the winters and horseback riding, mud pie making, and camp in the summers. A stream ran behind Simone and Betsy's home, which produced layers of mud and endless opportunities. Jane bought junk pie plates, pots, and pans, and the sisters spent many days making mud pies together.

Childhood activities: horseback riding, sledding, and Girl Scouts. *Private collection of Betsy Bailey*

When she was seven years old, Simone won "most sophisticated," for her costume at the fourth annual Hat and Boat Day at the New Castle Recreation Camp. Whereas the boys favored traditional sea captain, pirate, and naval officer costumes, the girls donned flapper ensembles. Simone pulled her costume together from a big box full of random clothing that her mother and grandmother had compiled over the years. She and Betsy also created their Halloween costumes from this bin. And, like most girls during this time, they sported Girl Scout and Brownie uniforms to showcase their badges, patches, and pins.

John was transferred to Massachusetts around 1970, and the family settled in the Boston suburb of Sherborn, a small and quiet rural community. There were no fancy French immersion schools in Sherborn, and in no time Simone lost her fluency for the language. However, the farming community boasted large parcels of land where the girls could continue their horseback riding lessons. Their new riding instructor informed Jane about a horse that would be great for the girls, so the family purchased Penuche.

Since Simone was younger and arrived home from school first, she spent her afternoons riding Penuche. Betsy arrived home later, just in time to clean out the stalls. This unfair arrangement and the fact that Penuche was a bit big for Simone prompted John and Jane to purchase a pony. From that point on, Betsy rode Penuche and Simone rode the new pony, Chocolate Sundae. The two girls were a team, riding trails all over Sherborn and even taking part in some small local showings.

Family cottage on Chappaquiddick. *Private collection of Betsy Bailey*

During summers, the family frequented their Vineyard cottage on Chappaquiddick. The home, which belonged to Jane's family, was a haven for the many cousins and aunts and uncles who arrived there throughout the summer months. Jane's father had owned the land for many years and finally built the cottage when he retired. The home contained three bedrooms, a living room, kitchen, and bathroom. Instead of using electricity, the family lit the home with kerosene lamps. When it was time to wash dishes, they pulled a string attached to a pump (like those used to start lawnmowers) in order to start the water pressure. They also used a propane-powered refrigerator. And they loved every minute of it. They brought books and puzzles to keep themselves entertained when they weren't swimming, sailing, or playing with cousins.

The family began vacationing on Chappaquiddick—still rural with only one paved road—long before its name became synonymous with Senator Edward Kennedy and the tragic death of Mary Jo Kopechne, and they were used to the inconvenience involved in traveling to the small island. Once they moved to Massachusetts, the ride to Woods Hole was shorter—about an hour and forty-five minutes. They arrived at the ferry—a carload of kids, dogs, linens, and other household necessities, with their Sunfish strapped to the top—in time for the forty-five-minute boat ride across Vineyard Sound. They usually docked in Oak Bluffs, the Flying Horses Carousel in the distance officially signaling

Simone on Chappaquiddick. *Private collection of Betsy Bailey*

their arrival to the Vineyard. From there, they sometimes drove (and sometimes thumbed) the twenty minutes to Edgartown, a historic seaport village on the eastern end of the island. Then they sailed on a three-car ferry, 527 feet across to Chappaquiddick.

They usually spent at least a couple of weeks every summer on the island and many long weekends. One year, they spent an entire summer on Chappaquiddick. In addition to swimming and clamming, the girls also learned to sail. Once John taught them, he sent the sisters out in the surf to sail the sea in the family Sunfish. Betsy remembers midnight sails with her father when the light of a lantern they had set on the beach was the only beacon to guide them back home to their cottage on the bluff.

Sometimes they would head over to the other side of the island where the Atlantic Ocean ran free. Jane would test the tides to see if it was safe to swim while the rest of the family unpacked their picnic sandwiches. One year, while John and Betsy prepared for a peaceful morning in their secluded spot, they were interrupted by a flurry of Jeeps, folding tables, and strangers.

"Don't mind us!" the catering crew for the *Jaws* film called out.

Betsy noted the mechanical shark in the distance. The small island, known affectionately as Chappy, was certainly never dull and furnished the girls with many happy days during their childhood, yet those days of summer and childhood seemed to move by quickly.

Before they knew it, Simone and Betsy were attending Dover-Sherborn High School. Whereas Betsy was the quiet one, Simone was a free spirit with a rebellious streak. Very bright, she bored easily and ignored authority. Still, she was a popular girl. Betsy described her sister during this time: "She was the one in school everyone knew because she was friendly. You were her friend immediately, even before you knew her."

When they returned to Chappaquiddick during the summer, they spent more time in Edgartown or Oak Bluffs, hitching rides to visit friends and boyfriends—their childhood days of shell searching and clam digging firmly behind them. Soon they would even outgrow their high school experience. At about this time, John and Jane decided to part ways. Their relationship had not been good for some time, and

John moved to Holliston, Massachusetts. Betsy moved in with friends. Simone remained with Jane.

At the same time, Betsy recalled that Simone simply stopped showing up for school. She received detentions for skipping school, and then detentions for skipping detentions. Each day, Betsy listened as Simone's name was called over the intercom. Though only a sophomore, Simone decided to drop out. Betsy admits that authority was a problem for Simone, and, as a result, she could get into trouble. Her assistant headmaster agreed that Simone "seemed to be rebelling against something" and that she simply "wasn't fond of school," though he, like everyone else, found Simone to be "a delightful girl." The result was that Simone decided to pursue her GED instead. Betsy wasn't exactly excited about attending school every day, either, so she completed her studies, graduated early, and began working for her father. Shortly thereafter, she moved in with him in Holliston.

During the summer after Simone dropped out of school, she also moved away from home. She and Jane searched for a suitable apartment, and they found a bottom-floor unit situated on a quiet street near the library in Framingham. Jane cosigned the lease for Simone, who secured a job in the neighboring town of Natick at the Rainbow Restaurant, a breakfast and lunch cafe where she worked as a waitress. She also enrolled in her GED program to earn her high school equivalency diploma. Though only seventeen years old, Simone was certainly an independent young woman. She enjoyed living her own life, but she still spent a great deal of time with her family, splitting her days among work, home, friends, and loved ones.

THE HITCHING CRAZE

Simone was not one to sit in her new apartment for long. She was adventurous and outgoing. She enjoyed spending time with people and making new friends, and she trusted people. In order to get to work, to meet up with friends, to buy necessities, and to visit family, Simone hitched rides. She hitched all over. She wasn't alone. Most young people hitched rides during the 1970s. Betsy recalled that even their own mother hitched rides when they were desperate to get to Edgartown from Oak Bluffs.

With the advent of the automobile, hitchhiking evolved based on the needs of each generation. During the Depression, hitchhiking was often a necessity for men looking for work or transportation. In the 1940s, hitchhikers were also primarily men and usually GIs who needed to get home. Picking up hitchhikers was seen as patriotic. With the end of the war, hitchhiking fell off. It began to pick up again in the 1960s and ballooned in the 1970s. The new demographic featured high school and college-age girls and women from middle-class to upper-middle-class backgrounds who hitched for the thrill. They considered it a "groovy" and exciting practice.

In a 1969 *Parade* magazine article on the hitchhiking craze, author Lloyd Shearer interviewed the daughter of one of the hundred wealthiest men in the country about why she hitchhiked to campus. She explained, "I used to drive my Mercedes to campus all freshman year. What a drag! The sameness, the same, dull routine began to bug me, so I decided to thumb. Now, I drive my car about a half mile down the road and park it on a side street, so my parents don't know. Then I start thumbing. I just stand there with my books, and I sort of nod in the right direction, and motorists stop. Every day is a fresh adventure, not a drag."

Car advertisements, album covers, and films of the day illustrated scantily clad females in suggestive positions waiting alongside the road for rides. The implications were clearly sexual—as if young women were offering their bodies in exchange for rides. The tagline for the film *The Hitchhikers* begins, "They're just up the road. Waiting for you."

Hitchhiking was also a part of the hippie culture of adventure, freedom, and love. With Jack Kerouac's *On the Road* as their mantra, a generation of young people embraced the idea of the uncharted course and the strange characters who might get them there. They believed in peace, love, and the goodness in people.

Though the practice was still widely used by the time Simone was hitchhiking in 1977, young people were somewhat aware of the dangers. In 1971, Charleyce Whalen was raped and murdered after accepting a ride from Sacramento to San Francisco, California. Like Simone, Charleyce Whalen was seventeen years old. Also like Simone, Charleyce had been hitching rides for a long time and felt completely comfortable and confident doing so. Between 1972 and 1973, seven female hitchhikers were murdered in Sonoma County and Santa Rosa, California. Dubbed the Santa Rosa hitchhiker murders, these crimes involved girls as young as twelve years old.

Still, like most young people, if not most people, hitchhikers believed that the horror stories they heard would not happen to them. One of Charleyce Whalen's good friends told *Parade* magazine, "I still think it's a groovy way to get places. If they pass a law against it, I'll do it anyway and so will everybody else. I mean, I feel bad about Charleyce and all, but well, you know, I think I can take care of myself."

Simone might not have been aware of Charleyce Whalen or the Santa Rosa murders. It was also a different time, when people knew one another. More often than not, Simone knew the people who gave her rides. Also, she wasn't some rebel hitchhiker in her community. Everybody hitchhiked in the area. People felt safe, and it just didn't seem to be an issue.

Being a teenager in the 1970s, Simone adopted the free-flowing dress and sense of adventure inherent in the hippie lifestyle. Although she hitchhiked as a practical means to get to the places she needed to go, rather than out of some misplaced need for adventure, she did enjoy meeting new people and she did trust people. When Jane asked Simone to join her and her boyfriend on the Vineyard that Labor Day weekend in 1977, Simone did not think twice about hitching her way down to the Cape to catch the ferry.

CROSSED SIGNALS

Simone should have arrived on the island by Saturday evening on September 2. When she did not, Jane figured that Simone simply made other plans or missed the ferry. Without a phone or electricity, Jane had no means to check in with Simone. However, Jane wasn't worried. She figured that her daughter would eventually show up, as always.

Jane and her partner most likely remained on Chappaquiddick through Labor Day weekend, returning to the mainland around September 6. During that time, Jane continued to wait for her daughter's arrival, hoping to spend some holiday time with her at the family beach house. Still, she was not concerned by her daughter's absence. Maybe just a little disappointed about not having the chance to spend the last of the summer days together.

Back home, Betsy was not concerned either. With no way to contact the family on the Vineyard, she figured that Simone had made it to the island and was enjoying time at their family beach house for those last official summer days at the start of September.

And then everything changed.

When Jane arrived home from her trip, she looked for Simone. She went to Simone's apartment and found a note on the door, though what the note said is unknown. She called Betsy, asking, "Have you seen Simone? Have you heard from her?"

Betsy replied, "No. She's with you."

Jane, becoming increasingly worried, informed Betsy, "No. She's not."

Betsy and Jane both knew that Simone might go off for a couple of days, but she would never go away for any length of time without checking in. And Simone *always* called if she made other plans. They would have heard from her by now. Jane called Simone's friends. She called the diner. No one had seen her daughter. In fact, no one had seen Simone since September 2, when she left the Rainbow Restaurant.

WHERE IS SIMONE?

As soon as she realized that Simone was missing, Jane went to the Sherborn Police Department to file a report. Jane likely went to the station shortly after she returned home, but the initial report is not dated until Sunday, September 11 at 5:55 p.m., nine days after

Simone's disappearance. Officer George Stevens, who was on duty when Jane went to the Sherborn precinct that day, remembers that by that time, the "trail wasn't just cold—it was frozen."

Since Simone was seventeen, officers determined that she was most likely a runaway and would return home soon. Her family adamantly disagreed. She had her own apartment. Was she running away from herself? Her sister, Betsy, admits that Simone could get into trouble and believes that because the police were aware of her already, they figured she just took off. For these reasons, the family felt that there wasn't much investigation into Simone's disappearance in those very early days.

Betsy also describes the lack of coverage in those days—no newscasts, Amber Alerts, helicopter searches, or heavy police presence. Simone's family realized that they would have to look for their daughter themselves. Jane was a determined woman, and John had a number of connections. Under their leadership, family and friends came together to look for Simone.

They made posters and knocked on doors. Jane hired private investigators. She worked with the Salvation Army, who was able to investigate city leads that the family couldn't search on their own. She even consulted psychics. John arranged for CB radio clubs to drive to the Cape and search along the sides of the roads.

Jane delegated assignments, too. Betsy liked Jane's take-charge attitude. Her assignments kept everyone busy in those initial days when Simone went missing. Betsy spoke to some of Simone's friends and checked out spots in Framingham where they told Betsy that Simone liked to hang out.

MISSING — Simone Ridinger, 17, of Framingham, was last seen Sept. 2 when she left a Natick restaurant where she was a waitress. She is believed to have been hitchhiking to Cape Cod for a family weekend at Martha's Vineyard. She is 5 ft. 2 inches, 120 pounds with blonde hair and brown eyes.

Missing announcement.
Boston Globe, November 1977

Early on, Jane received a call from a young man, whom I'll call the photographer, who had taken a series of recent photographs of Simone. He thought that Jane might want them for posters. Jane sent Betsy to the man's house to retrieve the negatives.

The photographer's pictures of Simone are the most widely used images we have of her today. She looks beautiful in her dark tank top, long checkered skirt, brown cowboy boots, and naturally free-flowing strawberry-blonde hair. Her silver rings and bracelet are prominently displayed as she poses for the camera in both seated and standing positions.

The photographer did not know Simone. He had given her a ride and asked to photograph her in a rural location that investigators have since identified. Though the images are gorgeous, they were taken by a stranger shortly before Simone's death. Detectives did question the photographer, but they have not made the details of his interview public, and he has since passed away.

INITIAL INVESTIGATION

One of the first persons of interest in Simone's case was her ex-boyfriend, who was incarcerated at the state prison in Billerica, Massachusetts. He was concerned because Simone had stopped writing to him. In fact, she was supposed to visit him on the very day that police showed up to question him, September 17, since she had acquired special privileges to see him. Investigators waited for her arrival, but she never appeared, and she never contacted him again.

Detectives have since spoken to this man, who was older than Simone. He described their on-again, off-again relationship. Due to his incarceration at the time of Simone's disappearance, investigators were able to eliminate him as a suspect. He was also genuinely concerned about Simone and her whereabouts.

On October 4, 1977, the Sherborn Police Department took over the case and began to officially investigate Simone's disappearance. They distributed flyers to other police departments and worked with neighboring agencies on the case.

In 2017, Officer George Stevens talked about those initial days of the investigation. Though he was not originally assigned to Simone's case, he knew her and her family. She waited on him every morning at the Rainbow Restaurant. He recalled that police initially went to the restaurant to investigate, though there are no records of them speaking to employees at the time. They also consulted with State Police in the case and visited area pawn shops to find links to Simone's jewelry. One aspect of this investigation that is unclear is whether detectives searched Simone's apartment. At some point, the apartment was cleared out, but investigators today are not sure who cleared or took Simone's belongings.

At first, witnesses suggested that Simone walked to the bus stop after she left the restaurant; however, police could not corroborate these statements. Other information suggested that Simone hitched as soon as she left the restaurant. Stevens felt that they had no place to start.

"She simply disappeared," he told a local newspaper.

The few leads in the case fizzled out early on, and the case grew cold, though officers like Stevens did not forget Simone. He told reporters that he continued to search for her years after he left the force, even traveling to North Dakota to follow up on a lead. Simone's family, too, continued to search for her.

"That's what you do," Betsy explains. "I'm still doing it."

Media plays a large part in keeping Simone's story alive. As long as Simone's case remains in the public eye, people are aware and continue to look for her. After an article appeared in the *MetroWest Daily News* in 1986, an elderly man called the Sherborn Police Department. He informed them that he had given a ride to Simone on September 3, 1977, the morning after she was last seen. Within minutes of his phone call, the seventy-nine-year-old retiree walked into the Sherborn police station. Since he enjoyed building clocks as a hobby, he will be known as Mr. C. The story he told was baffling and bizarre.

According to Mr. C., he was heading to Cape Cod to purchase clock parts on the morning of September 3, 1977, the day after Simone disappeared. As he was traveling down Route 128 in Westwood around 6:45 a.m., a state trooper pulled him over at Route 109 for a traffic violation. He told the officer that he was heading to Osterville, a village in the town of Barnstable on Cape Cod. Upon learning this information, the officer motioned toward his squad car and pointed out a teenage girl in the back seat who needed a ride to the Cape if Mr. C. would take her. Mr. C. agreed, and the teenager, who Mr. C. swore looked exactly like the photograph of Simone in the *MetroWest Daily News* article, hopped into his car.

The old man began to describe the girl for detectives. He said she was between sixteen and eighteen years of age, about five feet seven, and 135 pounds, with curly brown hair. She was wearing a blue shirt, ripped jeans, and "grubby" white sneakers. He also said that she wore a lot of gaudy jewelry and carried a gray duffel bag. He stated, "She smelled as if she needed a bath."

During the hour-and-half ride to the Cape, Mr. C. and the girl chatted. She informed him that her name was Sissy. He told her that he was from Framingham, and she disclosed that she was from the next town over. When she proclaimed that she hitchhiked often, he lectured her about the dangers.

"You never know who you are going to meet," he warned her.

"I have met a lot of nice people that way, though."

Mr. C. told police that he dropped the girl off at the Hyannis Rotary Club. The last he saw of her she was heading toward a Ground Round restaurant and a Howard Johnson hotel. After he dropped her off, he never saw her again.

Mr. C.'s description did not offer much to the investigation at the time. Simone had never used the name Sissy. She was five two, not five seven, and she weighed less than 135 pounds. According to the missing persons description developed shortly after her disappearance, she was last seen wearing a leather hat, brown or purple boots, and an Indian print skirt. It's unclear why this outfit was originally given as the outfit in which Simone was last seen, unless it's because the outfit is similar to what she is wearing in the photographs that were disseminated at the time of her disappearance.

Still, much of Mr. C.'s description rang true. Simone did grow up in a town that bordered Framingham. She was a frequent hitchhiker, and she did exhibit a trusting and friendly nature. She also wore a lot of silver and turquoise jewelry, with a ring on every finger. She particularly liked spoon rings, which fit with Mr. C.'s description of "gaudy jewelry."

For a second time, detectives pulled out Simone's picture and placed it down before Mr. C. Pointing to Simone, they asked Mr. C. if he was certain that she was the girl he picked up that day. He insisted that he was absolutely sure. The police took copious notes on Mr. C.'s story and added them to Simone's file, which, even after ten years, contained only a couple of pages or so. They never followed up with Mr. C., and the case went cold again.

COLD CASE

When a case goes cold, we imagine that everything stops. If we could envision this phenomenon, it would be a vast lake of ice—no sound, no movement, no light. Yet for the families of these missing people, cases never go cold. Their loved ones are reflected in this lake, awaiting justice. Families must continuously search.

Even when the original blitz of calls and tips subsides, media events and anniversaries elicit spurts and drips of information. Though most leads never pan out, they supply just enough hope for families to keep moving, to keep searching.

Simone's parents continued to search for their daughter for the remainder of their lives. On Labor Day twenty years after Simone disappeared, her mother Jane suffered a minor cerebral hemorrhage. She passed away the following month never knowing what happened to her daughter. Simone's father, John, died ten years later. Many of Simone's friends have since passed on as well. Still, Simone's disappearance remains a mystery.

Simone's sister, Betsy, occasionally received calls from police asking questions about Simone or offering comments about her case—Did she have a tattoo? We think there might be something . . . —but for the most part, her phone remained silent. The days passed and her sister remained missing. She would meet new people, and they would ask if she had siblings. She would wonder how to answer. She really didn't have an answer.

One day in 2014, she walked right into the police station and decided to ask. She told them that she was Simone Ridinger's sister, and she inquired about the state of the case. That's when she met Sergeant James Godinho.

NEW HOPE

Sergeant James Godinho was a newly appointed detective when he first opened Simone Ridinger's case folder in 2013. His first step was to read through all of the information in the case. Sadly, that was the easiest part. There simply wasn't much information in Simone's file. Instead, Sergeant Godinho was left with questions—a lot of them. He explained his initial thoughts and steps in those early days when he moved to reopen Simone's investigation: "After being moved into the detective role, I was provided the file and out of sheer curiosity I reviewed the case file and was left with many, many, questions, which is why we reopened the case. I began officially reviewing the case in 2014 and initiated a follow-up investigation in 2015 after concluding my review and determining the need for extensive follow-up."

Sergeant Godinho put together a list of what he called common-sense questions—the questions you ask about every case you tackle. Who saw Simone last? Was she dating anyone? Was she hanging out with anyone? Who were her friends? Where did she hang out? Where did she live? From these questions, Sergeant Godinho formulated a plan of investigation to breathe new life into what was at that time a nearly forty-year-old case.

According to the case file, the waitresses who worked with Simone at the Rainbow Restaurant were the last people to ever see her. The file, however, did not contain the names or contact information for any of these workers. Sergeant Godinho began the first of many media outreach campaigns in Simone's case to find the people who saw Simone that day or who knew Simone at that time. He knew that they could provide the valuable information he needed. The Sherborn Police Department published an article in the *MetroWest Daily News*. From that article, he was able to connect with people who waitressed at the restaurant with Simone. Strangely, they had never been interviewed at the time of Simone's disappearance.

Sergeant Godinho spoke with three former employees who provided enlightening information about their final hours with Simone as they finished up their lunch shifts and closed the cafe. They talked about Simone's Vineyard trip and her intention to hitchhike to the Cape. They all hitched, and normally it wouldn't be a big deal. The girls were concerned about the length of the trip—an hour and a half—which didn't seem like a good idea. Simone, who was not worried, changed out of her uniform. They told Sergeant Godinho about their practice of changing their clothes before leaving the restaurant because of how much they hated their uniform. Simone, they remembered, always carried a gray duffel bag with the same change of clothes—a white T-shirt, ripped blue jeans, and white high-top sneakers. The waitresses then reported that Simone headed southbound on Route 27 and was picked up immediately. That was the last they saw of her. They put the time at about 2:00 or 2:30 in the afternoon.

When the detective reviewed Simone's file, he was struck by the nearly identical descriptions of Simone's outfit provided by Mr. C. and the waitresses. What were the chances that they were reporting nearly identical descriptions when they had never spoken? The police department had never issued any public descriptions. It was hard to believe that it was a coincidence. The detective felt that perhaps, after all of these years, he had stumbled on his first real clue in this cold case.

In addition to establishing a new clue, Sergeant Godinho was also able to confirm existing information through his interviews with the waitresses at the Rainbow Restaurant. He confirmed that Simone did not in fact take a bus to the Cape on the day she disappeared. The other waitresses watched Simone exit the restaurant and begin thumbing for a ride immediately. With further investigation, Sergeant Godinho also confirmed that these waitresses were actually the last people to see Simone. There was a reference in Simone's file to a police officer's daughter who supposedly had given Simone a ride two weeks after her disappearance; however, that timeline proved incorrect. She gave Simone a ride *prior* to Simone's disappearance.

With the advance in DNA testing and the advent of genetic genealogy, Sergeant Godinho worked with agencies throughout the United States to share Simone's DNA in the hopes of finding Simone through Jane Doe matches. Prior to Sergeant Godinho's work on the case, the previous detective met with Simone's uncles and extracted their DNA for comparison, which is the DNA they currently are using. Unfortunately, they did not have maternal DNA; however, Betsy supplied them with greeting cards that Jane sent her. They extracted Jane's DNA from the stamps and have submitted these samples to the FBI and are currently awaiting the results. The hope is to create a full DNA sequence for Simone to strengthen her profile and match options.

Using DNA, detectives can work with other agencies to compare Simone's information to Jane Does throughout the country by sending her information to the National Missing and Unidentified Persons System to cross-reference. When they feel that a description might connect to Simone, perhaps by the jewelry or the age, for example, they submit Simone's DNA. If there is the chance, no matter how small, for a possible link to the case, detectives take it. So far, they have compared Simone's information with more than thirty Jane Does, not just in Massachusetts but in states across the country, such as California, Virginia, Ohio, Georgia, Pennsylvania, Arizona, Tennessee, Illinois, North Carolina, Arkansas, and Kentucky.

Though he used technological advances in Simone's case, Sergeant Godinho also relied on old-fashioned detective work. He realized quickly that he would need a team of investigators working full time to investigate Simone's case properly. Through a retired Natick detective, he connected with Detective John Haswell of the Natick Police Department. Soon Detective Haswell joined Sergeant Godinho on the case. Together, they conducted as many media interviews as possible and followed the leads. One of the major hurdles in the case is the question of whether Simone made it out of the Natick/Sherborn area at all. Mr. C.'s 1986 interview has become important in the current investigation.

THE PROBLEM WITH MR. C.

It is entirely possible that Mr. C. misidentified Simone's picture when he saw her image in the 1986 *MetroWest* news article. Perhaps he had the misfortune of being pulled over on his way down Route 128 that morning in 1977. Maybe the state trooper who pulled him over even asked him to ferry a teenager to the Cape. This theory suggests that the girl was not Simone Ridinger. Many travelers wear jeans and carry duffel bags. It is more likely that Simone disappeared closer to home, somewhere in the towns of Natick, Sherborn, or Framingham.

Coincidences are not usually likely though. Mr. C.'s description of Simone's outfit seems too similar to be a coincidence. If he did give her a ride on that Sunday September morning, though, his story raises far more questions than answers. The involvement of the state trooper poses many questions alone. First of all, what was Simone doing in the back of a police car at 6:45 in the morning the day after she intended to be on the Vineyard? Why wasn't she already on the island? Had she gotten sidetracked the day before? Had she decided to stay with friends? Had she gotten into trouble?

Another question, and one that is even more difficult to answer, is why an officer of the law would hand over a teenager to a complete stranger. Would a state trooper ever do such a thing? Sergeant Godinho asked retired police officers that very question to get a sense of the times. He discussed his thoughts on the matter during an interview on an episode of the podcast *Murder Sheet* in February 2022: "I talked to some troopers, some officers, who were on the job back in the 70s, and even they were kind of skeptical about that. . . . It's mind-boggling by today's standards to think an officer or a trooper would do that. Back then, I suppose, I could see it happening as at least not outlandish. . . . He's an older gentleman heading to the Cape, seems harmless . . . and maybe he feels comfortable enough letting this girl who was at the time seventeen take a ride down there. Could have happened. I'm skeptical, but I don't see it as outlandish back in 1977 as it would be today, and I think everyone would probably agree with that."

In an effort to confirm Mr. C.'s story, Sergeant Godinho reached out to the State Police, who searched through their records, but they could not find the traffic stop to which Mr. C. referred. It is possible that officers did not report every traffic stop they made at the time. Sergeant Godinho also considered that perhaps Mr. C. mistook a local officer for a state trooper, and he researched traffic records for area precincts with no luck. At this time, he has not been able to confirm or deny Mr. C.'s story.

Mr. C. had long since passed away by the time Sergeant Godinho picked up Simone's case, leaving only his 1986 interview behind. In an effort to uncover more information, Sergeant Godinho found and interviewed Mr. C.'s son. Unfortunately, Mr. C. never told his family about the incident. Many commenters on threads concerning Simone's case find it odd that Mr. C. never told his family; however, when you consider the fact that Mr. C. lived alone at the time, his omission doesn't seem unusual. His wife had passed away and his children were grown and living elsewhere. Perhaps he even intended to tell them, but he never did.

Stranger perhaps is the fact that he didn't tell them that he visited the police station in 1986 and provided a statement for an ongoing case. Neglecting to mention to your children the fact that you were pulled over by the police isn't surprising, especially for an older driver. However, when you realize that you gave an hour-and-half ride to a girl who has been missing for a decade and were possibly the last person to see her alive, that seems like a story worthy of sharing with your adult children. Still, everyone is different, and some people are private.

Others wonder how Mr. C. could remember the details of Simone's outfit after ten years. He even recalled the fact that her sneakers were "grubby" and that she smelled like she "needed a bath." Most of us have difficulty remembering what we wore yesterday, so how could Mr. C. remember what a hitchhiker wore nearly ten years earlier?

If a significant event happens on any given day, we are more likely to remember all of the details from that day. According to Mr. C., two significant events happened that day. He was pulled over early in the morning by a state trooper. No one likes to be pulled over. I can remember each and every time I have been pulled over in specific detail. The trooper then asked Mr. C. for an unusual favor—to give a ride to a teenager. The ride was not a quick ride down the street; it was an hour-and-half ride with a stranger. There is no doubt that this would have been a highly unusual day—one that Mr. C. was not likely to forget.

Other people suggest that Mr. C. did not go to Cape Cod that day because of Labor Day weekend traffic. Though there is certainly heavy traffic heading to the Cape at the start of the Labor Day weekend, he was traveling on Sunday, when most people already would be on the Cape. What's more, he was traveling early in the morning. He was not likely to run into much traffic that morning.

Mr. C.'s story seems unbelievable and unlikely. It's tempting to dismiss it altogether. The problem is that he described his passenger as wearing the same outfit that the waitresses described Simone wearing. How could these two sources, who had never interacted, describe virtually the same outfit when the description was never made public? Chances are, they couldn't. If Mr. C. was lying, he was probably only lying about parts of his story.

The most unbelievable part of his story? That a state trooper asked a stranger to take a teenage girl to Cape Cod, an hour and a half away. There is no record of Mr. C.'s traffic stop, and no record of Simone's arrest. If Simone hadn't been arrested, what was she doing in the back of the police car? Why would Mr. C. lie to detectives in 1986 about being pulled over by a state trooper in 1977?

Perhaps Mr. C. picked up Simone while she was hitchhiking. Mr. C. lived only 2.4 miles from Simone's Framingham apartment. Maybe she hitched a ride back to her apartment after leaving the Rainbow Restaurant to grab a few things for the Vineyard and decided to spend the night. The note on Simone's door, which Jane would later find, implies that maybe Simone went back to her apartment at some point after she left the Rainbow Restaurant. The next morning, she might have hitched from her apartment, and that's when Mr. C. picked her up.

If Mr. C. had innocently picked up the teenage hitchhiker ten years before, why would he lie about his role? Perhaps the elderly gentleman was worried about having been the last person to see Simone—and in his car no less. Maybe he felt that including a police officer in his story would lend legitimacy to his actions.

There is always, of course, the possibility that Mr. C. lied because he harmed Simone and is responsible for her disappearance. Maybe he picked her up on Saturday as she was heading to the Cape. When he gave his statement to the police almost ten years later, he invented large portions of the event—his trip to the Cape, the state trooper, the day on which he met and picked up Simone, where he dropped her off—to minimize his role in her disappearance.

If Mr. C. was responsible for Simone's death, why come to the police station at all? Sergeant Godinho wonders if he wanted to get something off his chest, put something out there, or protect someone else. He could have made the entire story up or been mistaken about the sighting.

At the end of the day, Mr. C. simply could have been a nice man who was excited about taking a Sunday drive to buy some clock parts on the Cape. Along the way, he did a favor for an officer of the law and a teenage girl. He further did his due diligence by going to the police and providing information when he learned that she was missing. Because he has passed away and detectives have had difficulty confirming or denying his story, we may never know.

Ultimately, according to the detectives working the case, the most important aspect of Mr. C.'s story is that it could help determine Simone's whereabouts. If they can confirm Mr. C.'s story, then they know for certain that Simone made it as far as the Hyannis Rotary Club. They can narrow their search to the Cape, which is a tremendous help to her case and their resources.

If Simone made it over the bridge—either the Bourne or the Sagamore to the Cape—there are a number of possibilities about what she might have done next. The first possibility is that she flew to the Vineyard on one of the chartered flights out of Hyannis. Her mother, Jane, who was a pilot, flew to the Vineyard the day before. Simone could have done the same. Unfortunately, there are no passenger manifests from that time period to confirm a flight.

Simone easily could have hopped on a ferry out of Hyannis to the Vineyard. The docks were not a far walk from the spot where Mr. C.

dropped Simone. However, despite detectives' best efforts, they have been unable to find passenger records from that weekend.

Since Simone had friends in Hyannis, she may have simply decided to stay and enjoy the bustle of the busiest town on the Cape, one of the only places where teenagers can find nightlife and activities catered specifically to them. In fact, one of Jane's first considerations when Simone failed to arrive on the Vineyard was that Simone had stopped in Hyannis. Detectives have been trying to track down some of Simone's Hyannis friends in order to confirm whether Simone ever made it to the Cape that day.

Another possibility is that Simone planned to hitchhike to Cotuit, where her aunt and uncle lived. The coastal Cape town known for its oysters and skiffs is situated halfway between Hyannis and Falmouth. The Ridinger family often visited Jane's brother Joe and his wife Anne on their way to the Woods Hole ferry whenever they traveled to the Vineyard. If Simone had planned to visit them, she never made it to their home.

A very real possibility is that she attempted to hitchhike to Woods Hole. From their first days of traveling to the Vineyard, Simone's family sailed out of Woods Hole. Simone's Uncle Joe worked for the Woods Hole Oceanographic Institution, and that was the ferry with which they were most familiar. Simone would have been able to hitchhike to Woods Hole from Hyannis along Route 28.

Without confirmation of Mr. C.'s story, however, detectives cannot definitely put Simone on the Cape that weekend. Sergeant Godinho explains their frustration, "That story is the hurdle in the whole thing."

THEORIES

Simone Is Alive

Detectives highly doubt that Simone is alive. Still, they have done their due diligence to follow up on this theory. Sergeant Godinho researched her banking and social security records. Everything stopped in 1977. According to her records, Simone Ridinger ceased to exist when she disappeared, unless she changed her identity. Because anything is possible, detectives have partnered with the National Center for Missing and Exploited Children and the FBI since Sergeant Godinho took over the case in 2014. The National Center created age progression images, and the department uses the media to disseminate Simone's picture on a national scale through these resources.

Simone Was Murdered

Detectives fear that foul play may have been involved in Simone's disappearance. They have concluded that Simone hitchhiked and was likely picked up immediately after she left the Rainbow Restaurant on Saturday afternoon. Perhaps, for the first time during her many years of hitching rides, she met the wrong person. Maybe on the day she disappeared, as Simone's sister Betsy points out, she trusted someone she shouldn't have. She may have met with trouble immediately. She also may have hitched a number of rides toward her destination, meaning that she could have made it to the Cape and possibly beyond before running into harm's way. In addition to their investigations into Simone's ex-boyfriend, Mr. C., and the photographer, detectives are currently following up on many other persons of interest who require more investigation. They are not necessarily suspects, simply individuals who might be able to help detectives with information.

Simone Died as the Result of an Accident

In the true crime podcast *Wicked Deeds*, Detective John Haswell noted that in 1977, the towns of Sherborn and Natick were still relatively small places where everyone knew one another. He suggested that Simone most likely knew the person who picked her up. Many people who were interviewed said that Simone often got rides with friends, and her friends acknowledged giving Simone rides when they saw her hitching. For these reasons, detectives suspect that it is likely that Simone was picked up by a friend that day. They may have decided to go to a party, which would have been commonplace for Simone and her peers. Both Sergeant Godinho and Detective Haswell posit that

Simone in 1977. *Private collection of Betsy Bailey*

an accident may have happened as a result of something Simone and her friends were doing—either in a car or at a party—that could have caused Simone's death. They think that it is possible that the people involved could have panicked and hid her body. In this scenario, they do not believe that Simone's death was intentional but they do believe that the people who were there might be too afraid to come forward.

With Detective Godinho's promotion to sergeant, Detective Andrew Richard of the Sherborn Police Department took over Simone's case in January 2023. With direction from Sergeant Godinho, he and Detective John Haswell of the Natick Police Department, in consultation with the FBI and other national and local agencies, continue to work on Simone's case.

EPILOGUE

When Simone Ridinger walked out of the Rainbow Restaurant on that late summer afternoon, it was her intention to walk through the door of her childhood vacation home that evening. The naturally beautiful, free-spirited, and independent Simone welcomed the afternoon adventure full of strangers, ferries, and islands that awaited her in between. Somewhere along the trip, this independent young woman encountered a greater force, whether malignant or natural, and lost her way.

For nearly fifty years, Simone Ridinger's whereabouts have remained a mystery, but she is still out there. Detectives are confident that there are people alive today who know what happened to Simone and where to find her. If someone, even just one person, comes forward to share what he or she knows regarding Simone, perhaps she can finally return home to her family, where she belongs. They deserve to know what happened to her, and she deserves a peaceful rest. She has been gone long enough.

HOW TO CONTACT AUTHORITIES ABOUT SIMONE'S CASE

Unlike the other cases in this book, Simone's case remains an active investigation. Detectives are looking for any information that will help them find Simone. They are also specifically seeking Simone's housemates on 29 Linden Street during the summer of 1977. She lived on the bottom floor, but they would like to know who lived in the other units or nearby during that time. They are eager to talk to people who knew Simone—housemates, classmates, friends, or coworkers. They believe that no piece of information is too small. Even if you did not know Simone but believe that you have information that may be helpful to her case, they want to hear from you.

Detectives on the case feel that people have been hesitant to come forward. Especially in the case of an accident, in which people may have remained quiet to protect one another, detectives urge witnesses to come forward. They remind witnesses with potential knowledge that the primary goal in this case is to recover Simone, bring her home to her family, and give her the proper rest she deserves. Anyone with information in this case can call the Sherborn Police Department (508-653-2424) or the Natick Police Department (508-647-9500) directly and ask to speak to the detectives regarding the Simone Ridinger case.

BIBLIOGRAPHY

CHAPTER 1: DOROTHY ARNOLD, 1910

"1910 United States Federal Census." *Ancestry* (Ancestry.com), database entry for Francis Arnold.

"American Consul at Naples Enters Hunt for Heiress." *Buffalo Courier*, 7 February 1911, p. 1.

"Arnold and Griscom Families Spend Day Dodging Reporters." *Los Angeles Times*, 17 February 1911, p. 1.

"Arnold Case Is Unsolved." *Poughkeepsie Eagle-News*, 30 January 1911, p. 1.

"Arnold–Culver." *New York Times*, 12 June 1911, p. 11.

"Arnold Discredits Tale of Buried Girl." *New York Times*, 18 April 1916, p. 6.

"Arnold Family Call Florence Clue Ridiculous." *Buffalo Times*, 5 March 1911, p. 14.

"Arnold Family Says Body Is Not That of Daughter." *Evening World (New York)*, 15 May 1911, p. 6.

"Arnold Girl Is Hiding in City Police Believe." *Times Union (New York)*, 28 January 1922, p. 1.

"Arnold Girl's Father Gets Threat Letter." *Buffalo News*, 2 February 1912, p. 13.

"Arnold Search at Sudden End." *Boston Globe*, 7 February 1911, p. 8.

"Arnolds Give up Hope." *New York Times*, 18 April 1911, p. 5.

"Arnolds Give up Hope That Dorothy Lives." *Evening World (New York)*, 13 March 1911, p. 9.

"Ask Griscom to Tell Everything." *Buffalo Enquirer*, 18 February 1911, p. 10.

"Ask Ransom for Rich Girl." *Kansas City Star*, 27 January 1911, p. 1.

"Ayers Denies Tale of Dorothy Arnold." *Evening World (New York)*, 9 April 1921, p. 1.

"A Baffling Mystery." *New York Tribune*, 10 December 1911, p. 53.

"Belief Is Family Knows Whereabouts of Dorothy Arnold." *Buffalo Courier*, 25 February 1911, p. 1.

"Believe Girl Is Hiding in City." *Fort Wayne News*, 28 January 1911, p. 2.

"Believes Daughter Has Been Kidnapped." *Buffalo Courier*, 28 February 1911, p. 1.

"Believes Girl Is Dorothy Arnold." *Press and Sun-Bulletin (New York)*, 21 December 1911, p. 1.

"Believes Sister Is Dead." *New York Tribune*, 7 February 1911, pp. 1, 4.

"Big Ransom Demanded for Dorothy Arnold." *Ashbury Park Press*, 27 January 1911, p. 1.

"Boardinghouse Keepers Beware." *Port Chester Journal*, 9 February 1911, p. 1.

"Bryn Mawr Girls Join Arnold Quest." *St. Louis Globe Democrat*, 17 March 1911, p. 1.

"The Case of Dorothy Arnold." *Columbia Record*, 28 February 1911, p. 4.

Chambers, Julius. "Walks and Talks." *Brooklyn Daily Eagle*, 31 January 1911, p. 19.

Churchill, Allan. "The Girl Who Never Came Back." *American Heritage* 11, no. 5 (August 1960).

"Clew to Dorothy Arnold." *Boston Globe*, 24 March 1911, p. 5.

"Close Search for the Missing Girl." *Ledger-Star (Norfolk, VA)*, 27 January 1911, p. 18.

"Co-eds Seek Missing Girl." *Star-Tribune (MN)*, 30 March 1911, p. 10.

"Creditors Swoop Down Again upon Griscom Junior." *Evening World (New York)*, 18 February 1911, p. 3.

"Demands for Ransom Not Seriously Taken." *Evening Star (Washington, DC)*, 28 January 1911, p. 1.

"Denial by Griscom." *Boston Globe*, 3 February 1911, p. 9.

"Denials by Griscom." *Washington Post*, 2 February 1911, p. 3.

"Denies Any Trace of Dorothy Arnold." *Brooklyn Daily Eagle*, 23 December 1913, p. 3.

"Deny Getting News." *Lincoln Star*, 5 March 1911, p. 4.

"Deny Miss Arnold Went Away by Boat." *New York Times*, 1 February 1911, p. 1.

"Disappearance of Miss Arnold Still Unsolved." *Buffalo Enquirer*, 28 January 1911, pp. 1, 9.

"Dorothy Arnold?" *New York Daily News*, 27 March 1932, p. 12.

"Dorothy Arnold, in Philadelphia, Wrote to Her Father." *Evening World (New York)*, 1 February 1911, p. 18.

"Dorothy Arnold Again." *Evening World (New York)*, 12 May 1921, p. 27.

"Dorothy Arnold Again." *New York Times*, 13 June 1913, p. 11.

"Dorothy Arnold Buried in Cellar, Man Confesses." *Buffalo Enquirer*, 17 April 1916, p. 1.

"Dorothy Arnold Case a Jumble." *Courier-Journal (Louisville, KY)*, 12 February 1911, p. 4.

"Dorothy Arnold Clew." *Boston Globe*, 8 March 1911, p. 20.

"Dorothy Arnold Clew Found." *Democrat and Chronicle*, 2 February 1912, p. 2.

"Dorothy Arnold Dead, Her Relatives Declare; Mother Scours Europe." *Evening World*, 31 January 1911, pp. 1, 2.

"Dorothy Arnold Diary Discovered." *New-York Tribune*, 3 January 1915, p. 12.

"Dorothy Arnold Hiding Police Now Believe." *Frederick Post*, 28 January 1911, p. 1.

"Dorothy Arnold in Albany." *Carbondale (IL) Daily News*, 11 May 1911, p. 8.

"Dorothy Arnold in Connecticut, Says New Story." *Daily News*, 29 April 1921, p. 2.

"Dorothy Arnold in Europe Belief of Investigators." *Post-Standard (New York)*, 31 January 1911, p. 1.

"Dorothy Arnold in Hiding Say Police." *Bridgeport (CT) Times*, 28 January 1911, p. 1.

"Dorothy Arnold Is 'Found' Again in Danville, VA." *Evening World (New York)*, 25 February 1911, p. 12.

"Dorothy Arnold Is Great Mystery." *Harrisburg Daily Independent*, 26 January 1911, p. 1.

"Dorothy Arnold May Be Home Today." *New York Times*, 28 January 1911, p. 1.

"Dorothy Arnold Mourned As Dead by Her Family." *Evening World (New York)*, 11 April 1911, p. 2.

"Dorothy Arnold Mystery Solved, Says Captain Ayres." *New York Times*, 9 April 1921, p. 1.

"Dorothy Arnold Not Found at Woodbury." *Philadelphia Inquirer*, 24 March 1911, p. 3.

"Dorothy Arnold Quarreled with Father and Fled." *Evening World (New York)*, 2 February 1911, p. 1.

"Dorothy Arnold Reported in Denver." *Times Tribune (PA)*, 27 March 1911, p. 1.

"Dorothy Arnold Said to Be in a Sanitarium." *Washington Post*, 6 February 1911, p. 3.

"Dorothy Arnold Sailed for Italy in January." *Evening World (New York)*, 3 February 1911, p. 2.

"Dorothy Arnold Seen after December 12th." *Press and Sun-Bulletin (New York)*, 7 February 1911, p. 9.

"Dorothy Arnold Sends Word to Griscom in a 'Personal.'" *Evening World (New York)*, 13 February 1911, p. 1.

"Dorothy Arnold's Family Expects Startling News." *Evening World (New York)*, 1 March 1911, p. 5.

"Dorothy Arnold's Father, Believing She Was Dead, Omitted Her from His Will." *Times Union*, 14 April 1922, p. 4.

"Dorothy Arnold's Father at Police Headquarters." *Evening World (New York)*, 1 February 1912, p. 13.

"Dorothy Arnold's Father Is Keeping up Costly Search." *Evening World (New York)*, 18 February 1911, p. 3.

"Dorothy Arnold's Mother Missing Adds to Mystery." *Buffalo Courier*, 30 January 1911, p. 1.

"Dorothy Arnold's Mother Will Search Near Home for Girl." *Morning Herald*, 28 February 1911, p. 1.

"Dorothy Arnold's Sister Married." *Courier-News (NJ)*, 10 September 1912, p. 10.

"Dorothy Arnold Still Missing." *Buffalo Times*, 13 February 1911, p. 1.

"Dorothy Arnold Suspect Sues." *Spokesman-Review*, 23 April 1911, pp. 1, 8.

"Dorothy Arnold Vanished before from Her Home." *Evening World (New York)*, 1 February 1911, p. 1.

"Dorothy Arnold Was Passenger, Say Ship's Crew." *Evening World (New York)*, 7 February 1911, p. 8.

"Dorothy Harriet Camille Arnold." *The Charley Project* (thecharleyproject.org), updated 23 September 2013.

"Doubt Griscom's Story." *New York Tribune*, 12 February 1911, p. 2.

"Dragging the Lakes." *Topeka State Journal*, 18 March 1911, p. 6.

"Explains 'Mary Martha.'" *New York Tribune*, 18 February 1911, p. 10.

"Exposing the Horror of Border Traffic in White American Girls." *Buffalo Courier*, 6 September 1925, p. 11.

"False Dorothy Arnold Tale." *New York Times*, 11 October 1911, p. 2.

"Family Abandons the Search for Dorothy Arnold." *Dayton Herald*, 13 March 1911, p. 1.

"Family Gets Letters Demanding Money for Return of Heiress Missing since Early December." *Akron Beacon Journal*, 28 January 1911, p. 1.

"Fate of Dr. Brand, Living Yet Dead, May Have Befallen Thousands." *New York Herald*, 18 January 1920, p. 23.

"Father Believes the Missing Dorothy Arnold Is Dead." *Tulsa Evening Sun*, 18 March 1914, p. 3.

"Federal Authorities Take Hand in the Poison Needle Mystery As a Clue to White Slavers." *Buffalo Sunday Times*, 7 December 1913, p. 25.

"Find Clew to Girl." *Washington Post*, 27 January 1911, pp. 1, 3.

"Find Woman in Harlem." *New York Times*, 1 June 1911, p. 20.

"Flat Denial from Arnolds." *Sun (New York)*, 14 February 1911, p. 2.

"Follow New Clue to Miss Arnold. *New York Times*, 27 January 1911, p. 3.

Foster, J. J. "Unraveling the Mysterious Disappearance of Dorothy Arnold." *Ninja Journalist*, 28 July 2019.

"Francis Arnold Asks Aid in Hunt for His Daughter." *Newark Star*, 26 January 1911, p. 4.

"Francis R. Arnold Dead." *New York Times*, 2 April 1922, p. 29.

"F. R. Arnold Denies Daughter Is Located." *Brooklyn Daily Eagle*, 29 January 1911, p. 1.

"Girl at Honolulu Says She's Dorothy Arnold." *New York Tribune*, 31 January 1917, p. 1.

"Girl Denies She's Lost Heiress/Prisoner Declared Dora Falk." *San Francisco Examiner*, 20 February 1911, p. 4.

"Girl Found Here May Be Missing New York Heiress." *Muskogee Daily Phoenix and Times*, 19 March 1911, pp. 1, 10.

"Girl in Hospital Not Miss Arnold." *Ledger-Star (NJ)*, 23 February 1911, p. 1.

"Girl May Be Here." *Baltimore Sun*, 28 January 1911, p. 1.

"Girl May Be Missing Girl." *Muskogee Times-Democrat*, 28 January 1911, p. 1.

"Girl Seeking Disguise May Be Lost Heiress." *Evening World (New York)*, 26 January 1911, p. 1.

"Girl Still Missing." *Washington Post*, 28 January 1911, pp. 1, 3.

"Griscom and Arnold Girl Meet in Boston." *Boston Globe*, 14 February 1911, p. 1.

"Griscom and Arnold Lawyers in Conference." *Standard Union*, 10 February 1911, p. 1.

"Griscom Expects to Wed Miss Arnold." *New York Times*, 12 February 1911, p. 1.

"Griscom Has Firm Belief She Is Alive." *Democrat and Chronicle*, 10 February 1911, p. 1.

"Griscom Here, Hopes to See Miss Arnold." *Sun (New York)*, 10 February 1911, pp. 1, 2.

"Griscom Impatient." *Boston Globe*, 18 February 1911, p. 4.

"Griscom Makes a Rush Trip to Atlantic City; Mystery in New Move." *Evening World (New York)*, 10 February 1911, p. 1.

"Griscom Meets Arnold." *Brooklyn Daily Eagle*, 10 February 1911, p. 1.

"Griscom Now Certain Dorothy Arnold Will Reappear Tomorrow." *Evening World (New York)*, 11 February 1911, p. 1.

"Griscom Still Hopes to Find Miss Arnold." *Buffalo News*, 12 February 1911, p. 1.

"Griscom Ventures Out." *York (PA) Dispatch*, 22 March 1911, p. 5.

"Hear Dorothy Arnold Started for New York but Fail to Find Her." *Brooklyn Daily Eagle*, 7 February 1912, p. 1.

"Hears from Miss Arnold?" *New York Times*, 22 February 1911, p. 1.

"Held for Arnold Blackmail." *New York Times*, 27 February 1911, p. 20.

"He Saw Dorothy Arnold Jan 29th." *Buffalo Enquirer*, 7 March 1911, p. 1.

"'I Am Waiting for You—Griscom.'" *Times Herald (New York)*, 22 February 1911, p. 1.

"Irma Munsell Goes to Bellevue to Be Examined." *Evening World (New York)*, 7 May 1912, p. 11.

"Jumped Overboard." *New Star and Chickasha (OK) Telegram*, 23 March 1905, p. 1.

"Killed Dogs for Husband." *Morning Call*, 3 December 1909, p. 1.

"Know Where Miss Dorothy Arnold Is." *Buffalo Enquirer*, 10 February 1911, p. 6.

"Leave Dorothy Arnold Alone." *Indianapolis Star*, 1 March 1911, p. 8.

Levins, Peter. "What Has Happened to Justice?" *Daily News*, 30 April 1944, pp. 14–15.

"Little Miss Fortune." *Daily News (New York)*, 11 May 1986, p. 153.

"Love Affair May Have Caused Girl to Quit Her Home." *Harrisburg Telegraph*, 27 January 1911, p. 1.

"Mail Addressed to Dorothy Arnold on Pacific Coast." *Buffalo Morning Express*, 10 February 1911, p. 1.

"Marjorie Brown Is Not Missing Dorothy Arnold." *Buffalo Enquirer*, 9 February 1911, p. 6.

"May Solve Arnold Mystery in Atlantic City by Night." *Star-Gazette*, 11 February 1911, p. 1.

McIntyre, O. O. "New York, Day by Day." *Buffalo Times*, 11 June 1931, p. 6.

"Millionaire Arnold Asked to Pay $5,000 for Missing Daughter." *Brooklyn Daily Eagle*, 27 January 1911, p. 1.

"Millionaire's Daughter Is Missing for over a Month." *Press and Sun-Bulletin.* 26 January 1911, p. 8.

"Millionaire's Daughter Is Underground." *Stockton Evening and Sunday Record*, 27 January 1911, p. 5.

"Miss Arnold Keeps Silence." *Sun (New York)*, 31 January 1911, p. 1.

"Miss Arnold Not Found." *Times Union*, 22 March 1913, p. 8.

"Miss Arnold Pawned Jewels in Boston." *New York Times*, 16 February 1911, p. 1.

"Miss Arnold Seen in Florence, Girl Writes Her Sister." *Evening World*, 3 March 1911, p. 3.

"Miss Dorothy Arnold Lost." *Sun (New York)*, 26 January 1911, p. 1.

"Miss Dorothy Arnold Reported in or near Long Island City." *Brooklyn Daily Eagle*, 28 January 1911, p. 1.

"Missing a Year $10,000 Reward Fails to Bring Word of Lost Heiress." *Buffalo Courier*, 12 December 1911, p. 3.

"Missing Dorothy Arnold." *Uncovered* (Uncovered.com), 20 April 2023.

"Missing Girl Back Who Disappeared Ten Months Ago." *Evening World (New York)*, 10 October 1911, p. 1.

"Missing Girl Expected Home." *St. Louis Star and Times*, 28 January 1911, p. 1.

"Missing Girl Held for Large Ransom." *Missoula Herald*, 27 January 1911, p. 1.

Monroe, Heather. "The Peculiar Disappearance of Dorothy Arnold." *Medium* (Medium.com), 19 December 2018 (accessed June 19, 2023).

"Mother of Lost Dorothy Arnold Left Secretly." *Buffalo Times*, 4 April 1912, p. 14.

"Mother of Missing Dorothy Arnold Dies." *Ithaca Journal*, 29 December 1928, p. 1.

"Mother Seeks Girl in Europe." *Daily Argus (New York)*, 1 February 1911, p. 5.

"Mrs. Arnold Home Again." *New York Tribune*, 5 June 1912, p. 3.

"Mrs. Arnold Home without Daughter." *New York Times*, 13 February 1911, pp. 1, 2.

"Mystery." *Buffalo Times*, 25 February 1911, p. 1.

"Mystery Veils Life of Latest Dorothy Arnold." *New York Tribune*, 30 April 1921, p. 9.

"New Angle in Girl Mystery." *Chicago Tribune*, 27 January 1911, p. 4.

"New Arnold Clues." *Brooklyn Citizen*, 2 February 1911, p. 1.

"New Hope That Dorothy Arnold Is Still Alive." *Buffalo Enquirer*, 22 February 1911, p. 9.

"Newspaper Chaff." *Daily Ardmoreite (OK)*, 28 March 1911, p. 4.

"Nine Years of Mystery." *Buffalo Times*, 13 December 1919, p. 6.

"No Clue to Girl, Arnolds Declare." *New York Times*, 6 February 1911, p. 3.

"No News, Says Father of Dorothy Arnold." *Buffalo News*, 23 October 1911, p. 13.

"Not Dorothy Arnold." *Evening World*, 9 December 1914, p. 3.

"Not Dorothy Arnold Says Attorney Keith." *New York Times*, 30 April 1921, p. 11.

"No Trace Found of Missing Girl." *Brooklyn Citizen*, 27 January 1911, p. 1.

"No Word from Miss Arnold." *Sun (New York)*, 29 January 1911, pp. 1, 2.

"O'Mara Declares Dorothy Arnold Will Return Soon." *Evening World*, 14 October 1911, p. 4.

"Our Point of View." *Journal*, 27–28 January 1911, p. 6.

Park, Edwin J. "Griscom and Arnold Girl Meet in Boston." *Boston Globe*, 14 February 1911, pp. 1–2.

Pasqualini, Kym. "Dorothy Arnold: Disappearance of a New York Socialite." *The Crime Wire*, (thecrimewire.com), 27 June 2023.

Pennsylvania, U.S. County Marriage Records, 1845–1963.

Phillips, Francis. "Gossip from Gotham." *Ottawa Journal*, 1 March 1911, p. 5.

Pietrangelo, Ann. "What the Baader-Meinhof Phenomenon Is and Why You May See It Again . . . and Again." *Healthline* (Healthline.com), 17 December 2019.

"Plans to Join Girl." *Washington Post*, 14 February 1911, 2.

"Police Abandon Hunt for Dorothy Arnold." *Intelligencer Journal (PA)*, 28 January 1911, p. 1.

"Police Angered by Secrecy of Arnold Family." *Washington Times*, 29 January 1911, p. 1.

"Police of Nation Asked to Find Missing Heiress." *St. Louis Post-Dispatch*, 28 January 1911, p. 1.

"Police of World Seek Dolly Arnold." *Lancaster Morning Journal*, 28 January 1911, p. 1.

"Police Still on Search for Girl." *Boston Globe*, 27 January 1911, p. 1.

"Postal Card from Missing Girl?" *Buffalo Commercial*, 6 February 1911, p. 2.

"Price Set on Girl's Return." *Boston Globe*, 28 January 1911, pp. 1, 5.

"Raid Brings News of Dorothy Arnold." *Sun (New York)*, 10 April 1914, p. 1.

"Ransom Demand Made on Father of Missing Girl." *Newark Star-Eagle*, 27 January 1911, p. 1.

"Ransom for Missing Girl Is Demanded." *Buffalo News*, 28 January 1911, p. 1.

"Real Romance from the Sunny South." *Bangor Daily News*, 27 April 1911, p.1.

"Reward up for Heiress." *San Francisco Examiner*, 27 January 1911, p. 2.

"Rich Girl Wanders Streets Two Days with $2 in Purse." *Evening World (New York)*, 6 May 1912, p. 3.

"Rumor That Heiress Landed in Brooklyn Today from a Steamer." *Brooklyn Citizen*, 28 January 1911, p. 1.

"Says He Saw Miss Arnold." *New York Times*, 29 January 1911, p. 2.

"Says She Never Said She Is Dorothy Arnold." *Buffalo News*, 17 May 1921, p. 13.

"Says She's Dorothy Arnold." *Sun (New York)*, 14 January 1915, p. 5.

"Search for Arnold Girl in the Capitol on Valuable Clew." *Washington Herald*, 8 March 1911, p. 1.

"Search in Vain to Find Missing Dorothy Arnold." *Allen County Republican-Gazette*, 31 January 1911, p. 7.

"Search Philadelphia for Missing Girl." *Barre (VT) Daily*, 27 January 1911, p. 1.

"Seek Miss Arnold in Flower Hospital." *New York Times*, 15 February 1911, p. 1.

"Seek Miss Arnold in River." *New York Times*, 15 May 1911, p. 1.

"Seizes Woman in Subway." *New York Times*, 23 February 1917, p. 11.

"Seven Detectives Shadow Suspected Dorothy Arnold." *Enid (OK) Daily Eagle*, 21 March 1911, p. 1.

"She Looked Like Dorothy Arnold." *New York Times*, 8 February 1912, p. 8.

"Silence of Death, Says Girl's Father." *New York Times*, 29 January 1911, p. 1.

"Society Girl Lost." *Evening Star*, 26 January 1911, p. 11.

"Sought Miss Arnold Last Thanksgiving." *New York Times*, 2 February 1911, p. 1.

"Still Seek Heiress." *Morning Post*, 27 January 1911, p. 1.

"Stranger Visiting Here Looks Like Missing Girl." *Harrisburg (PA) Telegraph*, 28 January 1911, p. 1.

"Subpoenas in Arnold Case." *New York Times*, 11 March 1911, p. 1.

"Suitor Watched in Arnold Case." *Washington Post*, 29 January 1911, p. 3.

"Swears to Death of Dorothy Arnold." *Brooklyn Daily Eagle*, 10 April 1914, p. 2.

"Tells of Girls Sold into Chinatown Slavery." *Sun (New York)*, 3 September 1912, p. 6.

"They Think They Saw Dorothy Arnold." *Democrat and Chronicle (New York)*, 6 February 1911, p. 3.

"Thinks He Has Found Missing Dorothy Arnold." *Democrat and Chronicle*, 26 October 1912, p. 19.

"Those Who Never Come Back." *Buffalo Times*, 31 March 1912, p. 76.

"Threats to Father of Dorothy Arnold." *New York Times*, 21 February 1912, p. 1.

Toomey, Elizabeth. "Anniversary of Mystery." *Times Record*, 12 December 1950, p. 14.

"To Philadelphia in an Automobile." *Boston Globe*, 3 February 1911, p. 9.

"To Torture Arnold Girl." *Butte Daily Post*, 28 January 1911, p. 1.

"The Trap That Awaits the Unwary Girl." *Buffalo News*, 12 January 1913, p. 26.

"U.S. Passport Applications, 1795–1925." *Ancestry* (Ancestry.com), database entry for George Griscom Jr., 6 January 1919.

"The Wealthy Mrs. Hayes-Dilworth and Rev. Craig Were Married." *Cincinnati Enquirer*, 2 December 1909, p. 2.

"Where Is Dorothy?" *Atchison Daily Globe.* 28 January 1911, p. 1.

"Where Is Dorothy Arnold?" *New York Times*, 11 December 1911, p. 10.

"Will Drag Lake in Central Park." *Boston Globe*, 30 January 1911, p. 3.

"Will of Mother Asserts Dorothy Arnold Is Dead." *Daily News*, 31 December 1928, p. 80.

"Woman Detective in Cruger Case, Girl Victim and One Who Escaped." *Parsons Daily Republican*, 1 July 1917, p. 6.

"Woman Gives New Clew to Missing Arnold Girl." *Brooklyn Daily Eagle*, 30 January 1911, p. 2.

"Woman Says Heiress Has Been Killed." *Buffalo Courier*, 9 February 1911, p. 1.

"Would Marry Dorothy Arnold." *The Los Angeles Times*, 17 February 1911, p. 1.

"Young Griscom Kept under Surveillance." *New-York Tribune*, 14 February 1911, pp. 1, 3.

CHAPTER 2: ANNA LOCASCIO, 1918

"1910 United States Federal Census." *Ancestry* (Ancestry.com), database entry for Anna Locascio.

"1920, 1930, 1940, 1950 United States Federal Census." *Ancestry* (Ancestry.com), database entries for Frank Locascio.

"9 Year Old Girl Hostile to Father at Murder Trial." *Daily News (New York)*, 25 May 1920, p. 30.

"Anti-Cabaret Bill Favored by Clergymen." *Atlantic City Gazette-Review*, 22 March 1918, pp. 1, 3.

"Barber Shop Entered at Ridgefield Park." *Record (NJ)*, 9 July 1913, p. 1.

"Brothers Are Indicted for Murder, Report." *Record (NJ)*, 5 March 1920, p. 1.

"Daughter Testifies against Her Father Case Depends on Story." *Atlanta Tri-Weekly Journal*, 29 May 1920, p. 8.

"Daughter Testifies against Her Father in Uxoricide Case." *New York Tribune*, 25 May 1920, p. 9.

"Frank & Salvatore Locascio of Ridgefield Park Charged with Death of Former's Wife." *Record (NJ)*, 24 May 1920, p. 1.

"Frank Locascio, Accused of Murder, Takes Witness Stand in Own Defense." *Record (NJ)*, 26 May 1920, p. 1.

"Frank LoCascio, Barber 65 Years." *Record (NJ)* 28 February 1972, p. 8.

"Freed of Murder Charge." *Daily News (New York)*, 27 May 1920, p. 4.

"The Great Arrival." *Immigration and Relocation in US History. Library of Congress.* (loc.gov), 23 February 2023.

"Hackensack's Barbers Strike Nearly Ended." *Record (NJ)*, 22 May 1913, p. 1.

"Italian-Americans and the 332nd Infantry Regiment." *The United States World War One Centennial Commission* (Worldwar1centennial.org), 19 April 2023.

"Italy Enters WWI." *The National WWI Museum and Memorial* (theworldwar.org), 19 April 2023.

"Jury Disagrees in Trial of Frank Locascio for Murder." *Record (NJ)*, 27 May 1920, p. 1.

"Locascio Jury Fails to Agree; Is Discharged." *Daily News (New York)*, 27 May 1920, p. 17.

"Locascio out on Bail." *Record (NJ)*, 29 May 1920, p. 1.

"Mrs. Grace Humiston, Woman Sherlock Holmes, Tells How She Solved Cruger Mystery." *Knoxville Sentinel*, 23 June 1917, p. 10.

"Mrs. Humiston, Whose Special Office Is Dissolved." *New York Tribune*, 6 January 1918, p. 56.

"Mystery Unsolved." *Record (NJ)*, 27 May 1920, p. 4.

"New York, U.S., Arriving Passenger and Crew Lists, 1820–1957." *Ancestry* (Ancestry.com), database entry for Pasquale Manfre, 4 January 1897.

"No Body Is Found Accused Slayer Is Freed." *Rutland (VT) News*, 29 May 1920, p. 2.

"One Brother Freed As Other Is Tried for Wife's Murder." *Daily News* (New York), 26 May 1920, p. 1.

"Raid on Ridgefield Park Still Follows Illness of Aged Customer." *Record (VT)*, 8 March 1923, p. 1.

"Ridgefield Barber Murder Suspect." *Daily Record (NJ)*, 31 January 1920, p. 1.

Ridgefield Park: 1685–1985. Ridgefield Park, NJ, Board of Commissioners, 1985.

"Seeks Writ of Habeas Corpus in Murder Case." *Record (NJ)*, 3 February 1920, p. 1.

"Tenements and Toil." *Immigration and Relocation in US History. Library of Congress* (loc.gov), 21 April 2023.

"Think Woman Left Home of Own Free Will." *Record (NJ)*, 31 January 1920, p. 1.

"Two Held for Murder of Pretty Italian Girl: Frank Locascio, Husband, and His Brother, Salvatore, Held in County Jail Here without Bail." *Record (NJ)*, 30 January 1920, p. 1.

"Wife's Body Not Found, So Husband Is Freed." *Buffalo Enquirer*, 28 May 1920, p. 18.

"Women in WWI." *The National WWI Museum and Memorial* (theworldwar.org), 19 April 2023.

CHAPTER 3: AGNES TUFVERSON, 1933

"1900, 1910 United States Federal Census." *Ancestry* (Ancestry.com), database for Agnes C. Tufverson.

Alexander, Jack. "The Still Unexplained Mystery of Agnes Tufverson's Disappearance." *St. Louis Dispatch*, 26 August 1934, p. 56.

"Avenging Fury of the Tufverson Sisters." *Daily News (New York)*, 4 October 1936, pp. 244–246.

Ayers, Captain John H. Letter to Olive Tufverson. 18 April 1935. Personal collection of David and Patricia Rupp.

———. Letter to Selma Tufverson. 31 May 1934. Personal collection of David and Patricia Rupp.

Blakemore, Erin. "Why Many Married Women Were Banned from Working during the Great Depression." *History* (History.com), July 21, 2019. www.history.com/news/great-depression-married-women-employment.

"Bludgeons Found in Cupboard." *Daily Herald (London)*, 23 June 1934, p. 1.

"Bride Missing Believed Slain." *Dayton Daily News*, 19 June 1934, p. 3.

Chirnside, Mark. "The Disappearance of Agnes Tufverson." *The History Press* (thehistorypress.com), 2023.

Chirnside, Mark, and Jack Wetton. "The Poderjay Case." *Mark Chirnside's Reception Room* (www.markchirnside.uk.com), 2004.

"Couple Held in Vienna Tufverson Mystery As Police of Two Continents Search for Clues." *State Journal (MI)*, 21 June 1934, p. 8.

"Crime Enigma in Abduction of Agnes Tufverson." *Philadelphia Inquirer*, 23 February 1941, p. 132.

"Dashing Foreigner to Leave Prison, His Secret Untold." *Birmingham News*, 18 January 1940, p. 5.

Doran, Dorothy. "Cuyahoga Falls Woman, Former Roommate, Remembers Oddities of Agnes Tufverson." *Akron Beacon Journal*, 27 June 1934, p. 16.

England and Wales Marriage Registration Index, 1837–2005, *FamilySearch* (https://familysearch.org), Ivan Poderjay and null, 1933; quarter 1, vol. 1A, p. 152, Paddington, London, England, General Register Office, Southport, England.

"European and American Police Seek a Missing American Girl." *Kansas City Star*, 22 June 1934, p. 17.

"Family Aids Police Hunt for Missing Lawyer." *Sentinel (Carlisle, Pennsylvania)*, 22 June 1934, p. 1.

"Fate of Bride Still a Puzzle." *Detroit Free Press*, 17 June 1934, p. 1.

Flowers, R. Barri. *Murder and Menace*. R. Barri Flowers, 2017.

"Fritz Kuhn Marked for Death in Prison." *Ogden Standard-Examiner*, 26 March 1960, p. 4.

Guilfoyle, Mary. Letter to Olive Tufverson. 5 March 1934. Personal collection of David and Patricia Rupp.

"Guilty Plea by Poderjay Is Rejected." *Daily News (New York)*, 31 January 1935, p. 443.

"His Bigamy Plea Deferred." *Daily News (New York)*, 31 January 1935, p. 510.

"Husband Held in Bride Hunt." *Evening Review (OH)*, 22 June 1934, p. 1.

"If It Was Murder, It Was the Perfect Crime." *San Francisco Examiner*, 17 March 1940, p. 99.

"Ivan Poderjay Loses Eye in Prison Battle." *Daily News (New York)*, 20 July 1938, p. 57.

"Ivan Poderjay to Leave Cell, Bride Never Found." *Herald-Press (MI)*, 31 January 1940, p. 4.

"Kin Believe Vanished Bride Dead." *Daily Times (Davenport, IA)*, 23 June 1934, p. 16.

"Lack of Scar Baffles Office." *Windsor (Ontario) Star*, 8 September 1934, p. 21.

Lane, Doris. "The Case of the Vanishing Bride." *Porchlight International for the Missing and Unidentified*, posted 23 August 2001, edited 20 December 2003.

Levins, Peter. "Honeymoon." *Atlanta Constitution*, 30 March 1947, p. 97.

———. "Mystery Problem of Missing Bride." *Pittsburgh Sun-Telegraph*, 30 November 1939, p. 17.

———. "Nothing Missing but Happy Bride in Poderjay Case." *Daily News (New York)*, 24 February 1935, p. 169.

Longin, Samuel. "Murders on the Olympic." *RMS Olympic*, https://rms-olympic.com/meurtres-sur-olympic/.

"The Man Who Laughed Last at the Law." *Miami Herald*, 10 March 1940, p. 97.

"Memoranda Pertinent to Disappearance of Agnes Tufverson Poderjay on December 20th, 1933." NYPD Missing Persons Bureau, 12 June 1934.

"Missing Adventurer's London Marriage." *Daily Herald (London)*, 8 June 1934.

"Missing Bride." *Evening Sun (Baltimore)*, 17 January 1940, p. 3.

"Missing Bride Dead, Sister Convinced As Brief Case Is Found." *Daily Brooklyn Eagle*, 19 June 1934, p 1.

"Missing Woman's Clothing Found in Vienna Flat." *Nottingham Evening Post*, 19 June 1934, p. 7.

"Mum on Missing Bride." *Brooklyn Daily Eagle*, 29 January 1935, p. 1.

"New York, New York, U.S. Marriage License Indexes, 1907–2018." 4 December 1933. Database for Agnes C. Tufverson and Ivan Poderjay IV.

"New York, U.S. Arriving Passenger and Crew Lists, 1820–1957." *Ancestry* (Ancestry.com), database entry for Agnes Colonia Tufverson, *Ile de France*, 4 July 1933.

———. *Ancestry* (Ancestry.com), database entry for Ivan Poderjay, *Ile de France*, 4 July 1933.

———. *Ancestry* (Ancestry.com), database entry for Ivan Poderjay, *President Polk*, 29 January 1935.

Norris, Kathleen. "Love-Starved Agnes Tufverson's Tragic Marriage at 43." *Des Moines Register Sunday Magazine*, 17 February 1935, p. 40.

"One Last Chance to Solve the Tufverson Disappearance." *Dothan (AL) Eagle*, 22 November 1936, p. 13.

"On Way Back." *Daily News (New York)*, 23 January 1935, p. 30.

"Ordered to U.S." *Chicago Tribune*, 7 December 1934.

Pellicer, Marlene Pardo. "An International Mystery." *Stranger Than Fiction Stories*, https://miami-ghost-chronicles.weebly.com/stranger-than-fiction/category/all.

"Perjury Charge Underway to Hold Poderjay." *Daily News (New York)*, 22 June 1934, p. 3.

Poderjay, Ivan. Letter to Olive Tufverson. February 1935. Personal collection of David and Patricia Rupp.

"Poderjay Denied a Parole in N.Y." *Detroit Free Press*, 3 February 1938, p. 1.

"Poderjay to Wed an 'Ex' in Exile." *Daily News*, 6 February 1940, p. 195.

"Poderjay-Tufverson Puzzle Becomes a Trunk Mystery." *Battle Creek (MI) Enquirer*, 18 June 1934, p. 1.

"Portia Comes East." *McCall's*, fall 1930.

Rapp, David, and Patricia Rapp. Personal interview, 19 February 2021.

Reynolds, Ruth. "Avenging Poderjay Sisters to See Foe Poderjay Go Free." *Daily News (New York)*, 7 January 1940, p. 353.

"Romeo Quizzed on Wife's State." *Globe-Gazette (IA)*, 20 June 1934, p. 1.

Roosevelt, Eleanor. "Advice to Women." *Woman's Home Companion*, October 1933.

"Search Spread for Woman Lawyer to Three Countries; Detain Husband at Vienna." *Evening News (PA)*, 15 June 1934, p. 1.

"Sister Awaits News of Missing Agnes Tufverson." *Chattanooga Daily Times*, 23 June 1934, p. 12.

Stein, John S. "Into the Nowhere." *Dayton (OH) Daily News*, 25 November 1945, p. 6.

"Swaggering Poderjay, Leaving U.S., Hides Mystery of Missing Bride." *Detroit Free Press*, 4 February 1940, p. 11.

"The Trunk Murder Mystery." *So Dead: A True Crime Podcast*. Scream Queen Productions, February 2020.

"Trunk Murder Victim Was Not Miss Tufverson." *Globe-Gazette (IA)*, 20 June 1934, p. 1.

"Trunk Stains Not Made by Blood, Claim." *Globe-Gazette (IA)*, 20 June 1934, p. 1.

Tufverson, Agnes. Letter to Selma and Olive Tufverson. 22 September 1933. Personal collection of David and Patricia Rupp.

Tufverson, Selma. Letter to Olive Tufverson. 13 September 1934. Personal collection of David and Patricia Rupp.

———. Letter to Olive Tufverson. 13 September 1934. Personal collection of David and Patricia Rupp.

"Tufverson Mystery Recalled." *Detroit Free Press*, 3 March 1949, p. 2.

"Tufverson Sisters and Father Mourn Attorney." *Lancaster (OH) Eagle-Gazette*, 21 June 1934, p. 10.

"U.S. City Directories, 1822–1955." Ancestry (*Ancestry.com*), database for Agnes Colonia Tufverson.

"U.S. Government in Formal Demand for Extradition Poderjay." *Evening Herald Courier (TN)*, 28 November 1934, p. 2.

"Wiles of a Bolting Banker." *John Bull (London)*, 12 May 1934, p. 23.

CHAPTER 4: JEAN SPANGLER, 1949

"200 to Comb Park for Corpse." *Colton (CA) Courier*, 11 October 1949, p. 1.

"An Actress, a Disappearance, and a Cryptic Note: What Happened to Jean Spangler?" Historybyday.com, accessed 20 April 2021.

"An Actress Is Missing: Police Troubled by Cryptic Note." *Kansas City Star*, 10 October 1949, p. 8.

"Actress May Have Called for Help at Filling Station before Disappearance." *Californian*, 12 October 1949, p. 21.

"Actress's Mother Believes Jean Spangler Alive." *Colton (CA) Courier*, 17 October 1949, p. 1.

"Ask Tot's Custody." *Marion Star*, 18 October 1949, p. 15.

Balsham, Casey, with Dylan Adler. "What the Hell Happened to Jean Spangler?" *Shady Shit Podcast*. 22 April 2021.

"Battle over Child of Actress Begins." *Los Angeles Times*, 4 April 1950, p. 31.

"Call off Mass Hunt for Missing Actress." *Los Angeles Evening Citizen News*, 12 October 1949, p. 7.

Charles River Editors, *The Disappearance of Jean Spangler*. Charles River Editors, 30 April 2021.

"Clues Fading in Hunt for Jean Spangler." *Los Angeles Evening Citizen News*, 13 October 1949, p. 25.

"Cohen Aides Mentioned in Custody Fight." *Daily News (Los Angeles)*, 3 April 1950, p. 10.

"Cops Probe Tips on Lost TV Girl." *Mirror News (Los Angeles)*, 14 October 1949, p. 4.

"Custody of Jean Spangler's Daughter Awarded Father." *Los Angeles Evening Citizen News*, 27 October 1949, p. 6.

"Daughter of Lost TV Girl Goes to Dad." *Mirror News*, 26 October 1949, p. 2.

"Disappearance." *Troy Messenger*, 20 October 1949, p. 1.

"Disappearance of Jean Spangler Is Still Hollywood's No. 1 Mystery." *St. Louis Globe Democrat*, 15 February 1950, p. 11.

"Early Issue." *Mirror News Los Angeles*, 10 June 1958, p. 13.

"Father Again Sued over Spangler Girl." *Daily News (Los Angeles)*, 15 January 1953, p. 34.

"Father Gets Missing Actress's Child." *Daily News (Los Angeles)*, 26 October 1949, p. 18.

"Fear Missing Actress Met Black Dahlia Fate." *Brooklyn Daily Eagle*, 11 October 1949, p. 3.

"Fear New Dahlia Death: 200 in Hunt." *Daily News (Los Angeles)*, 11 October 1949, p. 1.

"Fears Missing Daughter Slain." *Daily Reporter*, 18 October 1949, p. 4.

"Fight Settled over Lost TV Star's Child." *Mirror News*, 17 December 1949, p. 5.

"Find Jean Spangler; Oops. Wrong One." *Los Angeles Evening Citizen News*, 21 October 1949, p. 7.

Fisher, Rachel, and Desi Jedeiki. "Jean Spangler." *Hollywood Crime Scene Podcast.* Episode 86. 16 April 2019.

Fleming, Erin. "The Disappearance of Jean Spangler." *Redrum Blonde Podcast.* 4 February 2021.

"Former Husband of Missing Actress Asks for Daughter." *Wilmington Daily Press Journal*, 14 October 1949, p. 7.

"Gambler Tired of Jailing Whenever a Girl Vanishes." *Daily News (Los Angeles)*, 13 October 1949, p. 57.

"Glamour Girls Ok'd as Fit Mothers." *Lodi News-Sentinel*, 14 August 1948, p. 6.

"Griffith Park Area Scoured for Clues to Missing Actress." *News-Pilot*, 10 October 1949, p. 1.

Hoover, Marc. "The Disappearance of Actress Jean Spangler." *Clermont Sun*, 20 June 2020.

"Hunt Missing Film Actress: Purse, Strange Note Found." *Daily News*, 10 October 1949, pp. 2, 41.

"Hunt Renewed for Body of Actress. *Los Angeles Evening Citizen News*, 12 October 1949, p. 5.

"Hunt Widens for Film Player." *Pittsburgh Sun Telegraph*, 10 October 1949, p. 3.

"In Serious Condition." *Santa Cruz Sentinel*, 13 October 1949, p. 5.

"Jean Spangler Body Sought." *The Times (San Mateo, CA)*, 12 October 1949, pp. 1, 2.

"Jean Spangler Child Talks with Judge." *Los Angeles Times*, 5 April 1950, p. 2.

"Jean Spangler's Hubby Asks Order." *Whittier News*, 25 September 1952, p. 18.

"Jean Spangler's Mother Fights for Custody of Child." *Valley Times*, 13 December 1949, p. 20.

"Jean Spangler's Mother Requests Custody of Child." *Colton (CA) Courier*, 12 December 1949, p. 1.

"Jean Spangler Still Missing." *Lexington Herald-Leader*, 11 October 1949, p. 18.

"Jean Spangler Thought Alive." *Los Angeles Times*, 17 October 1949, p. 4.

"Judge Blasts Dad, Granny in Tot Fight." *Mirror News (Los Angeles)*, 28 April 1953, p. 25.

Kilgallen, Dorothy. "Voice of Broadway." *Shamokin News-Dispatch,* 19 October 1949, p. 6.

———. "Voice of Broadway." *The News Herald (PA),* 22 October 1949, p. 4.

Lenker, Maureen Lee. "The Missing Star Spangler Girl: Inside the Chilling, Still Unsolved Disappearance of Jean Spangler." *Explore Entertainment,* https://ew .com/celebrity/true-crime-jean-spangler-unsolved-disappearance, accessed 24 March 2021.

Lyons, Arthur. "The Mysterious Disappearance of Jean Spangler." *Palm Springs Life,* 6 November 2014.

"Man Quizzed in Missing Actress Hunt." *Los Angeles Evening Citizen News,* 10 December 1949, p. 1.

"Manufacturer Faces Fifteen Day Jail Term." *Lubbock Evening Journal,* 28 April 1953, p. 14.

"Missing Actress May Be Slain." *Republican and Herald,* 11 October 1949, p. 1.

"Missing Dancer Sought by Police. *Los Angeles Times,* 10 October 1949, p. 2.

"Missing Movie Player Sister of Local Man." *Lexington Herald-Leader,* 10 October 1949, p. 1.

"Mother Posts Reward in Spangler Case." *Mirror News (Los Angeles),* 3 December 1949, p. 5.

"Mother Sure Film Player Murdered." *Daily News (Los Angeles),* 12 October 1949, p. 1.

"Movie Actress Reported Missing by St. Louis Relative Visiting Her." *St. Louis-Post Dispatch,* 10 October 1949, p. 1.

"Mrs. Spangler Scouts Report Daughter Seen." *Los Angeles Evening Citizen News,* 23 March 1950, p. 3.

"Mrs. Spangler Upheld in Grandmother Rights." *Los Angeles Times,* 11 April 1950, p. 14.

Muir, Florabel. "Florabel Muir Reporting." *Mirror News (Los Angeles),* 8 March 1951, p. 6.

"Patricia MacCauley Fetes Popular Bride-elect." *Evening Vanguard (Venice, California),* 25 June 1942, p. 7.

Pearson, Nick. "The Dancer and the Movie Star: Unsolved Mystery Fascinates Hollywood 71 Years Later." *9News,* 24 December 2020.

Pickett, Russ. "Biography of Edward Spangler." Findagrave.com, accessed on 3 May 2021.

"Police Believe Jean Spangler Missing on 'Own Volition.'" *Pomona Progress Bulletin,* 18 October 1949, p. 1.

"Police Drop Case of Lost Spangler Girl." *Daily News (Los Angeles),* 17 October 1949, p. 16.

"Police Find List of Lost TV Girl's Pals." *Mirror News (Los Angeles),* 12 October 1949, p. 4.

"Police Seeking Dexter Benner." *Los Angeles Evening Citizen News*, 9 December 1953, p. 2.

"Police Tackle Five Missing Persons Cases." *Whittier (CA) News*, 22 October 1949, p. 1.

"Proves to Be Sack of Cans." *San Bernardino County Sun*, 19 October 1949, p. 10.

"Prowler Seen Near Missing Girl's Home." *Mirror News (Los Angeles)*, 15 October 1949, p. 3.

"Relative from Here Fears Foul Play." *St. Louis Globe Democrat*, 10 October 1949, p. 1.

Rossner, Richard, and Molly Brandenburg. "Jean Spangler." *Gone Podcast*, 15 June 2020.

Rule, La Reina. "Mother Heartbroken over Daughter's Disappearance." *Valley Times*, 13 August 1952, p. 14.

"Seek Missing Actress. Torn Purse Clue." *Los Angeles Evening Citizen News*, 10 October 1949, p. 23.

"See Trunk Victim Lost Showgirl." *Tribune (Scranton, Pennsylvania)*, 30 October 1951, p. 8.

"Spangler Girl Custody Plea Denied." *Daily News (Los Angeles)*, 6 October 1952, p. 14.

"Stepmother Loses Fight for Child of Jean Spangler." *Daily News (Los Angeles)*, 7 March 1951, pp. 3, 4.

Stokes, Chris et al. "Hollywood Case File #11: The Disappearance of Jean Spangler." *Mystery on the Rocks Podcast*. 3 September 2020.

"Torn Handbag Clue to Missing Actress." *Los Angeles Evening Citizen News*, 10 October 1949, p. 1.

"TV Actress Feared Sex Murder Victim." *Mirror News*, 10 October 1949, pp. 3, 18.

"TV Actress Feared Victim of Sex Fiend." *Long Beach Independent*, 12 October 1949, p. 1.

Valin, Edward. "Salvatore Piscopo: The Man Who Betrayed Johnny Rosseli." *The American Mafia*, https://mafiahistory.us/rattrap/salvatorepiscopo.html, 2018.

Warder, Robin. "Jean Spangler." *The Trail Went Cold—A True Crime Podcast*. Episode 164. 4 March 2020.

Wilson, R. J. "The Chilling Disappearance of Jean Spangler." *Stories from Classic Hollywood*, https://thelifeandtimesofhollywood.com/the-chilling-disappearance-of-jean-spangler-did-kirk-douglas-kill-her/, 29 June 2018.

Wood, Kyle J. Interview with Sophie Spangler. *YouTube*, www.youtube.com/watch?v=cXVa0XU33sY, 2001.

"Young Man Sought in Jean Spangler Case." *St. Louis Post-Dispatch*, 11 October 1949, p. 3.

CHAPTER 5: SIMONE RIDINGER, 1977

"Age Progression Image Shows Missing Sherborn Teen as 60th Birthday Approaches." *25 News Boston*, 3 January 2020.

Bailey, Betsy. Personal interviews. December 2022 and July 2023.

"Chasing Rainbows." *The Voice*, www.evaporatethemissing.com/post/chasing -rainbows, 23 October 2022, updated 21 June 2023.

Crimaldi, Laura. "Police, Group Renew Effort to Resolve 1977 Mystery." *The Boston Globe*, 5 January 2020, p. B1.

———. "Search for Teenager Last Seen in Natick in 1977 Is Renewed on Her 60th Birthday." *Boston Globe*, 4 January 2020.

Dabilis, Andrew. "Missing Persons: Questions and Anguish." *Boston Globe*, 14 May 1990, pp. 1, 16.

Genter, Ethan. "Cold Case: Where Is Simone Ridinger?" *Cape Cod Times*, 24 September 2017.

Godinho, Sergeant James. Personal interview. 15 July 2021.

Haddadin, Jim. "Sherborn Police Probe New Leads in Woman's 1977 Disappearance." *The MetroWest Daily News*, 20 May 2017.

Haswell, Detective John. Personal interview. July 2023.

"Lost Rainbow: The Disappearance of Simone Ridinger." *Murder Sheet*. www.youtube.com/watch?app=desktop&v=13T8waaSWFg, 8 February 2022.

"Missing." *Boston Globe*, 3 November 1977, p. 12.

"Missing: Simone Ridinger." *Uncovered* (Uncovered.com), 12 May 2023.

"New Efforts Underway to Solve 1977 Disappearance of Massachusetts Teen," *WCVB5 Boston*, 4 January 2020.

O'Brien, Charlie. "Whatever Happened to Simone Ridinger?" *Medium.com*, 18 June 2023.

O'Donnell, Brenna. "On Teen's 60th Birthday, Detective Still Holds Out Hope." *National Center for Missing and Exploited Children Blog*. 2 January 2020.

Richard, Detective Andrew. Personal interview. 26 July 2023.

Schwan, Henry. "Sherborn Police Still Working on 1977 Case." WickedLocal.com, www.wickedlocal.com/story/bulletin-tab/2020/09/27/i-think-theres-chance -sherbon-police-continue-to-look-for-clues-connected-to-simone-ridinger-who -we/42968927/, 27 September 2020.

"Simone Ridinger—1977—MA." *Wicked Deeds*, www.wickeddeedspodcast.com/ episodes/episode-thirty-four-simone-ridinger-197-ma. Episode 34. 3 May 2022.

"Simone S. Ridinger—Sherborn, Massachusetts." *ViCAP Missing Persons*, FBI.gov, www.fbi.gov/wanted/vicap/missing-persons/simone-s-ridinger

"Simone Stephanie Ridinger." *The Charley Project*, https://charleyproject.org/case/ simone-stephanie-ridinger, 24 February 2020.

"Whereabouts Still Unknown." https://whereaboutsstillunknown.wordpress.com, 17 March 2013.